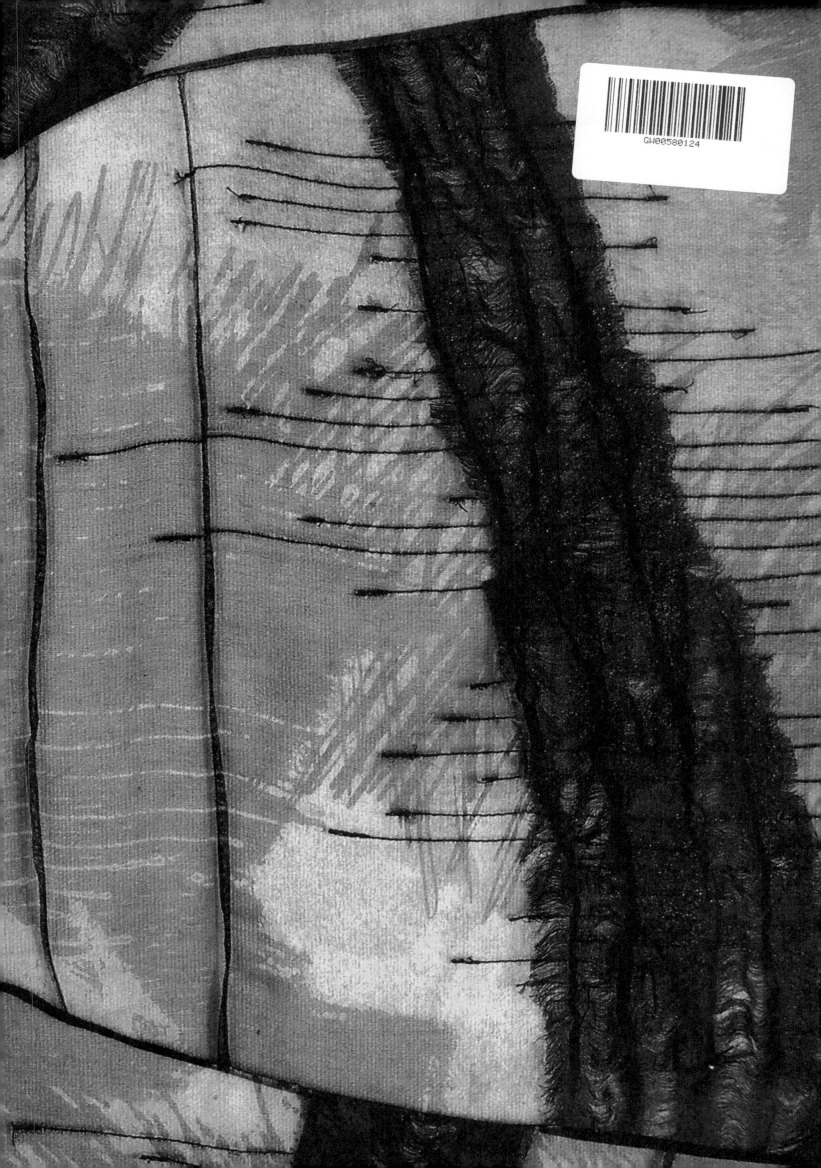

ralph rucci the art of weightlessness

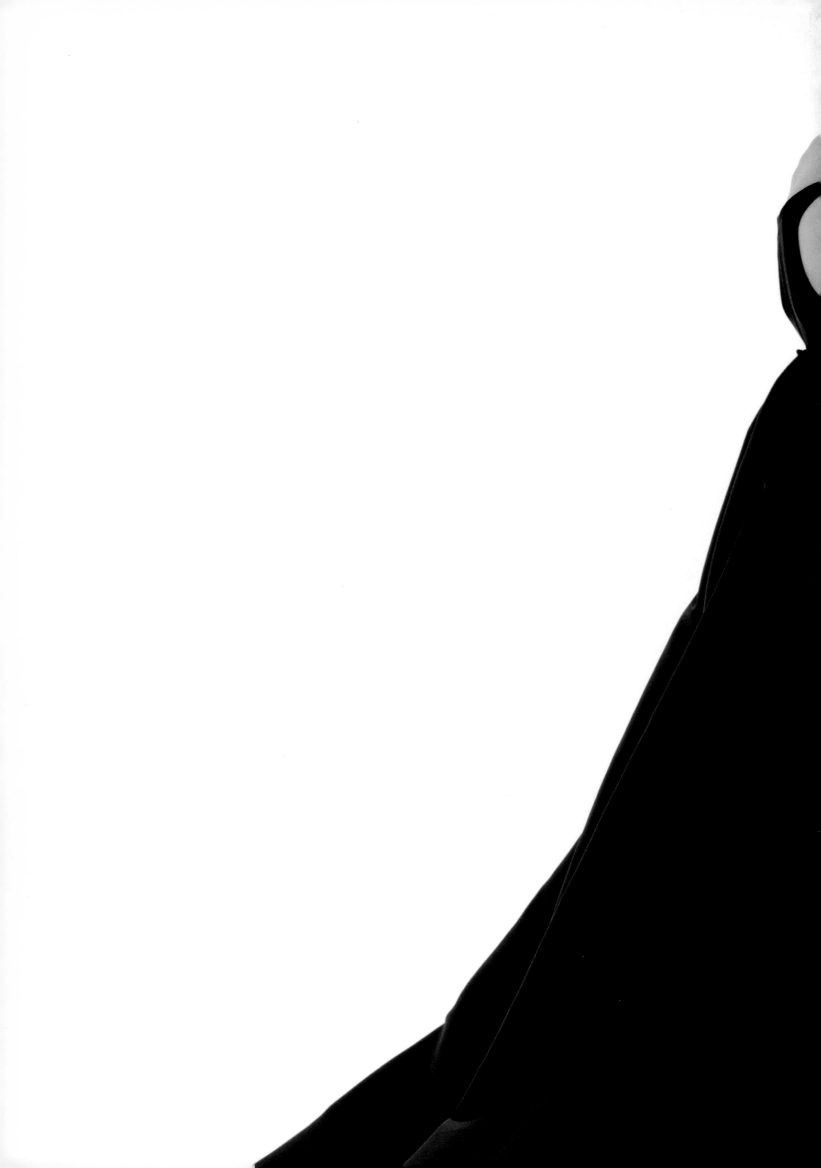

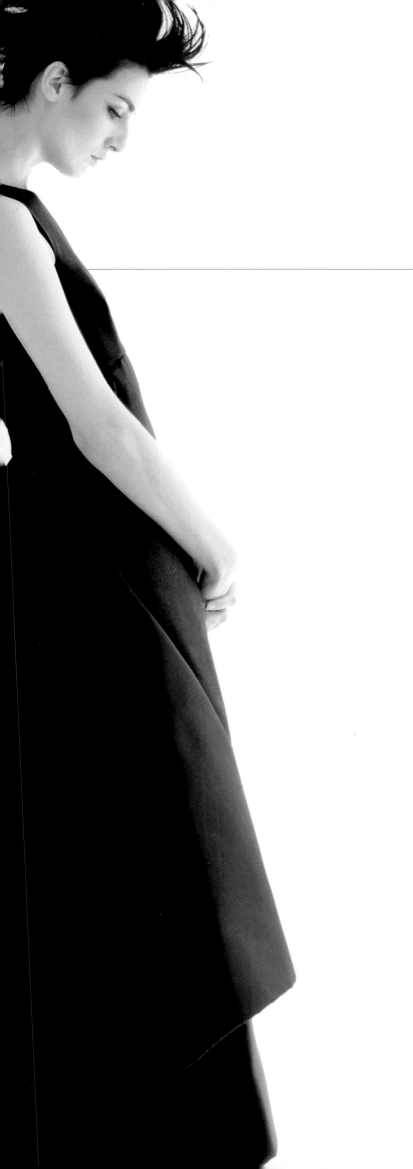

ralph rucci the art of weightlessness

yale university press new haven and london published in association with the fashion institute of technology, new york

Printed in Italy by Conti Tipocolor

Designed by Paul Sloman

Library of Congress Cataloging-in-Publication Data

Steele, Valerie.
Ralph Rucci : the art of weightlessness / Valerie Steele, Patricia Mears and Clare Sauro.
     p. cm.
Includes bibliographical references and index.
     ISBN 978-0-300-12278-7 (cl : alk. paper)
1. Rucci, Ralph. 2. Fashion designers–United States–Biography.
3. Fashion design–United States–History. I. Mears, Patricia. II. Sauro, Clare, 1972- III. Title.

TT505.R89S84 2007
746.9'2092–dc22
[B]
                         2006101177

Images on pp. v, viii–ix, 48, 94–5, and 192: Ralph Rucci, 2005 haute couture,
photographs by Iké Udé, courtesy of Iké Udé's *aRude* magazine.

Image on p. vi: silk jersey pleated bodice, fall/winter 2003 haute couture collection,
photograph by William Palmer.

Images on pp. 50–1, 52–3, 92–3, 170–1, 172–3, and 188–9: photographs by Sandi Fellman.

Images on pp. 58–63, 66–9, 72–5, 79, 81, 83, 85, 87, 89, 91: photographs by Dan Lecca.

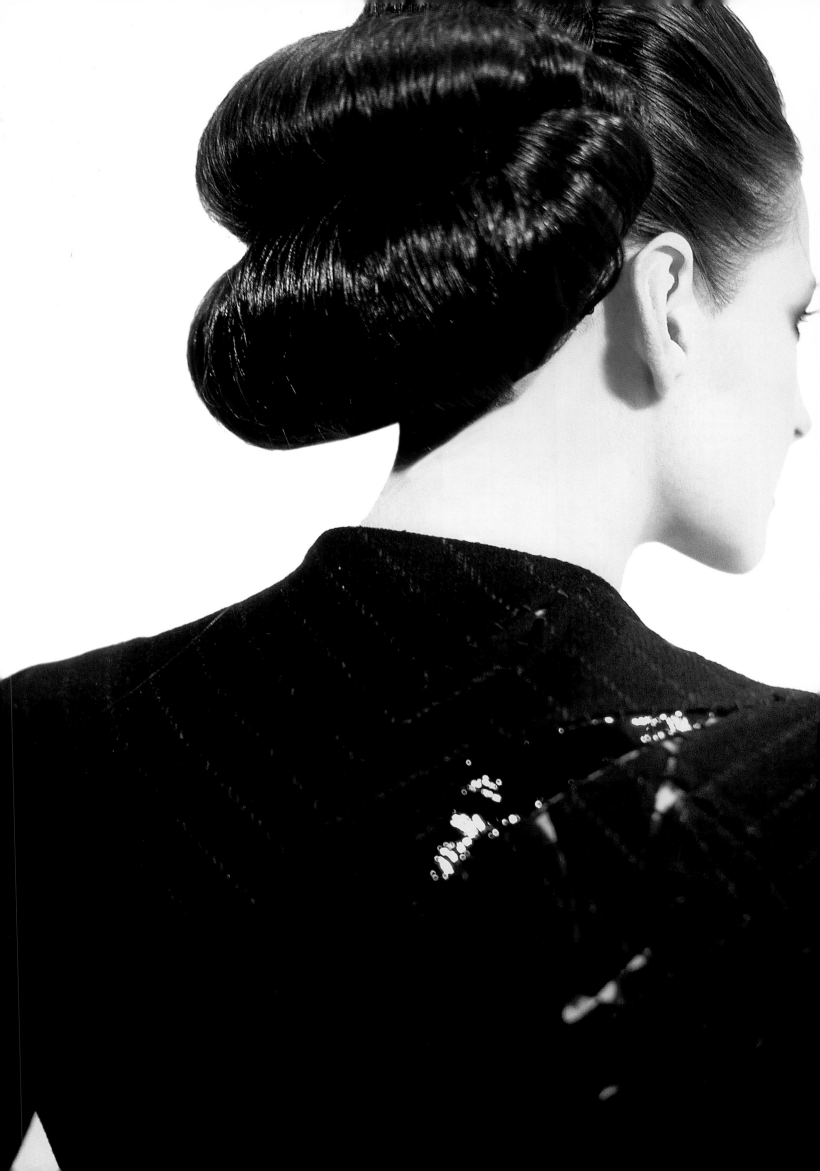

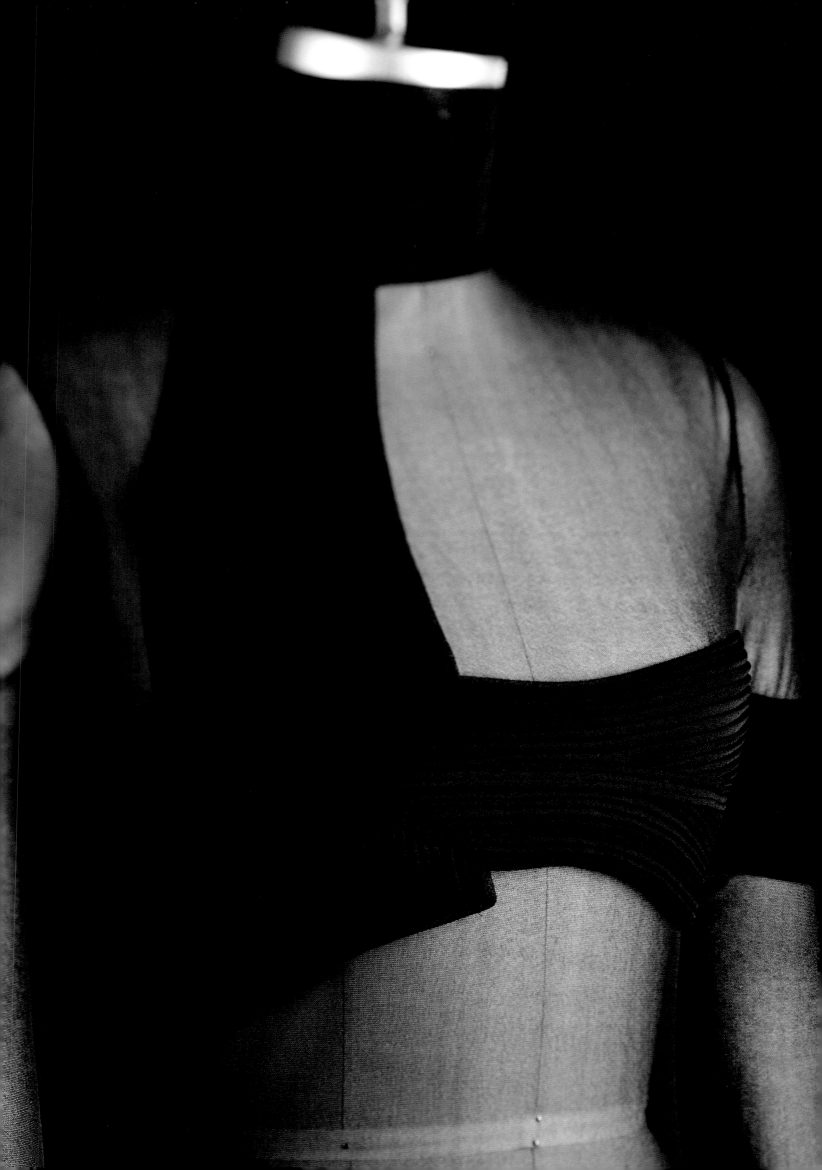

contents

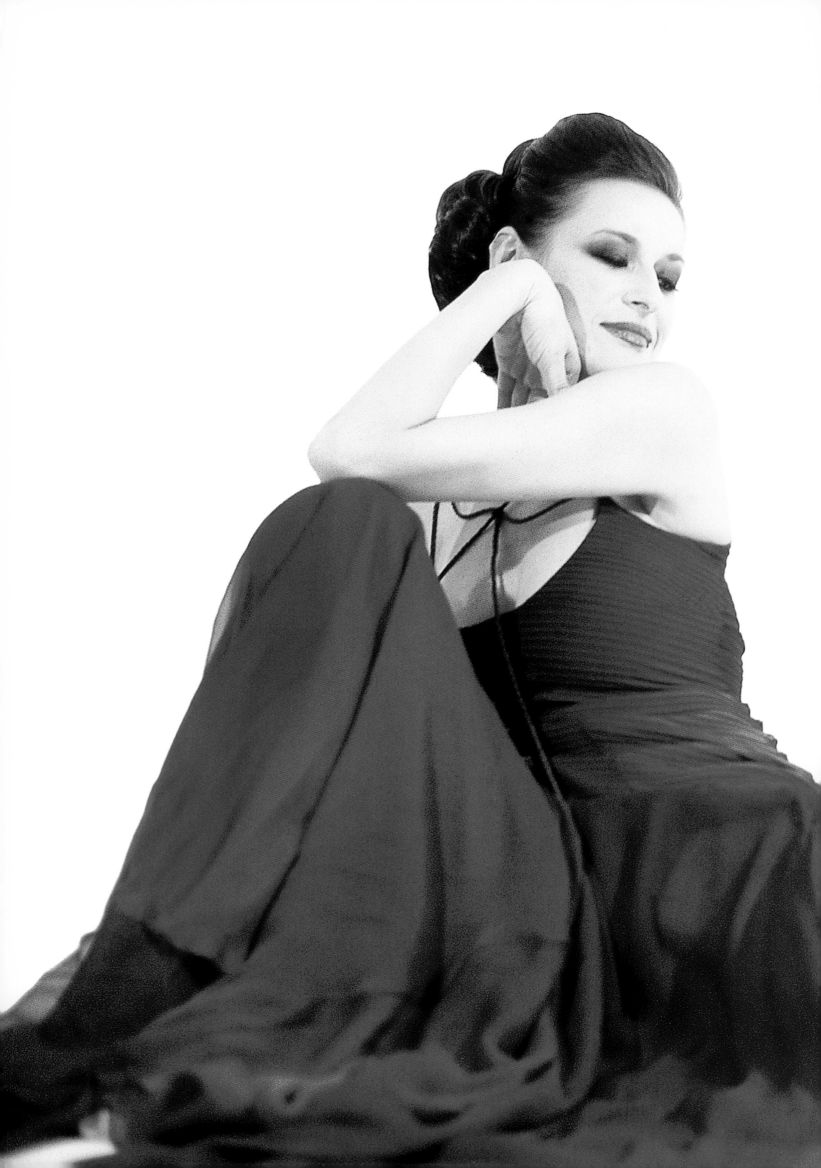

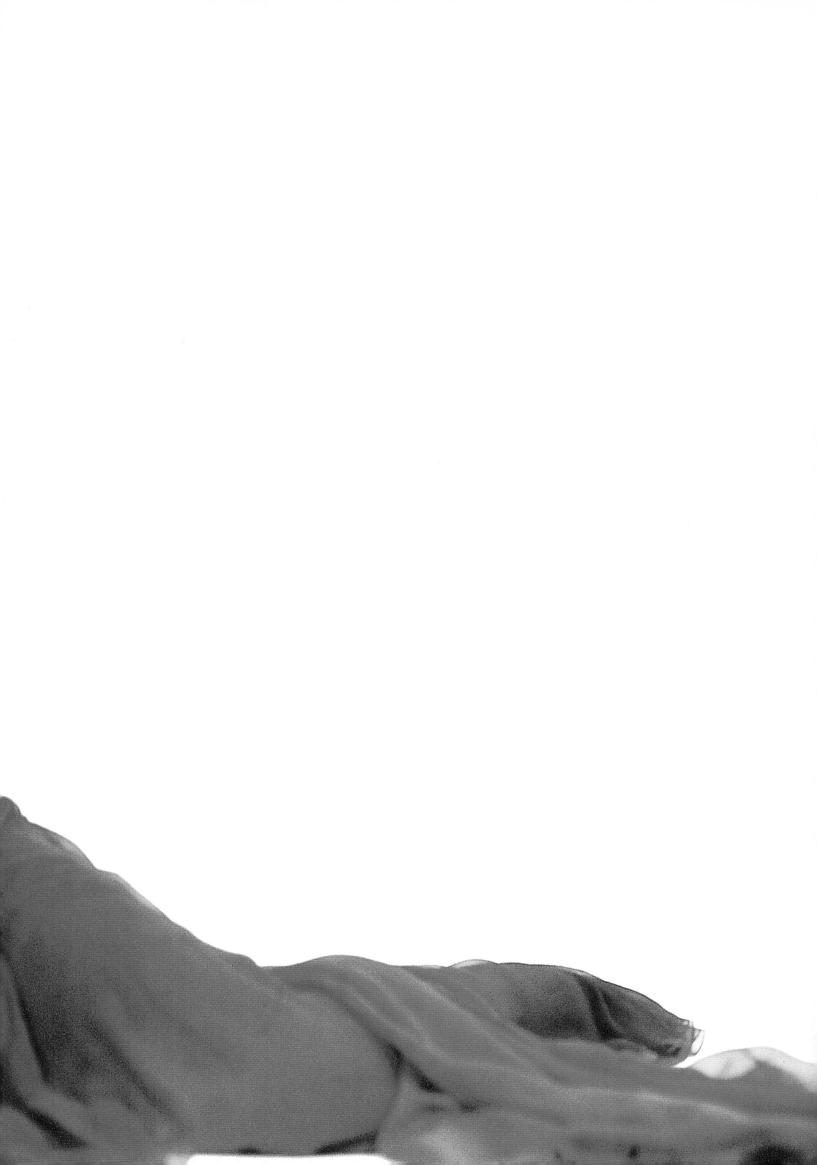

Ralph Rucci lives my idea of a perfect life. He's able to synthesize all his fascinations, heightened aesthetic sensibilities and global wanderlust and have it come through his hands and across workshop tables as a vision in cloth as unique as he is. There is no separation between his work and his life.

There is nothing derivative in Ralph's work. There is the purity of originality of someone who has the strength to listen to his own voice.

Linda Fargo

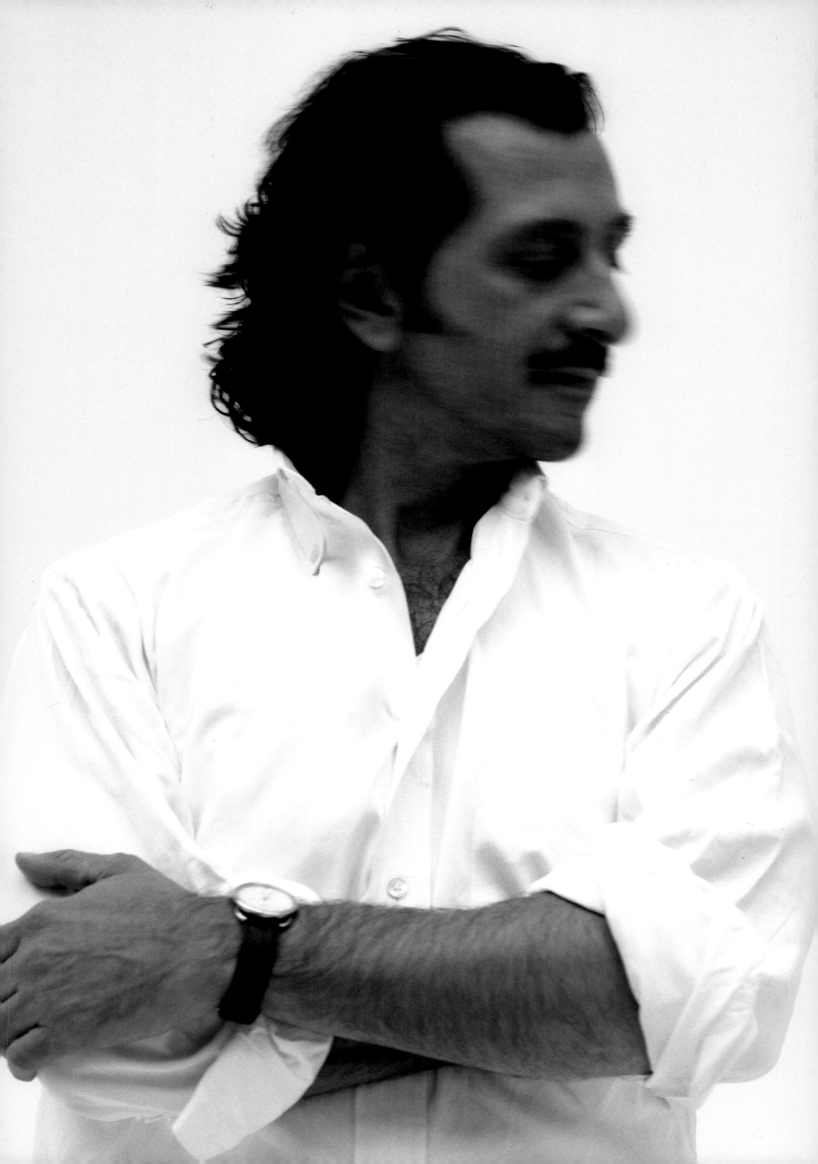

an american in paris

"One Day on Welfare, the Next He's Showing in Paris." The rags-to-riches headline was not entirely accurate: Ralph Rucci had never been on welfare, as he reassured his horrified parents. But he had certainly come close; once he was even reduced to standing in line at the welfare office, impeccably dressed, surrounded by crack addicts, to get help when he could not pay his rent because a client was late paying her bills. And then, suddenly, after years struggling in obscurity, going in and out of business, he was being lauded in the *New York Times* (May 7, 2002) as the first American since Mainbocher in the 1930s to show his own collection during couture week in Paris. When Cathy Horyn's article appeared, she assumed that most people's first thought would be: "Who is Ralph Rucci, anyway?"[1]

Yet Rucci had been working "under the radar" for more than twenty years, creating beautiful and luxurious clothes that received almost no attention in the fashion press. Although he began designing at the same time as Michael Kors and Marc Jacobs, Rucci's clothes had never been featured in a major fashion magazine. Since 1994 he had designed a ready-to-wear collection, which was already close to couture quality, but his clients learned about him mostly through word-of-mouth, since few journalists even attended his fashion shows. This began to change after the Chambre Syndicale de la Haute Couture Parisienne invited him to show in Paris.

"Suddenly there's all this talk about a designer named Ralph Rucci," reported *Vogue*'s André Leon Talley.[2] Readers were informed that Rucci created "fabulous" and very expensive clothes, inspired by great couturiers like Madame Grès, Cristobal Balenciaga and Charles James, artists like Cy Twombly, and fabled women of style like Pauline de Rothschild.

In the months leading up to his Paris fashion show, Rucci worked feverishly in his New York atelier. Always fanatical about using the best possible materials, he had acquired silk gazar (Balenciaga's favorite) from Bucol in Lyons, and he used exactly the same kind of jersey from Racine that Madame Grès favored. Even though the House of Lesage had recently been acquired by Chanel, Rucci had convinced François Lesage to produce some of his embroideries. "I was impossible to live with, because nothing was good enough," he recalls. "We were redesigning constantly. By the time we left for Paris, I was really nervous and excited."[3]

Rucci's first couture collection was scheduled for 3:30 in the afternoon on Friday July 12, 2002 – the last show of the last day of couture week. Karl Lagerfeld was first to show on Tuesday with his prestigious and extremely successful haute couture collection for Chanel. Then Jean Paul Gaultier, long the bad boy of French fashion, produced a couture collection that combined masterful tailoring with deconstruction. The American designer Oscar de la Renta took his final bow after a decade spent designing couture for Balmain. John Galliano of Christian Dior, Valentino, Christian Lacroix, and a handful of other designers showed to greater or lesser acclaim. Meanwhile, the Paris nightlife sizzled, as Sean Combs, Mick Jagger, Tom Ford, and some topless dancers partied at Les Bains Douches.

During the entire week before his show, Rucci left the Ritz Hotel only once. He slept poorly, and he spent most of his waking hours working on making his clothes as perfect as they could possibly be. As usual, Rucci had twice as many looks as she could possibly show. Stress levels ran high as he and his team started doing fittings in the ballroom of the Ritz Hotel. "All of us were so nervous and frightened that we were at odds with each other," he remembers. "I was exhausted, raw, worried about the financial part of it."

To make matters worse, people kept dropping by the hotel to see how things were going and to offer unsolicited advice. "André would pop in and say 'You can't put that coat with that' and I'd say 'Get out if you are going to critique it. I need to concentrate!'" When journalists from the French newspaper *Le Monde* appeared, Rucci told them he was too busy to talk, and they would have to come back when the collection was finished. "You did *what*?!" said André Leon Talley. "I can't believe you threw *Le Monde* out!" Anna Piaggi of *Italian Vogue* was deeply offended when she got the same reception. "And in the midst of all that we had CBS Sunday News filming."

"You know how seriously I take it, it's all very emotional for me," Rucci told CBS News. Television seldom produces a special program dedicated solely to a single obscure designer. "No, not Ralph Lauren – Ralph *Rucci*," explained the voice-over when the program was finally aired in October. The story of an American in Paris, the first in more than sixty years to show his own collection at the haute couture, "the big leagues," was potentially a major story in the American mass media.[4] But no-one then knew how the big-league fashion journalists would react.

Finally, in a small but elegant room at the hôtel d'Evreux in the Place Vendôme, Ralph Rucci presented fifty ensembles to a small but distinguished group of journalists, buyers, and individual couture clients. Represented in his first couture collection were Rucci's signature pieces, such as his famous "Infanta" evening gowns in duchess satin, cashmere "Dalai Lama" coats, and sculptural jackets with seamed arcs.

The first look to come down the runway was a white cashmere sweater and sable ski pants worn by the model Erin O'Conner. The African-American model Coco Mitchell, who is Rucci's primary fitting model, wore a sheered mink coat over a dress embroidered by Lesage with silk ribbons on a silk chiffon foundation. Colette wore a forest-green double-faced cashmere cape, tunic and trousers. Alek Wek wore a long skirt in chocolate broadtail sparkling with tiny stones. The last dress out, Rucci's favorite, was a black satin evening gown, accessorized with a Shang-dynasty ax-head as a necklace.

There were many outstanding ensembles, especially for day. A sleeveless dress in taupe-colored wool crepe bore the traces of gently curving seams and was strategically punctuated with tiny diamond-shaped holes. Accessorized with burgundy gauntlet gloves and a laquered evening bag shaped like a quiver, slung diagonally across the model's back, it was fit for a modern Amazon. A black wool jersey day dress had a leather yoke and Renaissance cartridge pleats falling from a dropped waist. An Asian-inspired jacket opened over a dress with an impossibly chic crocodile bodice. A long slender column of a dress was completely covered in delicate feathers.

Rucci's loyal clients, such as Joan Kaner of Neiman Marcus, were very happy, and he acquired important new clients. "I used to go to Givenchy and Balenciaga and Chanel," says style icon Deeda Blair. "And I received an invitation to Ralph's first couture collection in Paris. There was very quiet, almost celestial music, no hot rock and strobe lights. It was just extremely beautiful. Although there are intricate seams, the clothes are simple. Or, rather, they are deceptively simple, because there is great intricacy."[5] He also received major press coverage.

"Ralph Rucci closed the couture collections by realizing a dream of bringing to Paris his New York collection of clothes that explore volume and shape in an architectural way," declared Suzy Menkes of the *International Herald Tribune*. "It is rare to find a designer who is both a sculptor and a decorator, but Rucci has those skills, using ivory or black double-faced wool to make jackets that stand away from the body in a style reminiscent of the designer's hero, Cristóbal Balenciaga." Menkes mixed praise with criticism, suggesting that "these references to a past of grand gowns seemed too rarified" for contemporary life. She preferred his daywear, praising the way in which "geometric lines dissect[ed] a jacket into quadrants." All in all, she concluded "It was a quiet but polished debut."[6]

While acknowledging that Rucci "fills a void for casually elegant clothes," Cathy Horyn of the *New York Times* was clearly disappointed: There were "too many apostle odes to Balenciaga" and not enough "lightness." Although she pronounced his debut "a success," her review was cursory.[7] It was doubly disappointing for Rucci, since Horyn had been almost alone among major journalists in supporting his career.

Women's Wear Daily was negative, perhaps in part, because Rucci had made the mistake of telling their reporter that "working only in New York is too provincial." The New York-based industry daily responded by dismissing both Rucci's remark and his show as "pretentious." But *WWD* had never much liked Rucci's work. After complaining about the "excruciatingly slow pace" of the show, reporter Bridget Foley admitted that "the clothes looked quite beautiful," although they were "not for everyone." Indeed, for every word of praise – "dramatic and serene," "finely conceived and executed" – she slipped in a poisoned blade: "With their somewhat intellectual undercurrent . . . they will appeal to a mature woman."[8] This judgement was echoed in *W Magazine*: "Rucci's clothes looked rich and decidedly client-friendly, playing to a mature woman who likes to make her presence felt while retaining an aura of distinction."[9]

Rucci clearly had his own style, characterized by strong, sculptural shapes and beautiful details. His clothes were discreetly elegant, with a kind of "rigorous chic," as Hamish Bowles put it.[10] Some observers liked it, others did not. Godfrey Deeny of *Fashion Wire Daily* thought the clothes were "an exercise in subtle perfection."[11] Noting that Rucci's work was reminiscent of Madame Grès and Balenciaga, *Le Figaro* concluded: "It's perfect, but do we still want it?"[12]

But at least Rucci was finally getting press coverage, and the French, especially, were pleased to observe that Rucci honored the techniques and luxury of the couture tradition. The Associated Press published an article, "American in Paris," which was syndicated around the world. The Agence-France Press surmised that Rucci's wearable, well-cut, and luxurious clothes "might well attract well-heeled customers with nowhere to go since Saint Laurent's withdrawal."[13] *Vogue* published nothing from Rucci's first couture collection, but *Harper's Bazaar* printed one photograph, soon to be followed by more extensive coverage of his work.[14]

"Perhaps I am the James Baldwin of fashion," said Rucci later. "It wasn't until I went to Paris that I had any recognition."[15]

"The son of an Italian butcher from South Philadelphia, Ralph Rucci did not take the direct route to Paris," reported the voice-over on "Runway Success," the CBS News program about his life and work, which brought images of his first couture show to millions of viewers. In one of a series of extensive interviews, Rucci told me that he came from "a very conservative Italian family. They were very loving – I was totally indulged – but they were also very fearful of the new and different."

He knew he was gay from an early age. "I was a little boy that was gay." However, "coming from a very conservative Roman Catholic family, sex was never discussed." It was in primary school, a private Catholic boys' school, that he first remembers "being categorized as a faggot." He remembers feeling "alienated, alone, different. Not being able to speak about it to anyone, I began to internalize all this negative energy . . . But there was another aspect to it, that within this space where I felt I had to hide, I started a process of self-discovery, of developing an aesthetic sensibility."

"Because my childhood was so introverted, I started *looking*." His first memory of anything related to color and fashion dates from the age of about four, when he used to run to the window every day to watch a neighbor shaking out a dust mop, which he described as a brilliant "Vreeland red." The color was "so seductive" that he begged his parents to buy him one just like it, which he kept in the corner of his room. He also remembers going with his mother to her dressmaker, John, "who would make her Dior copies in heavy duchess satin, and I would always get involved: 'You have to have a hat with that, Mom'." By the age of six, he had created his own personal uniform of black trousers with a black-and-white checked shirt. Soon he was selecting his mother's wardrobe, "selecting everything in the house."

His primary school was run by The Sisters of Mercy, whose "Chanel-esque" nuns' habits greatly impressed him. To this day, he sees "an association between nuns' habits and the greatness of Madame Grès' taffeta dresses." Grade school was "a lovely experience." He was elected school president, and the nuns encouraged him to paint and write. By contrast, the Jesuit preparatory school that he attended was "the worst experience of my young life." In retrospect, however, "it gave me enormous strength, [because] it fortified my sense of self." When school became too much, he would escape, making day trips to New York City to visit boutiques like Granny Takes a Trip that carried clothes from London. "It was the Antonio Lopez moment, the gay appearance, with calypso shirts and platform espadrilles. That's how I dressed."

"The bug had already bitten me about fashion. I was already doing my research and clippings. But it was still in the closet." Fashion was not an acceptable career goal. Because he had excelled in school, he was accepted at New York University where he planned to study philosophy. But once there, he suffered from severe anxiety attacks, and retreated to Philadelphia, where he enrolled in Temple University to study literature and philosophy. Even today Rucci says, "I never approached my work as a fashion designer," by which he meant that he did not begin by looking at trends. "I approach it as an academic. I begin with my research. That is the most important part of my work." By "academic," he means that "you conceive a thesis and draw your conclusions." In other words, "I try to translate the ideas into wearable clothes. It's not just sketching." Even more important is the art of "note-taking," a process that he calls "the metaphysical side" of design.

icons of fashion

"I was in the library doing a paper for an aesthetics class," recalls Rucci, "when I came upon two photographs – of a black cape and a trapezoidal gown. They were shot from the back, and looked very sculptural. Like Japanese Noh costumes. I looked down and saw that they were designed by a man named Balenciaga. It went straight to my heart." These photographs by David Bailey for *Vogue* (July, 1967) are still displayed on the wall of Rucci's atelier. As soon as he saw them, Rucci's mania for research went into high drive. Already engaged in making his own art, as well as studying the history and philosophy of art, he wrote a term paper called "Beyond Aesthetics: The Relationship of Yves Saint Laurent, Balenciaga, and Robert Motherwell." It received an A, and his professor encouraged him to pursue his interest in fashion.

"I started buying fabric, cutting directly into it, draping it on my sister, researching – how do you make this flat cloth three-dimensional with one seam? I began thinking I *am* a fashion designer, not I'm going to become one." While researching Balenciaga, Rucci also discovered that "one of his prophets was in New York: Halston." This discovery, too, would bear fruit.

For many years, Rucci proudly told journalists that Balenciaga was his idol. But too often journalists concluded from this that his work was merely derivative of the great couturier. This is not the case. "I first went to Balenciaga in 1958 or '59, so I know Balenciaga's work very well," says couture client Deeda Blair, "and of course Ralph knows it very well. Ralph appreciates it, but he doesn't do the same thing. He is inspired by the purity and the architectural quality of Balenciaga, but I don't see it as duplication in any way." Curators who have examined the work of the two designers agree that it differs significantly in numerous ways. What Rucci *does* have in common with Balenciaga is a rigor of technique and an obsessive perfectionism, an unwillingness to let go until every detail is exactly as he wants it.

Rucci rushed through Temple University in three years and applied to the Fashion Institute of Technology in New York City. "My family gave me a very hard time," he recalls. "They didn't want me to do this." But Rucci was determined. He designed and made a black sequinned jumpsuit and a set of evening pyjamas, which he nervously presented to members of the fashion design faculty at FIT. He was immediately accepted, moved into the school's dormitory, and began taking classes in draping and pattern-making. The year was 1978.

"I didn't like him at first," recalls Vivian Van Natta, a former classmate. "I thought he was arrogant and pretentious. He kept talking about people like Balenciaga and Charles James, who I'd never heard of. He was really serious about his work. He even ironed his muslins, and he was really into draping." But one day she said something that made him laugh, and they ended up becoming close friends and, eventually, colleagues. "Ralph was so talented. By the third semester, I told him 'Some day I'll work for you'."[16]

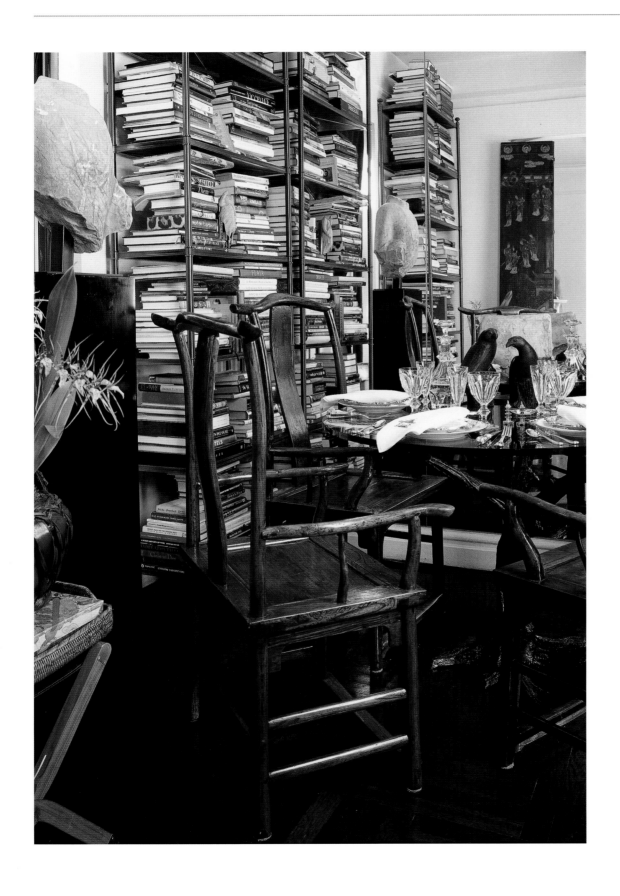

Views of Ralph Rucci's apartment.
Photographs: Dan Mayers.

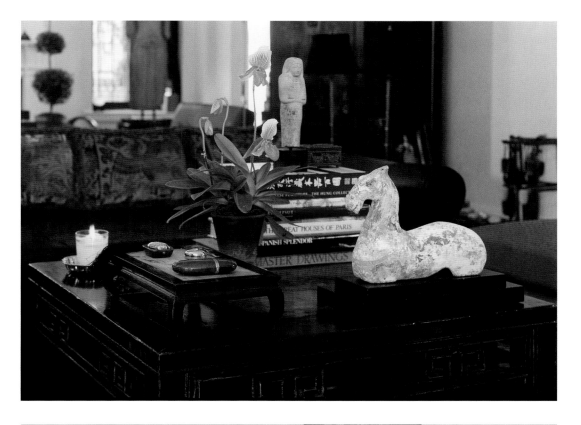

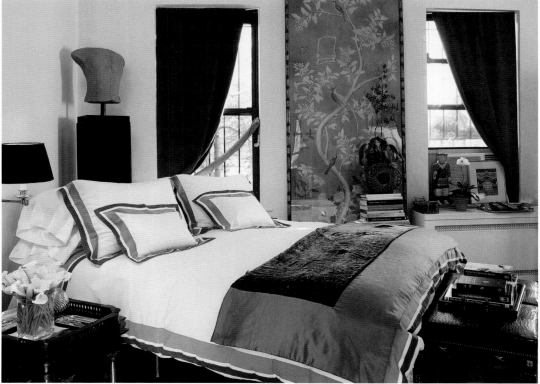

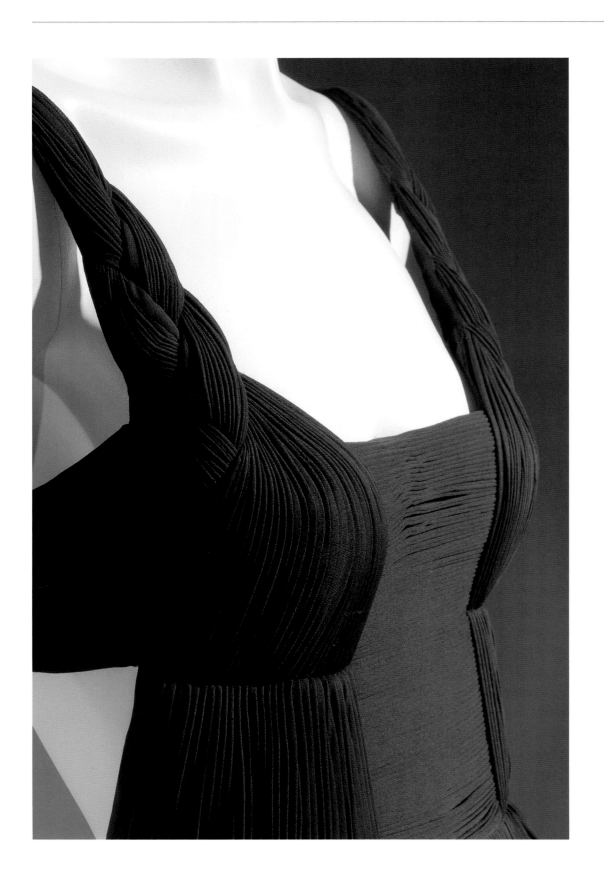

Detail, navy blue fluted silk jersey
evening dress by Madame Alix
Grès, 1972, Museum at FIT.
Photograph: Irving Solero.

Rucci carefully analyzed many of the dresses, including all of the Balenciagas, in the permanent collection of The Costume Institute of The Metropolitan Museum of Art. He also did research at The Museum at FIT, then known as The Design Laboratory, where he examined the dresses by Madame Grès and Charles James. Grès, in particular, was a great influence. Although based in Paris, she held several fashion shows in New York as charity benefits. One year, Rucci worked backstage as a dresser. "The dryness of black paper taffeta!" he recalled. "I was injected with the drug that day, and it never left me." Still a student, he had the temerity to ask Madame Grès for a job. She said: "You must work in the couture for twenty years. Then come and see me."

Rucci was also deeply impressed by Elsa Peretti's biomorphic jewelry designs, which responded to the lines of the body in a radically new way. She crafted a silver cuff so that it moulded the wrist, emphasizing the wrist bone, and she took a lima bean shape and made an indentation so the thumb would fit perfectly in the hollow. "I had a job after school, working as a salesman in a menswear shop," Rucci recalls. "I saved all my money, and I bought a cuff [which he wore] as a symbol of the design philosophy I was embracing," which he describes as one of "respect for the body." Years later, he became friends with Peretti, and her silver cuff remains on Rucci's front desk.

Another great inspiration was Pauline de Rothschild, "who dressed with enormous style but a deeply personal style, even a somewhat eccentric style."[17] The Baltimore-born socialite designed for Hattie Carnegie before marrying into the French branch of the Rothschild family. Rucci loves to talk about her sense of style, and the way she combined a very avant-garde sensitivity to new trends with a complete disregard for fashion pieties. Even the way she moved, on the balls of her feet, almost floating, was unique. Not only did she have a deeply personal style, she was obsessively perfectionist about achieving exactly the effect she wanted. These were all traits that appealed greatly to Rucci, who already "dressed perfectly all the time."[18]

●

While studying at FIT, Rucci started keeping a series of scrapbooks devoted to Halston, who seems to have been a kind of role model for him. "Halston recreates a Frank Stella painting on a float of sheerest chiffon," declares the copy on an advertisement, over which the young Ralph Rucci drew a pen-and-ink sketch inspired by Halston's dress. Other headlines – "Halston: Quiet Quality" and "Halston: More Elegant Understatement" – also seem to look forward to Rucci's own aesthetic. Halston believed that "fashion comes from fashionable people," such as his friends and clients Mrs. Agnelli, the Vicomtesse de Ribes, Babe Paley, Elsa Peretti – all women that Rucci admired.

"I wormed my way into Halston's shows through a vendeuse," he remembers.[19] Carefully pasted into one scrapbook is an invitation to see Halston's fall collection at his boutique on Madison Avenue; a note on the back kindly tells the young student: "Dear Ralph, If you have free time, I know you like to see everything Halston." He carefully listed the people who attended or modeled in Halston's shows: Elsa Peretti, Victor Hugo, Bill Dugan, Karen Borjenson, Chris Royer, Liza Minelli, Elizabeth Taylor, Diana Vreeland, Martha Graham, Lily Auchincloss, Lee Radziwill, Andy Warhol. He also listed the colors Halston used. ("purple, lilac, lemon, red, navy, cobalt blue, green, black, gray, white") and the fabrics ("crepe de chine, charmeuse, chiffon, silk jersey, ultra-suede, cashmere").

Rucci's handwritten accounts of Halston's runway shows became increasingly detailed: "Monday February 13, 1978. New York. Today, 12:00 at 645 Fifth Avenue, the Olympic Tower, Halston presented his spring summer made-to-order collection/We arrived at about 11:30, when we went up the elevator with a lynx-clad tour de force of some of Halston's devoted customers . . . One woman said to another, "Let's go see what our boy has to show us." Of Halston's show-room, Rucci observed, "It is truly magnificent and terribly modern. Ultra-ultra modern . . . 18-foot-high ceilings are all paved with mirrors. Deep ox-blood carpets . . . with ox-blood lacquered Parsons tables and potted calla lilies . . . Chrome folding-chairs lined the runway three deep."

"The audience fell silent when Mrs. [Empress] Vreeland arrived in total Halston: black cash-mere T-shirt, slacks, and red cashmere scarves, one tied around her waist and one around her neck. Her ivory tooth and ivory cuff were the only jewelry items. And she had the most magnifi-cent sable coat that I have ever seen . . . Andy [Warhol] was in his usual jeans and ski parka." The anticipation before the show was "intense," Rucci wrote, and the clothes, when they appeared, were "breath-taking." Rucci was thrilled to see such complicated, inventive cuts, with everything on the bias. "There has never been anything like this. It was an historic day in fashion." Even today he looks back on Halston's flying saucer collection as one of the pivotal experiences of his life: "Vionnet done in a new way." It makes him "angry that Halston is remembered for his evenings at Studio 54 rather than for his body of work."

The notebooks document the way Rucci moved from school at FIT to the world of Halston, his focus constantly on fashion: "December 14, 1978. After sewing for over 20 hours, it was about 7:30 a.m. as I 'finished' my garments. I ran out to buy *WWD* and have breakfast . . . I ran back to my room, grabbed my things and went to the classroom. My garments looked great: A plain black wool faille dress with a bias silk crepe de chine scarf in black around the waist and my black-and-red double-faced wool jersey cape. Red and white cotton gabardine suit. Small shirt tail jacket in red and faced inside in white. Entirely reversible in white. Straight red skirt; bias red camisole with peplum and white sash. Everyone went wild.

"I ran back to the room, and began to get dressed: black slacks, black cashmere T-neck and cardigan. Then I met Rosina [his sister] at the station – red cashmere shirtdress and cardigan, Peretti belt, cuffs, pearls, white coat. We took a cab [uptown to Halston's showroom] . . . Red silk taffeta treated for rain blouson jacket and straight slacks – incredible! *No* set-in sleeves in the entire collection. . . . On Carla in the finale: Halter with wrapped waist and *huge full* skirt – all in ombré silk chiffon – yards and yards."

Believing then and now that Halston was "one of the really great designers," it is not surpris-ing that Rucci wanted to work for him. Dressed entirely in black cashmere, like the designer him-self, Rucci walked in off the street and asked Halston for a job. The year was 1980. "Halston was intimidating as hell, wearing those dark glasses, so you couldn't see his expression," Rucci recalled. "I showed him my portfolio. There was a sketch of a red dress. He said 'How is that made? What is the pattern for this like?' I said, 'Like an X-shaped sculpture by Ronald Bladen'. Then he said,' 'See Mr. Cardello'."

Salvatore Cardello had apprenticed with Balenciaga before going to work for Halston. Now he passed on his knowledge to Rucci. "I thought he was sadistic. He made me do things over and over. But he said, 'If you want to do couture . . .' I draped and cut under Mr. Cardello." Ultimately, however, working at Halston proved too "crazy," and Rucci left after less than a year. He then worked briefly for Stanley Platos on Seventh Avenue, gaining additional practical experience. But he really wanted to create his own collection.

an homage to couture

In 1981, Rucci left Halston. His aunt loaned him $10,000 to create and show his first collection. He remembers that Vivian Van Natta urged him to "make the entire collection in taupe hammered satin – it would be so chic!" That proved far beyond his budget, but they bought remnants of couture fabric in cocoa brown, pearl gray and ivory from Abraham, the best fabric supplier in New York.

Rucci designed, draped, cut, and fitted the entire collection, working in his studio apartment, assisted only by a draping model and two sample-makers who arrived after their day jobs. Van Natta came every day after work, bringing food and useful gifts, such as a pair of basketball player's kneepads, since Rucci was spending hours on his knees, cutting things on the floor. "He was so driven," she recalls. "That collection was the biggest labor of love ever."

Rucci's first collection, *An Homage to Couture*, was an experiment in cut, inspired by Madame Grès. Every piece was cut on the bias – tunics and trousers, silk rainwear, and body-worshipping evening dresses. The *pièce de résistance* was a dress with a hand-sculpted bodice attached to a skirt made from 109 yards of ivory silk chiffon, entirely hand-fluted by Rucci himself. Impressed by the dresses, the models agreed to work without pay.

The show was held on 4 November 1981 in the ballroom of the Westbury Hotel, where Madame Grès had shown. The music was Thomas Newman's "Variations on a Theme." Rucci invited everyone who had been listed on the program for Madame Grès's benefit fashion show, and he had also acquired a list of Valentino's clients. Van Natta addressed every envelope by hand and telephoned every person invited: "Hello, is Mrs. Onassis there?" It was a 'who's who' of the history of couture: Doris Duke, Gloria Guinness, Jacqueline Onassis, Diana Vreeland. None of them came. Family, friends, and one journalist attended. Rucci sold one dress. But it was an undeniably beautiful collection.

For the next few years Rucci freelanced wherever he could. He designed a collection for an Italian Contessa, who failed to credit him and tried to wriggle out of paying him. His great friend Eve Orton, the fur and fabrics editor at *Harpers Bazaar* under Diana Vreeland, helped him get a job ghost-designing a hat collection for Joan Collins. These jobs helped support his tiny one-man business, custom-designing garments for individual clients.

Then in 1984 he opened his own ready-to-wear company, working initially in two fabrics: black or ivory wool knit, mixed with black, chocolate, or flesh-colored double-faced satin. Within a year, one of his dresses entered the permanent collection of the Victoria and Albert Museum in London.

"Rucci, 29, loves to intellectualize about his elegant ready-to-wear collection," reported *Women's Wear Daily* (December 31, 1985). "He cites Elsa Peretti and Pauline de Rothschild as his influences, the first for her 'biomorphic nature' and the second for 'creating harmony out of disorder'." Throughout his career, Rucci's attempts to analyze his work have frustrated fashion journalists accustomed to a very different kind of discourse. But he was serious about his work and his inspirations. "The clothes are understated," Rucci said. "But my version of understated is dramatic, so that you know the woman is an individual."

"Seventh Avenue's other Ralph lets his quality do the talking," said Cathy Horyn in her first article on Rucci, published in *The Detroit News* (June 28, 1987). "For every Calvin Klein, there are probably one hundred Ralph Rucci's, relatively anonymous but ambitious [designers] with a refined sense of taste and not a whole lot of money." Yet according to the young reporter, Rucci "hasn't veered from his original ideals of understatement and superb workmanship. Nor has he been willing to sacrifice quality for lower prices. His clothes are priced from $380 to $3,700 – not exactly a steal, but certainly in line with better-known labels."

Buyers, as well as journalists, were discovering Rucci's clothes. The famous retailer Martha not only carried Rucci's clothes, but decided to feature them in the windows of her store on Park Avenue. Coming home from work late at night Rucci came upon the windows by accident.

Then everything fell apart. A major department store placed a large order in 1987, but cancelled in mid-production after the stock market crash, leaving Rucci $200,000 in debt. He went out of business.

a subway couturier

For the next few years, Rucci struggled to survive as a designer, while he paid off all his debts. "I was sort of a lobby, subway couturier," he recalls. "I would meet my pattern-makers in lobbies of the buildings where they were working full time. I would meet sample makers on subway stops with silk chiffon gowns."[20]

Even as he struggled to survive financially, Rucci continued to pursue his aesthetic vision. "Seams no longer decorate; they are there for cause and subliminal effect," Rucci noted to himself in 1987. "Seams become relief, and cut echoes thought." A year later, he reminds himself: "Seams to be used as etchings and in some way to create a bas-relief." His design philosophy focused on cutting clothing "biomorphically," to follow the lines of the body," and create the appearance of simplicity.

Finally in 1994, he scraped together enough money to start over. He called his new company "Chado" after the elaborate Japanese tea ceremony of the same name. Consisting of 331 steps, the ceremony was designed to create a feeling of grace and serenity. Rucci decided not to name the company after himself, because he felt that multiple attempts to relaunch his business under

Below and following page:
Views of Ralph Rucci's atelier.
Photographs: Dan Mayers.

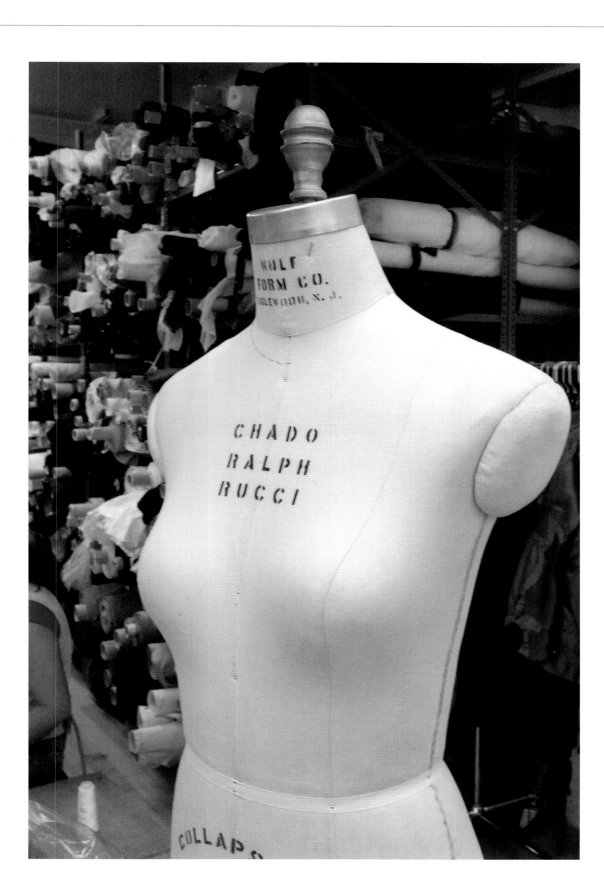

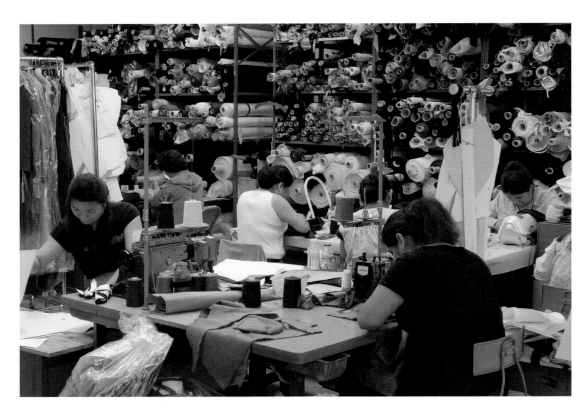

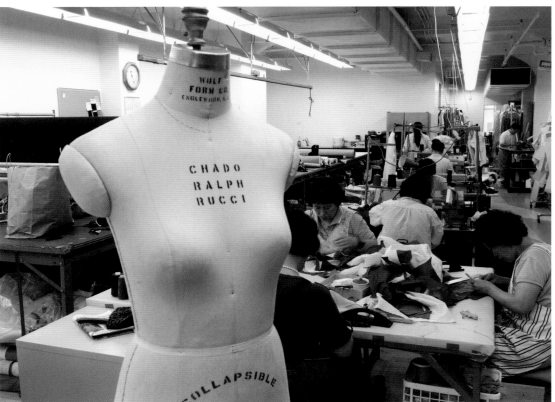

his own name had led the industry to perceive him negatively. He also wanted to acknowledge his small team of skilled workers: "We had to include all these genius technicians." For despite his financial ups and downs, Rucci's single-minded dedication to the craft of fashion had attracted some highly skilled collaborators. Later, Neiman Marcus convinced him to add his name to the label, so that the company became Chado Ralph Rucci.

Joan Kaner, then Senior Vice President and Fashion Director for Neiman Marcus, greatly admired Rucci's signature style, based on quality and craftsmanship, and featuring virtuoso cuts and exquisite curvilinear seams. She wore Rucci's clothes everywhere in Europe in an effort to convince her colleagues that he was a designer worth supporting. Kaner was convinced that there was a market for special clothes and clients for whom money was no object. Eventually she convinced the Dallas branch of Neiman Marcus to carry Rucci's clothes, and soon they were selling briskly at stores across the United States.[21]

If he was ignored by the press, he could go directly to the consumer. "He's got a great head for business," says Van Natta. "Everyone else has a Pierre Bergé." (Her reference, of course, is to Yves Saint Laurent's brilliant business partner. Unwilling to compromise on quality, Rucci gradually achieved considerable financial success. Twice a year, during New York Fashion week, Rucci showed his luxurious ready-to-wear collection, initially in his showroom, and later in the tents at Bryant Park. Soon he was selling not only at Neiman Marcus, but also at Saks Fifth Avenue and at Bergdorf Goodman in New York City.

Regional newspapers, such as *The Philadelphia Inquirer*, *The San Francisco Chronicle*, *The Houston Chronicle*, and *The Palm Beach Daily News* began to run enthusiastic articles about Rucci's clothes. As he traveled around the country, Rucci explained his design philosophy. "I don't do trends"; the important thing was the cut, the execution, the metier. He quoted Mies van der Rohe: "God is in the details." It was all about the make: "A seam is there for fit, not pretty lines," Rucci told one reporter. "I might as well use a piece of rick-rack if I only wanted a visual effect."[22]

•

"Ralph Rucci is one designer, working almost anonymously and with a word-of-mouth following around the country (he does the trunk show circuit), who concentrates on the product," Cathy Horyn reminded readers of the *New York Times*. "He keeps evolving without fanfare."[23] Rucci is "totally underplayed," she reminded *Women's Wear Daily*; "he has a great workroom that is the equivalent of anything in Europe."[24]

Looking at his "incredibly well-made clothes," she asked herself: "Why aren't people responding to this?" Looking back, she concludes: "There is no excuse for why journalists didn't go to see [Rucci]. There were lots of things about his work that should have attracted attention. It was monastic, strict, minimalist, luxurious." Journalists were "lazy," and also "it was Tom Ford Time, and Ralph was the opposite. He was so serious."[25]

"When he started Chado, in the mid-1990s, it was the era of Tom Ford at Gucci," agrees Vivian Van Natta. Whereas Gucci produced flashy clothes that screamed sex and money, Rucci was all about discretion. Van Natta says that she never even bothered to try to show Chado to women carrying Gucci bags. "Ralph's clients all have Hermès bags, or else something very individual. They are cultivated women who want to look elegant. They are not fashion victims."

"He had the yearnings of any great designer," says Horyn, "but he had the pressure of the clients and the need for money." As a result, she believes, he made too many "client clothes," such as "store suits" in double-faced cashmere. "He hurt himself using those heavy fabrics. The clients may have wanted it, but it was out of step with what was going on in fashion." Rucci disagrees with this assessment, insisting that he believes in these materials, but he would probably agree with Horyn's conclusion: that then "two big things happened: He went to Paris, and he got attention."

"I'm not for everybody," Rucci told *The Houston Chronicle* in 2001. "I make the most expensive clothes in the United States, not because I want to, but because I want the best."[26] Indeed, it was precisely because he "couldn't do a less expensive collection" that Rucci decided to do haute couture. "So the ready-to-wear becomes the less expensive collection, even though it's so expensive."[27] Even his simplest ready-to-wear often includes couture touches, such as lambskin inserts in a wool crepe dress, but Rucci's emphasis on luxurious fabrics and imaginative details has resulted in truly extraordinary couture ensembles.

the lightness, the memory

"Being able to participate in the haute couture, I feel more confident to express additional eccentricity and luxury in my ready-to-wear collection," Rucci observes in one of his many notebooks. At another point, he muses: "The HC becomes the essence – distilled into RTW. Would I feel accomplished? – *No*. The HC and the RTW must be separate." It was, of course, twice as much work. No sooner had he shown his first haute couture collection in Paris in July 2002 then he had to design and show his ready-to-wear Chado Ralph Rucci collection in New York in September. Indeed, even while he was in Paris, he was busy faxing sketches of ready-to-wear designs back to his workroom in New York. Then he was back to Paris again for his next couture show in January 2003.

Rucci's second haute couture collection (spring/summer 2003) was his all-white collection, featuring every shade of white, cream, ecru, and ivory, darkening to beige. There were deceptively simple dresses, delicately ribbed with leather or tacked with ribbons. An alabaster silk jersey gown featured an airy hand-knotted bodice. Silvery-white trousers were paired with a matching shirt-jacket. Materials ranged from cashmere to chiffon, with touches of alligator. An ivory silk organza gown was hand-painted and embroidered for an abstract effect, inspired by one of Rucci's own paintings that "had to do with existing in one realm and aspiring to a higher realm." The dress featured a message written upward and embroidered in black mohair yarn, the "words with hair growing out of them."

"His technical virtuosity promises him a beautiful future," declared *Libération*. His graphic cuts and expressive surface decoration inspired by Cy Twombly conveyed a welcome "modernity" that compared favorably with the "historicism" typical of many European couturiers, declared another French journalist.[28] Suzy Menkes was one of many journalists who found the collection to be "younger and fresher" than his first collection.[29] Rucci's work has "impeccable grace," and belongs to the same "school of elegance" as Jackie Kennedy's style (then on display at the Musée de la Mode), noted *Le Figaro* (24 January 2003), adding: "Welcome to Paris."

L'Officiel (February 2003) proclaimed Rucci's second collection "in line with the greats, equal to Valentino . . . His collection is splendid, refined, and sophisticated." *Madame Figaro* (February 15, 2003) described Rucci as "the anti-show-off par excellence, but [with] a hyper-elegant silhouette and incredible workmanship and materials . . . the chic-est style." Even *Le Monde* (February 1, 2003) praised the work of his atelier, while still noting the "sometimes icy sophistication" of his work.

In a gallery on the Avenue Matignon on Thursday, July 10, Rucci presented his third haute couture collection (autumn/winter 2003). Erin O' Conner walked the runway in a dark-brown ostrich-skin coat with matching trousers and an over-sized satchel. As *Le Monde*'s reporter observed, since Yves Saint Laurent's departure, few couturiers were continuing the tradition of elegant day clothes, such as a safari jacket in alligator or a cigaline trench "light as breath." "In his third couture outing, Ralph Rucci struck a home run," declared André Leon Talley on vogue.com. "What a difference from the High Mass Balenciaga severity of his first two efforts!"[30] Rucci himself told a journalist from *Le Monde* (July 12, 2003): "The difference between ready to wear and couture is the lightness, the memory."

Working with Parisian embroidery houses, including Lesage, Le Marie and Jean Pierre Olier, Rucci was able to create extraordinary pieces, such as a jacket knotted in leather that took 600 hours of skilled work. But it was not just that the sheer luxury and workmanship was breathtaking. Rucci's experimentation with handwork brought a new and "very specific vision" to the couture. Traditionally, embroiderers simply worked on the surface, but Rucci's knotted leatherwork was "integral to the structure of the garment," says Hamish Bowles. "I've never seen anything like it anywhere," agrees Deeda Blair, "and it was totally part of his aesthetic."

"I feel that this was my best collection ever," says Rucci today. The elements were "severe, yet light," with "abstracted cultural references." A pleated gown of tobacco-colored chiffon was surmounted with a sexy crocodile bodice. Equally dramatic was a black silk satin skirt with a design of hand-painted brush strokes of bleach under a bodice of sheer black chiffon. A brown cashmere skirt suit was delicately embroidered with leather. There was a knitted sable jacket and another decorated with ostrich feathers, a petrol silk raincoat over a dark petrol silk faille blouson and trousers. The last look that came down the runway had a black lace and silk chiffon appliqué bodice worn with a black silk marquisette skirt trimmed with mongolian lamb and coq feathers. "Grand luxury . . . magnificently executed," declared *Le Figaro*. (July 11, 2003). "It is so perfect that it is almost cold."

In January of 2004, Rucci presented his couture in a magnificent hotel particulier complete with the original boiseries, stunning chandeliers, and (as Suzy Menkes observed) "a big showing of enthusiastic clients." Alek Wek was first to come down the runway in a dress with a wood-beaded, cut-away bodice. Another look consisted of an organza skirt by Olier and a bodice embroidered by Lesage to resemble little pieces of ice. The image of a Pompeian fresco was silk-screened on a third dress. Suzy Menkes described Rucci as "the heir to the codes of tradi-

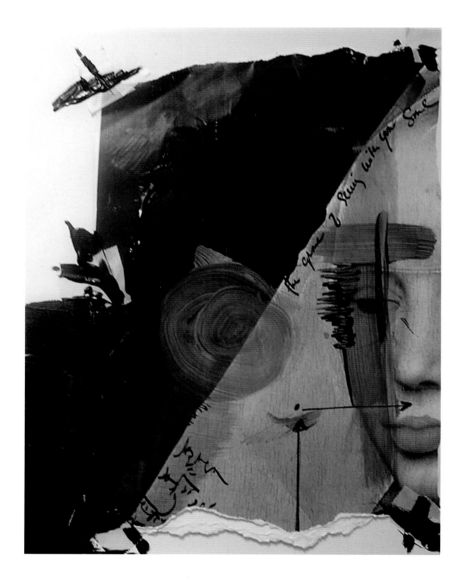

Left: *Reconciliation*   18
Ralph Rucci
Mixed media on canvas
Photograph courtesy of Serge
Sorroko.

Facing page: *X-Infanta*, 2005
Ralph Rucci
Mixed media on canvas
Photograph courtesy of Serge
Sorroko.

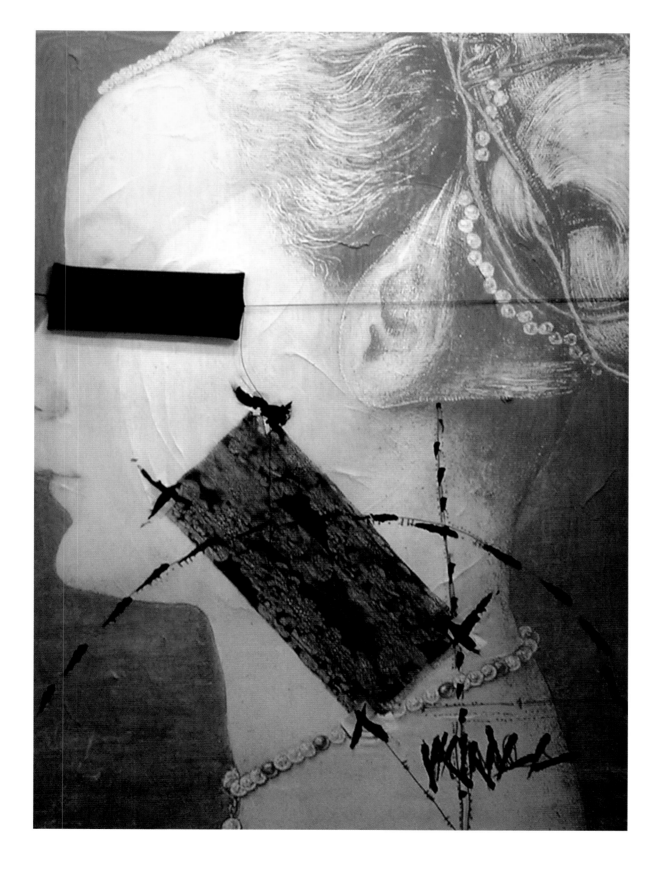

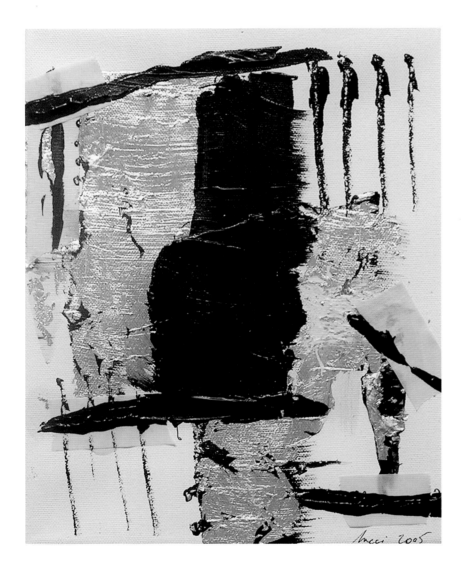

Left: *Witness*
Ralph Rucci
Mixed media on canvas
Photograph courtesy of
Serge Sorroko.

Facing page: *Suspended
Destination*
Ralph Rucci
Mixed media on canvas
Photograph courtesy of
Serge Sorroko.

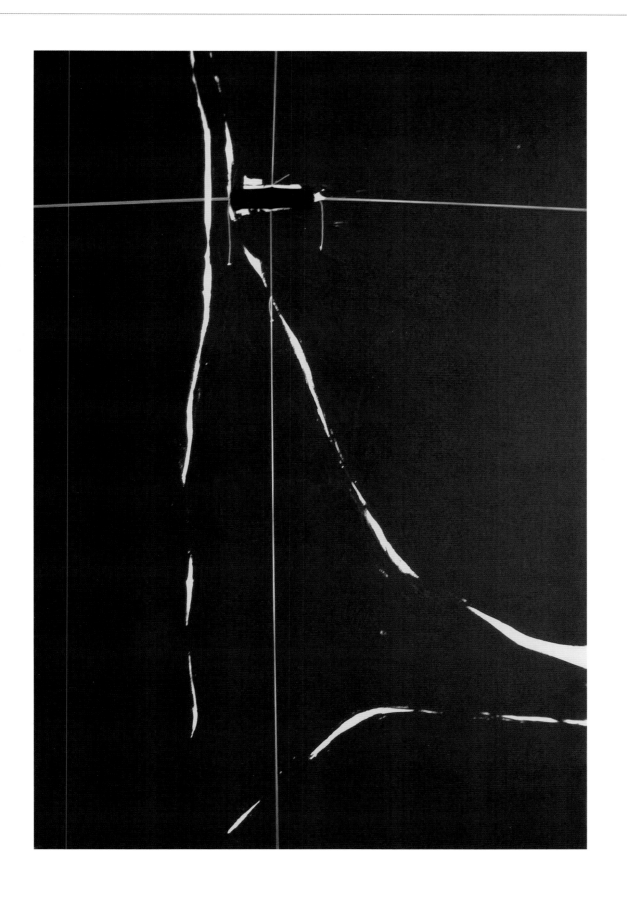

tional haute couture – and not just in the stiff swish of faille, organdy and duchess satin. Those Balenciaga-inspired sculptures, though finely done by Rucci, inevitably look as though they belong to another era. His more contemporary tailored pieces had a fresh feeling."[31] Certainly, a sleeveless evening dress lightly embroidered with ostrich feathers from the fourth couture collection seems almost supernaturally light.

"Haute couture is often justified as a laboratory in which designers test ideas that might eventually cross over to the ready-to-wear mainstream," wrote veteran fashion journalist Tim Blanks. "In Rucci's case, this is actually true." Already "one of America's technically most accomplished designers," Rucci's experience in Paris has resulted in many new ideas for his ready-to-wear collections.[32] Beginning in 2005, Rucci's ready-to-wear collection in New York has also featured some ensembles from his haute couture collection.

"Reports of Couture's Death were Exaggerated," announced the *New York Times* in one of those articles that periodically assesses the viability of an industry with only a few hundred clients worldwide. "With so many couturiers focusing on red-carpet clothes, Ralph Rucci... has found a niche with his day suits and coats which range from the quietly sublime. . .to the coolly possessed." As Horyn noted, the Paris couture had given Rucci tremendous exposure, while also liberating him in terms of what he could create.[33] But it is a very expensive proposition to show at the couture in Paris, especially on top of showing in New York, and without the benefit of perfume or accessory sales. In 2005, when his mother died, Rucci decided not to show in Paris, at least temporarily.

the dress of thought

"I can only suggest clothes that dress a person's mind," Rucci wrote in one of his notebooks in 1987. "This may seem philosophical, but . . . clothes are just another language we use to help communicate the structures and contents of our minds." "I am attempting to dress individuals who know that clothes are merely an outward expression of the inner self." His ideal woman is someone "who is in the state of developing and refining her own self and mind."

What does it mean to dress a woman's mind? "His clothes make an emotional connection to a woman's intelligence," explains veteran trend-forecaster David Wolfe.[34] They are thoughtful clothes, because a great deal of thought and emotion went into creating them. "It doesn't come easily," admits Rucci. "The eye is so discerning, and it has to connect with the heart."

"These are not 'career clothes' or 'social' clothes – just strong clothes for strong women," Rucci writes.[35] Words that recur again and again in his vocabulary are grace, poise, femininity, strength. "What inspires me constantly is the most lasting, modern, and timeless quality in a woman . . . Grace." For a Roman Catholic like Rucci, grace may imply a spirtual state, but grace is also a physical characteristic. As a designer, Rucci necessarily dresses bodies, as well as minds. In 1987, he writes: "There is also a sexual side, which I hope I have muted in such a way as to produce a quiet sensual intensity, as opposed to an overt statement. The clothes, I hope, add femininity to women only insofar as they are mirrors which echo a woman's gestures."

Like the poet Charles Baudelaire immortalizing a passerby, Rucci envisions an indissoluable relationship between the woman and the dress. "You cannot have style or chic in a garment," he says. "A garment [alone] can not possess these qualities. It must be like a marriage between a woman who has these qualities, which then become attached to the garment. On its own, the garment could be seen as some kind of thought piece. Notice that I did not say 'a work of art'." But, he implies, the garment only really comes alive when it is worn by the right woman. "I want to create clothes that allow a woman's style to merge with the garment, so that they become one," he explains. "The way to do this is not through minimalism or decoration, but by making clothes in a new way so that the cut and construction become like the scent of a woman's perfume. So that when people see women in my clothes, they are captivated by the totality of what they sense."

"Many designers make beautiful, chic, elegant clothes. What I try to do is empower the woman through her experience of the clothes." When the chemistry is right between the woman and the dress, something extraordinary happens. "The clothes ignite, I think, a sense of spiritual awareness. The woman realizes: it's not just the garment, it's her *self* that is brought forward, empowered, elevated."

"He wants to make the world a better place," says Rucci's colleague, Vivian Van Natta. "How do you do that by making a jacket?" She admits that women do get "emotional" about Rucci's clothes, and say they feel "good" and "confident" in them. By wearing clothes that are undeniably special, clothes that have "integrity," the wearer may, perhaps, feel elevated. Hamish Bowles suggests, though, that the very "perfectionism" of the clothes may "make demands of the wearer." If so, this could be a double-edged sword, since not everyone wants to live up to her clothes. Certainly, in practical terms, Rucci's clothes do not make demands on the wearer. Quite the contrary, they are extremely comfortable and flattering. One woman even told me that she vacuumed and loaded the dishwasher while wearing a Rucci dress.

From an early age, Rucci has been doing what he calls "research," collecting images and ideas. "I carry an inventory of people in my mind, who are touchstones for my work," he says. Some of these people he has known personally; others he only met through his research – a distinction he refers to as "lived experience" versus "felt experience." But in both cases, he says that he learns from them. "I use my memories of their characteristics and apply this to designing the clothes." There is thus a circle: from the original inspiration (say, Pauline de Rothschild) to the designer, to the garment he creates, to the woman who wears it, who, in turn, may become an inspiration for the designer (although, obviously, he only meets a few of the people who wear his clothes).

"There are things that he has seen, that linger with him, and that he interprets in his own way," says Deeda Blair. Rucci's notebooks are filled with photographs, sketches, and images clipped from magazines. Not surprisingly, many are photographs of his icons: Balenciaga, Grès, Pauline de Rothschild, Diana Vreeland. There are also images of architectural interiors, such as Elsa Peretti's living room in Rome designed by Renzo Mongiardino. Many of the rooms that he admires seem to exhibit a nostalgia for the past, without being literal reproductions of past styles. They may be grand, but they are also highly individual spaces – much like the people he admires, and the clothes he designs.

"Editing is the key," reads a type-written note on the wall of Rucci's office. "Elegance is a state of mind that carries you through absolutely every situation – problems, happiness, depression – it has absolutely nothing to do with money. Elegance is the quiet, secret cloak . . . that separates those who have it from those who do not."

Art is very important to Rucci, who lives and works surrounded by paintings and sculpture – especially Asian art (a Shang-dynasty ax-head, a Khmer torso, a Southeast Asian Buddha, a Tang dynasty tomb sculpture), as well as modern and contemporary works by painters such as Francis Bacon, Antonio Tapies, and Cy Twombly, as well as sculptors such as Yves Dana. Rucci himself is a painter, whose abstracts have been exhibited, and have sometimes seved as an influence on his fashion designs. Once when he was inspired by a Cy Twombly painting, Rucci's studio created a drawing that was sent to the House of Lesage to be embroidered on a dress. "Today Mr. Lesage called and asked if I wanted the brush strokes to be angry or calm," Rucci told Cathy Horyn. "That's why I go to Europe."[36]

"Pure minimalism I find very dull, one-dimensional and lacking any spark of psychological edge," says Rucci. By contrast, "Asian art may be minimal, but there is a beautiful sound that goes through it." This applies both to the "stark shape" of a kimono and, for example, "the glazes on Sung dynasty ceramics." There are "elements of calligraphy," he suggests, that are like "beautiful stepping stones into the world of Franz Klein" or Cy Twombly. "If I took out my [contact] lenses, a Cy Twombly could look like calligraphy."

His notebooks include many pictures of works of art, which range widely in style. There is a a Mannerist painting, a Venetian masquerade by Pietro Longhi, classical statues – both nudes and figures clad in drapery – as well as examples of applied art, such as furniture. Some of these images have a clear relevance to his work. For example, an abstract sculpture by Xavier Corberó consisting of a group of vaguely neo-classical columns recalls the abstract shapes and subtle variations in form and texture characteristic of Rucci's fashions. Another image of an abstract modern sculpture triggers a pen-and-ink sketch of a jacket and skirt.

Throughout his career, Rucci has gravitated to a palette of black, white, beige and taupe, although he constantly tries to evolve beyond the comfort of neutrals. "I can make an entire collection in taupe; it is the shadow and the mystery of the mind's eye. But just because I like taupe, I cannot expect the public to only want taupe," he told the artist Iké Udé. "Halston taught me that super-rich women want color."[37] For his spring 2004 ready-to-wear collection, "Woman as Monolith," Rucci's notebooks list the following colors: beige, ecru, white, taupe, apple green, wet green. The following season, he favored gray, taupe, dark green, and black. For haute couture he mixes achromatic colors like black, ivory, pearl and dusk with bright apricot, violet, acid green and cinnabar. His signature color is cinnabar, because "it expresses everything from the Orient to Russia." Black is also central to his vision, being associated with deep space and "the movement of time," which he sees as being "directly related to the spiritual structure of the mind."

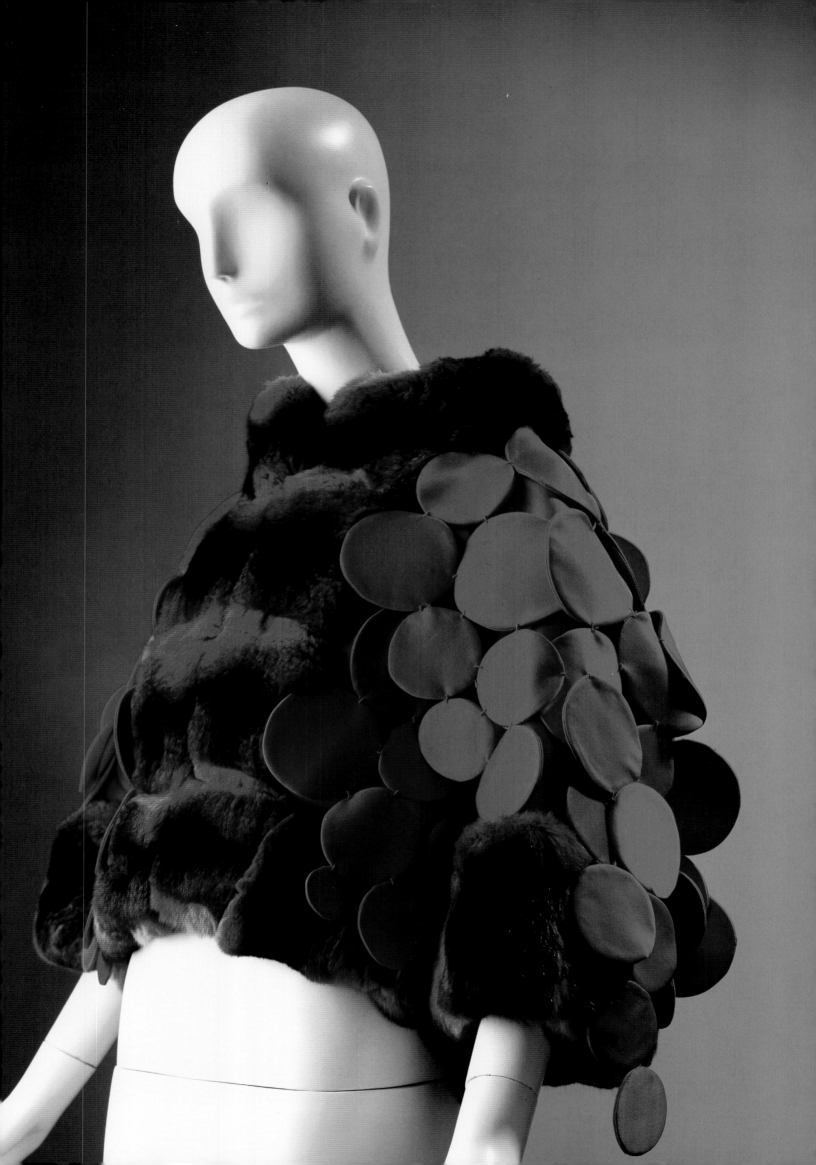

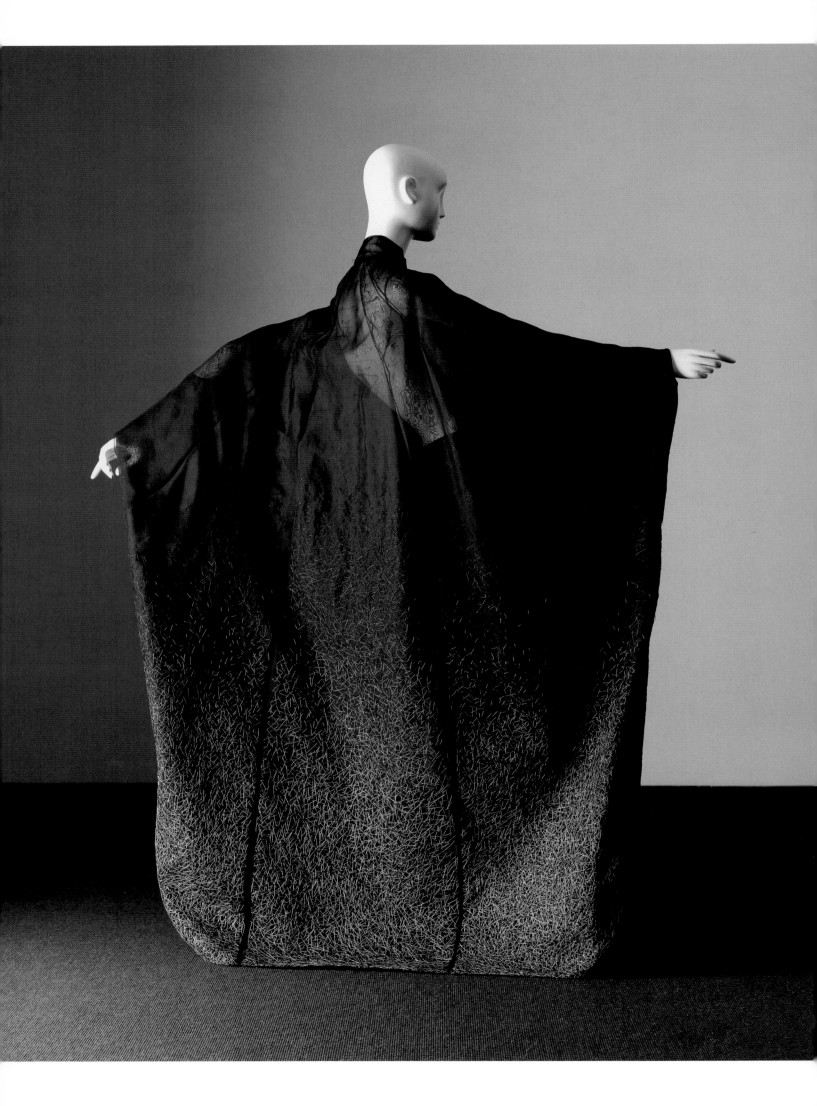

Facing page: silk organza caftan and
pants with embroidery, fall/winter
2005.
Photograph: William Palmer.

Below: hammered silk satin
pajamas, 1981.
Photograph: William Palmer.

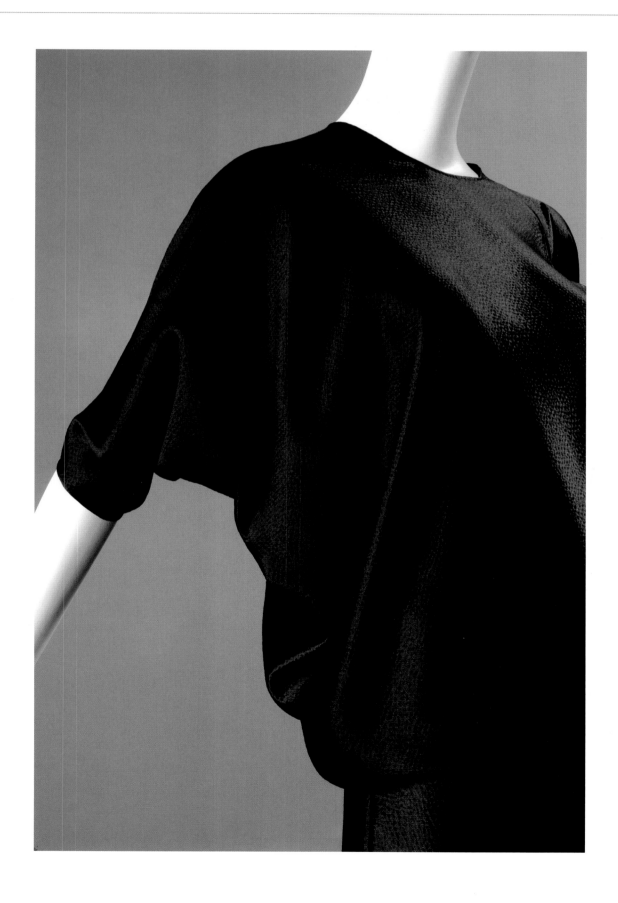

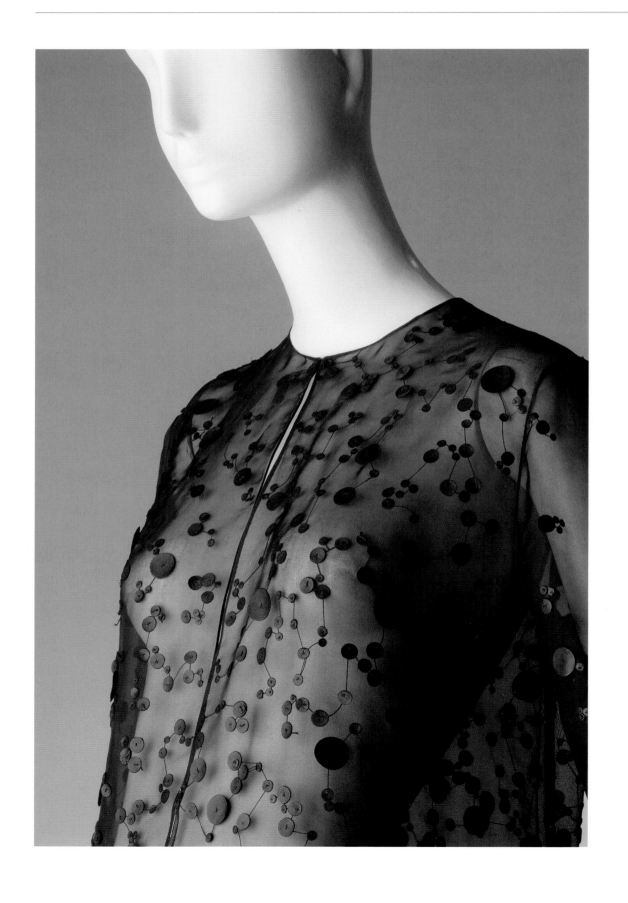

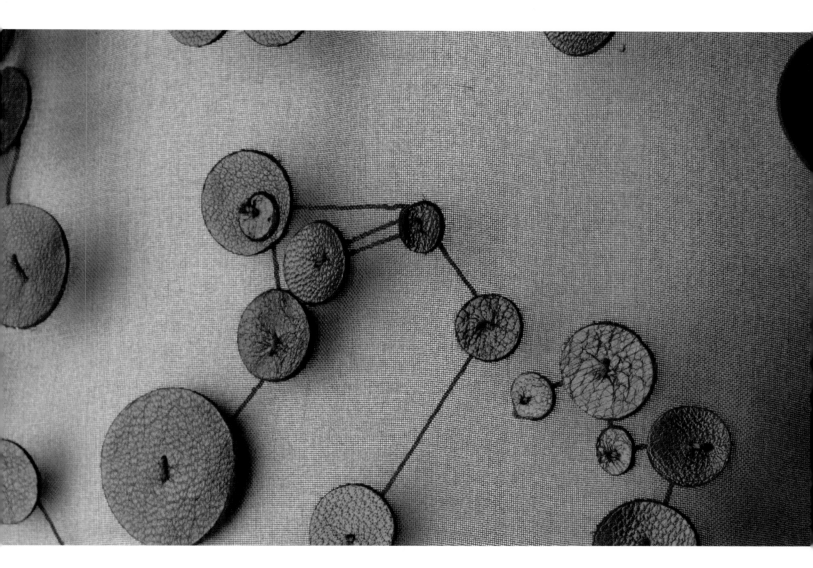

Silk organza jacket embroidered
with leather paillettes. Collection of
Tatiana Sorokko.
Photograph: William Palmer.

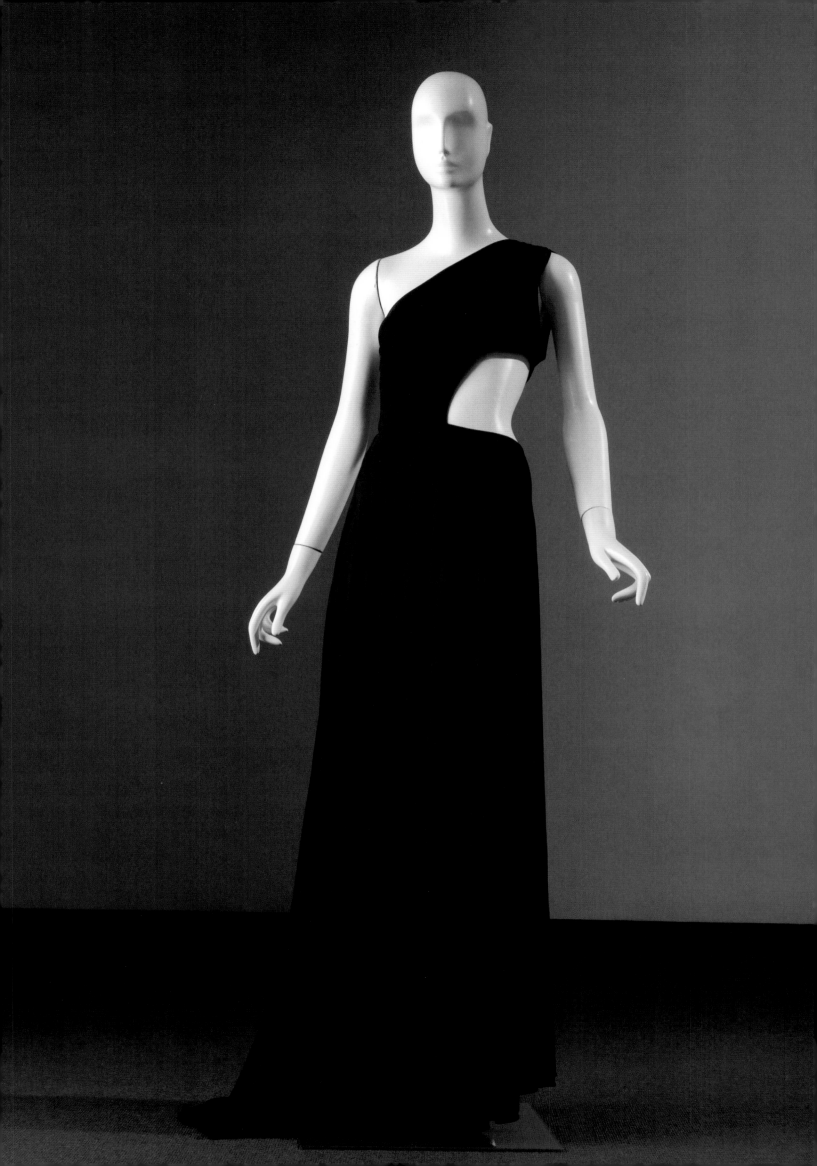

Black silk jersey
evening dress, 1981.
Photograph: William Palmer.

Detail of black lace and silk chiffon
appliquéd bodice and silk
marquisette skirt embroidered with
Mongolian lamb and trimmed coq
feathers, fall/winter 2004, haute
couture collection.
Photograph: William Palmer.

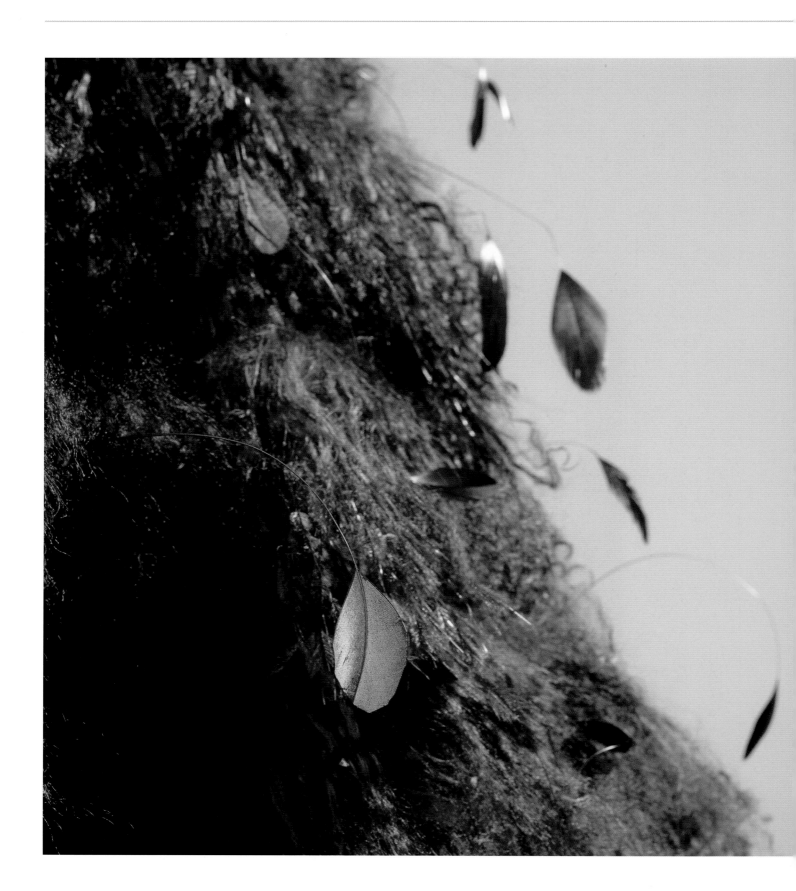

Detail of black cashmere coat
with silk floss embroidery, collection
of Tatiana Sorrokko.
Photograph: William Palmer.

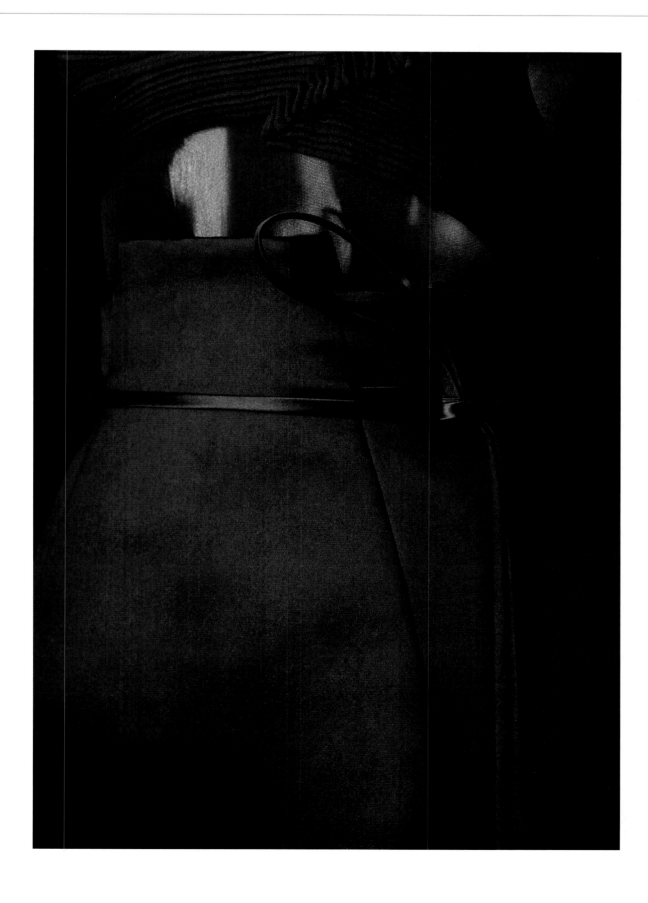

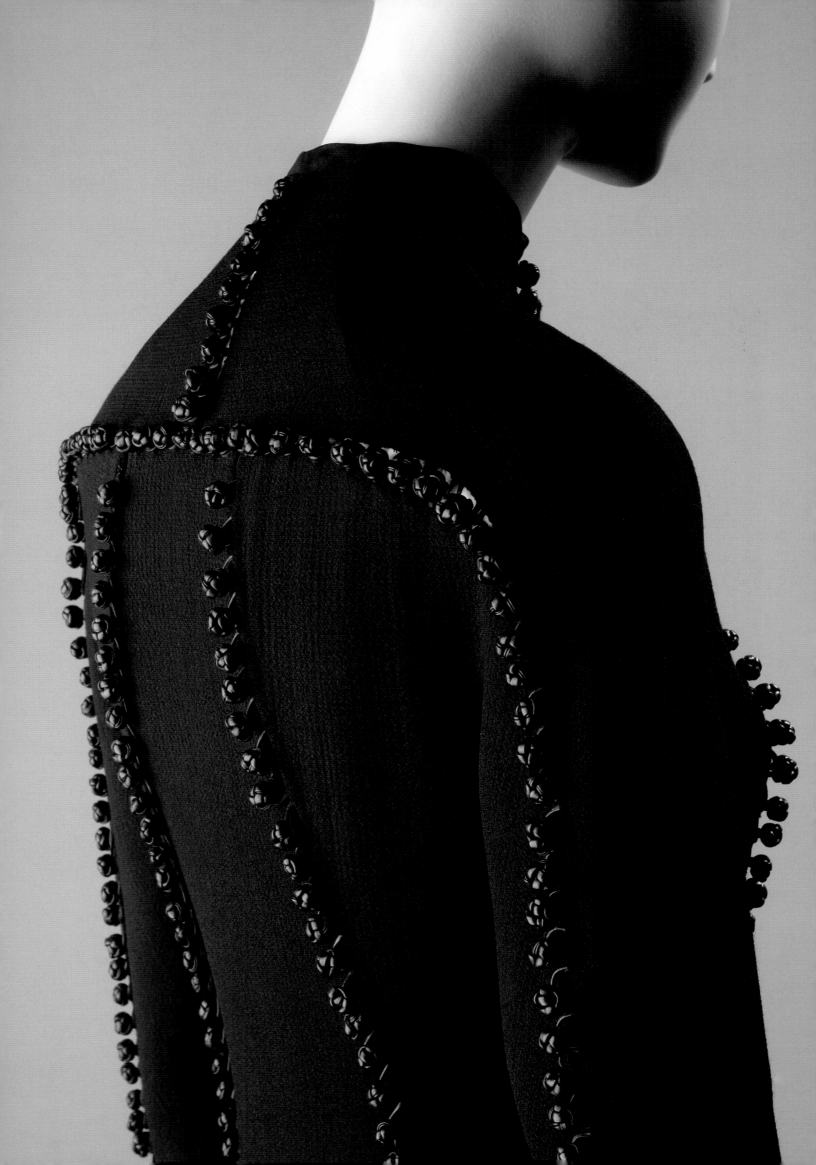

Button details, pieced black wool
crepe coat, haute couture fall/winter
2004.
Photograph: William Palmer.

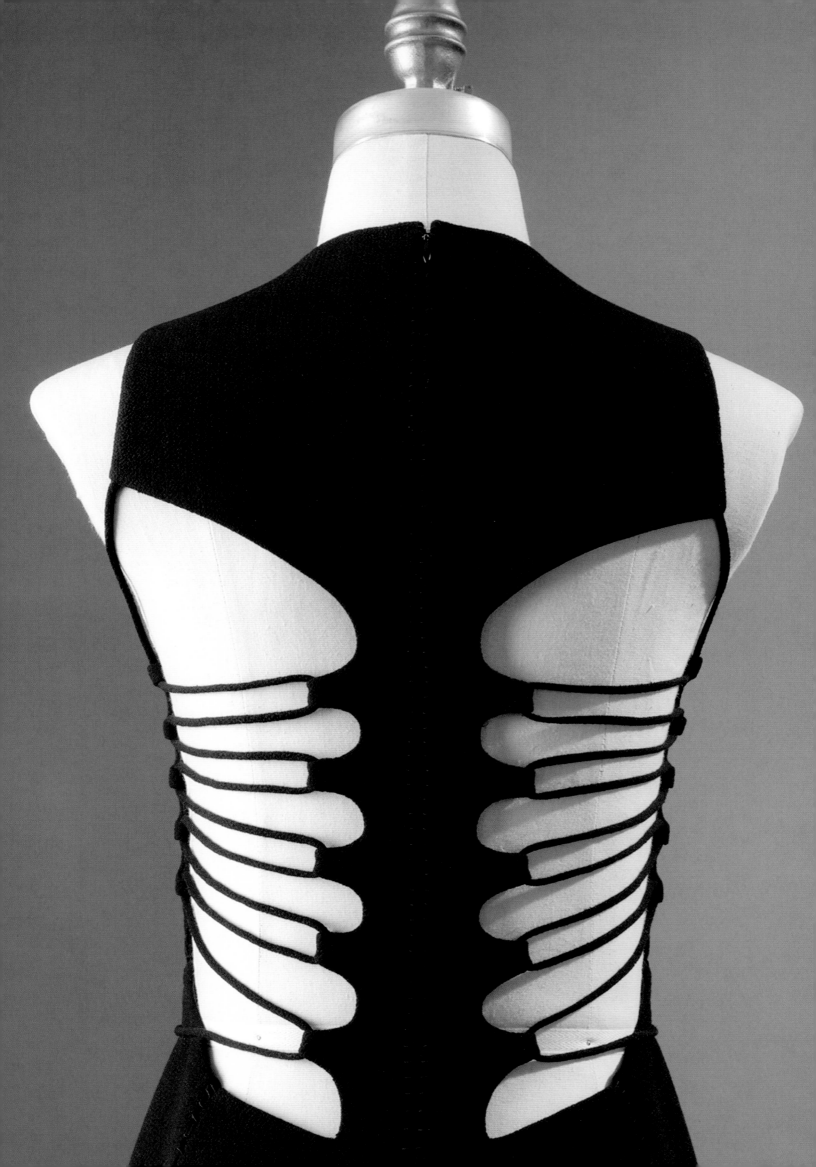

Black wool crepe "Vertabrae
back shift," ready-to-wear
collection, fall/winter 2004.
Photograph: William Palmer.

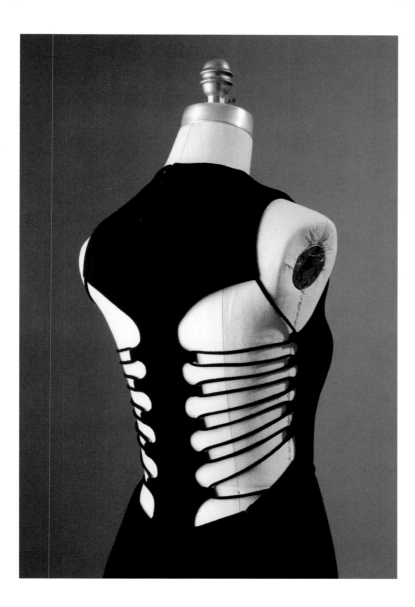

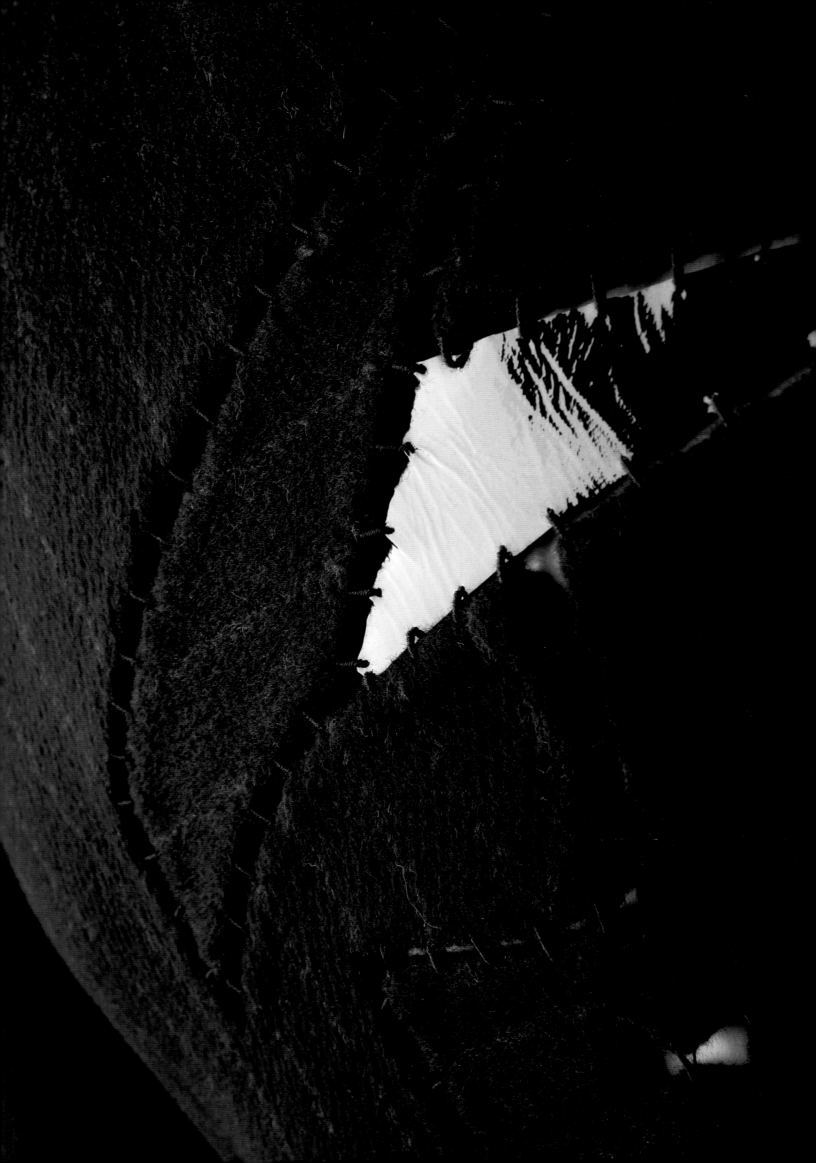

Facing page: suspension coat
detail, pinstriped vicuna, fall/winter
2006 ready-to-wear collection.
Photograph: William Palmer.

Below: detail of yarn embroidery.
Photograph: William Palmer.

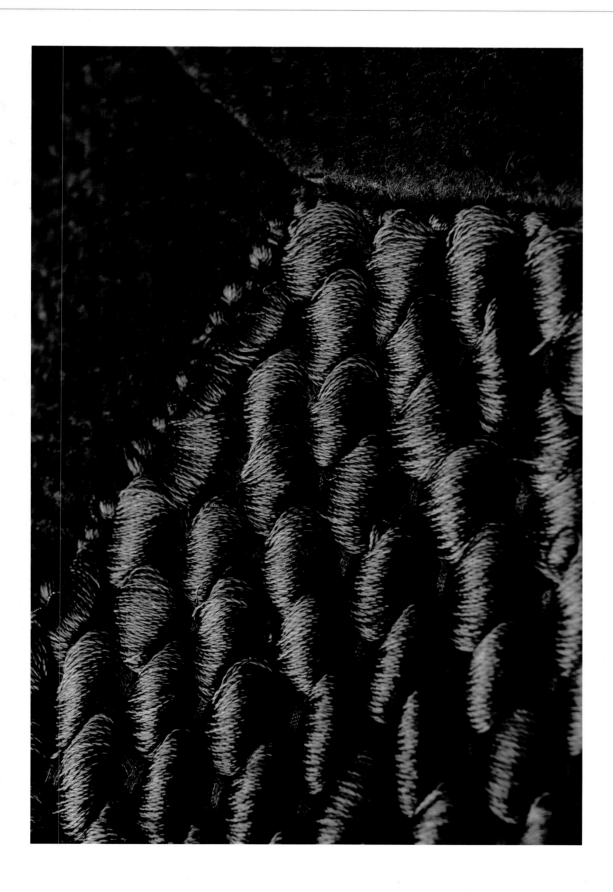

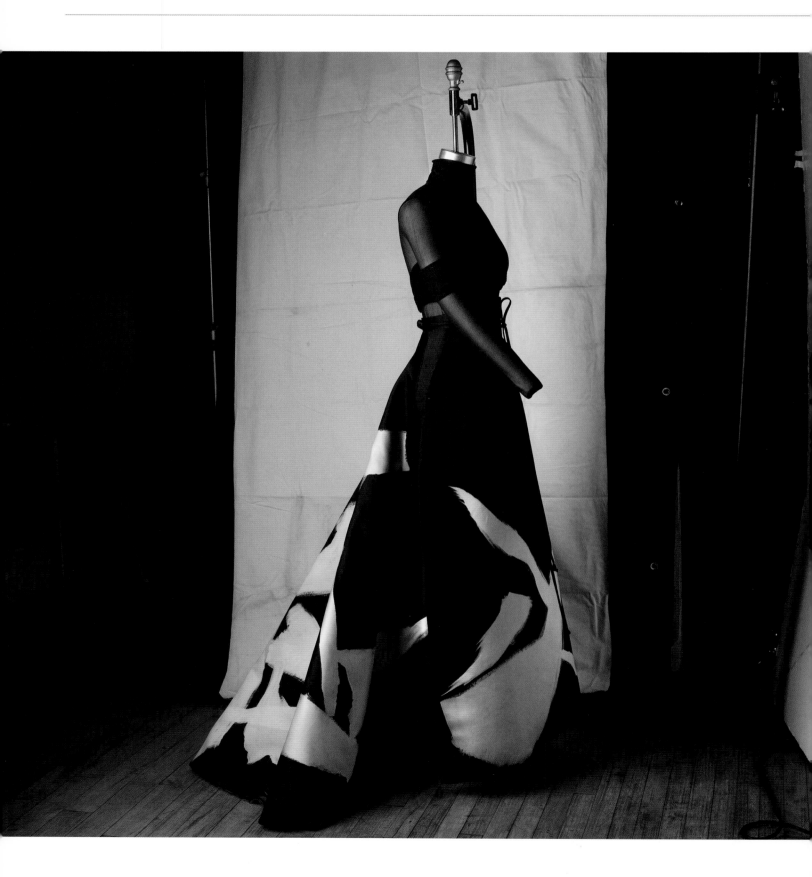

Black silk jersey fluted top, duchess
satin skirt with bleached
brushstroke, fall/winter 2003 haute
couture collection.
Photograph: William Palmer.

The notebooks also contain fashion images, both those clipped from magazines and his own fashion sketches. But what is intriguing are the juxtapositions. In one notebook, for example, several pages of fashion imagery from the 1920s to the 1960s are followed by a number of erotic photographs. A photograph of a white coat is overlaid with hand-drawn seams. On the facing page is a photographic close-up of a man's arm, the muscles and veins prominent. Seams and veins echo each other.

The anatomy of fashion is central to his vision. "All of my cuts come from what's beneath the skin," he says. "I think about how to cut clothes in three-dimensional ways – from the musculature to the veins beneath the skin. Balenciaga didn't do that. The first impetus I had to do this came from Elsa Peretti's biomorphic jewelry. It's the idea of the biomorphic respect for the woman's body."

There is in Rucci's work an intriguing combination of physicality and spirituality. On one side, there is a kind of mystic marriage between the woman and the dress. The woman is viewed with respect, even a kind of veneration. He dresses her mind. Yet on the other side, there is a real, and growing, emphasis on physicality. Rucci's clothes for women are becoming sexier, although never in a vulgar way. He believes that this evolution in his work stems from his growing comfort with his own sexuality.

"My physical attraction was always to men, but my intellectual stimulation came from women. I prefer the company of women intellectually," says Rucci. "Over the years, the clothes have become so much more sexy and feminine, and I think that's partly because I've become more accepting of my sexuality."

"I am dressing *women*," Rucci writes in one of his (undated) notebooks. "Femininity is perceived subliminally through their gestures and visibly through their figures, their legs, necks, breasts, hips. Overtly feminine touches on clothes do nothing but make a woman *effeminate*. A modern woman of the twenty-first century does not need a petticoat. We (as designers) cannot go to the eighteenth century for Watteau fantasies of milkmaids *à la polonaise*. Modern feminine clothes are about sensuality and fluidity. The cloth is closer to the body." Yet he can certainly be inspired by images of women from the past. "Think of a woman from the court of China or Japan," he says. "The poise, the grace, and the female dignity. It's just so seductive!"

The process of design remains somewhat mysterious, even miraculous. "It's not about sketching a coat and saying 'Here' . . . It's about *finding* it," Rucci says. "Suddenly, you get a thought – as though someone has spoken to you. That moment of receiving an idea is so joyous and empowering. It's like taking dictation from God." Religion is an important part of Rucci's life. Just as Kandinsky proposed the spiritual in art, so Rucci believes that fashion can be spiritual, and certain designers, such as Balenciaga, seem especially close to God. As for himself, "I don't feel that I do this all alone."

In the material world, material plays a crucial role. Both his couture and his ready to wear utilize luxurious, often extraordinary, fabrics. "I would close the door if I had to use synthetics," he says. "We have to allow the fabric to speak and synthetics do not have a wonderful vocabulary."[38] "When you hear the sound of a faille or the whoosh of taffeta or the oomph of a cashmere or the ahh of a chiffon, there is such mystery! And if you really hear it, the fabric tells you what to do, where to go. It's a handle on adjectives like intensity, dignity, sensuality. When you pull a length of taupe petral silk faille from the roll, the sound and the scent transport you to every atelier on the avenue Montaigne. It's that history, that secret church of the couture. I can't use synthetic fabrics. Many people think I'm obstinate, but I've tried and you cannot achieve the best result with synthetics. And fabric is so important, because it gives you the silhouette."

Not usually thought of as a "conceptual" designer, Rucci nonetheless begins by working with abstract concepts, such as the monolith, the black hole, the meaning of time and, recently, the idea of shadows and smoke. Once he has the concept, he begins research – looking at images, touching fabrics, thinking, and sketching. "I have to go back to a space inside to go forward." Of a collection inspired in part by prehistoric and ancient art, he writes in his notebook: "The ravages of time – weathered palette – architectural fragments – are these not part of history and antiquity which stimulate us most of all? – They move us – allowing new forms to emerge – strange fascination."[39]

Nature can also be a source of inspiration. One day Rucci saw a photographic magnification of an ant. The insect's thorax reminded him of crustaceans such as lobsters and horseshoe crabs. He began sketching rapidly. Suddenly he realized that when he sketched the places where four right angles met, and then cut them away, the division into quadrants produced a sense of movement. It came to him in a flash that he could apply the same principle of articulation to fabric draped over the female body.

Later the idea of articulation morphed into suspension, whereby the fabric is fragmented into parts, which are suspended by small chains of threads called "worms." In the beginning, Rucci and his team were only able to suspend a few strategically placed pieces, at the neckline, for example, or on the sleeves. But as time went on, the technique was increasingly applied to more and more of the garment, resulting in an extraordinary mosaic-like effect. Some of his suspension jackets require thirty hours of skilled labor.

It is through such techniques that Rucci gives lightness and ease of motion. Like his curved seams, these labor-intensive techniques are designed to improve the way the clothes fit and the way they feel on the body. They may look decorative, but they are integral to the construction of the garment. Technique merges with concept when "the idea of energy moving" inspired him to insert tiny flashes of orange in a white background.

For Rucci, creation is not a question of reproducing the *look* of something that inspired him. Instead, he asks himself: "How do you convey the *emotion*?" One of the things he admires about Cy Twombly is the way he "took the myths of ancient Greece and Rome, and reduced them to scribbling. But his works still have the majestic quality of the original subject matter."

a revisionist view

Rucci's work is difficult to characterize because it does not fit into any conventional category. The American fashion industry has always been about mass-produced clothes. The number of people who understand and appreciate cut and construction is limited, and diminishing. Today, even many expensive designer clothes are not particularly well made. Meanwhile, the haute couture,

Dress and short jacket, woven silk
ribbon, punched leather, cotton
piqué, spring/summer 2006 haute
couture collection.
Photograph: William Palmer.

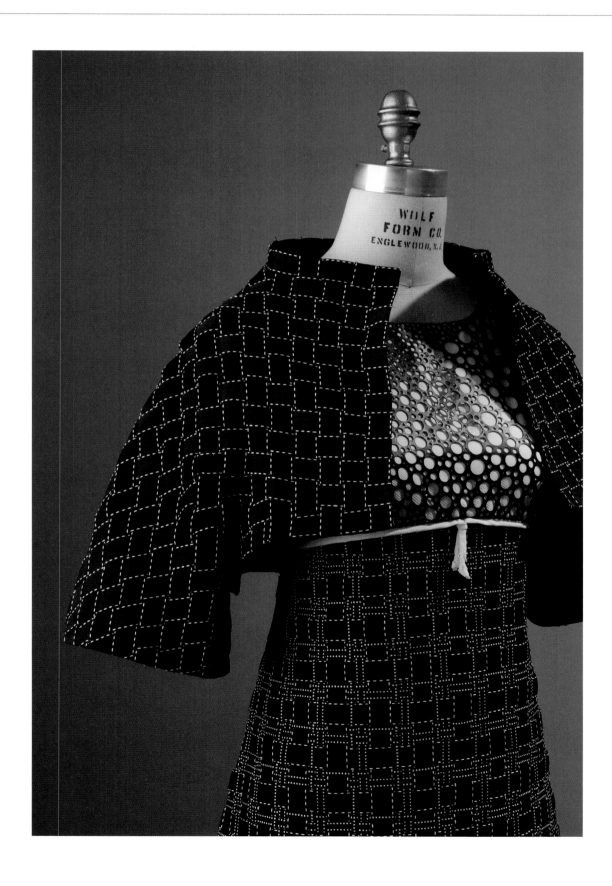

like the upscale ready to wear, has increasingly become a publicity-driven machine, where the focus is on the development of a strong brand identity. Theatrical shows featuring extreme fashions create headlines, which sell accessories and perfume. Rucci's emphasis on technique is meaningless for most people, while the gradual evolution of his style makes him less-than-newsworthy, from a journalist's perspective.

Because Rucci has "never played the game" and has "never been part of the trend-oriented fashion industry," journalists find it "difficult to fit him in," explains Hamish Bowles. "So much of fashion today is about constantly changing trends, and his fashion is more evolutionary, less revolutionary." Even journalists who are "awed by his technique" tend to believe that his style is "essentially conservative and lady-like."[40] Rucci is aware that many journalists see him as "representative of the old guard." Many compare him to classic American fashion designers, like the late Bill Blass and Geoffrey Beene.

Some of Rucci's supporters imply that there is a conspiracy to ignore him, that certain key figures in the fashion world deliberately leave him out of the picture. "It's like *Women's Wear Daily* ignoring Geoffrey Beene for all those years." Perhaps. But other factors are also probably at work. Rucci almost never advertises, for example, and editorial coverage tends to be closely related to advertising revenue. Nor does he cater to the editorial desire for trend-oriented looks. Rucci once said, "It's not about an editor's judgement, it's about my judgement."[41] Over time he has begun to acknowledge that at least some editors and journalists have a significant body of knowledge, and he respects their opinions, even if he does not always follow their advice.

On the other hand, Rucci has inspired tremendous loyalty and enthusiasm from his clients. "Ralph's clothes are never trendy or flamboyant," says Deeda Blair. "They are totally timeless. Many are extremely discreet, but they have a lasting and enduring quality to them. So many other designers create clothes that are so overwrought. Ralph's clothes look as though he made them with excitement and enthusiasm, but at the same time he has the discipline to be very exacting. "

Deeda Blair is the kind of cultivated and elegant woman who feels no need to impress other people with her clothes. "Rucci doesn't advertise or dress celebrities for the red carpet," she says. "He's not a household name. But he has an enthusiastic following." The reason, she implies, is because Rucci creates wearable, beautiful clothes that work perfectly in women's lives. For example, when she chaired "a really important dinner in Washington for the NIH," she had to give a public speech. "If you don't like to speak, wearing something wonderful can give you confidence. Ralph had made a wonderful white double-faced wool sleeveless dress, quiet and understated, which was just right for this occasion."

Rucci has said that he does not believe in designing clothes only for tall, thin, young women. His years of working directly with private clients has made him aware, as few designers seem to be, that women come in all sizes and ages. Marjorie Fisher, for example, says that she is a little over five feet tall and, although she has said that she plans to come back in her next life as a model-tall woman, she is able to wear many of Rucci's designs. As a woman of a certain age, the first time she saw Rucci's work, she thought "Here's the next Galanos!" Later she was lucky enough to be present when the couturier James Galanos came to "pay his respects" to Rucci.[42]

Galanos subsequently became a close friend and flew to Paris to attend Rucci's first haute couture show. Hubert de Givenchy and Philippe Venet are other great designers of a previous generation who admire Rucci's work.

Not that Rucci fails to cater for tall, young clients, too. Tatiana Sorokko met Ralph Rucci in the 1990s when she was a runway model. At that time, she had only recently emigrated from Russia, and her English was far from perfect. Rucci likes to tell the story of how she came to a fitting and showed her the dress he wanted her to wear, to which her reply was a blunt "Tatiana no like." Today she insists "Tatiana like very much!" – and she has an extensive personal collection of his work to prove it. Sorokko regards Rucci as "the greatest American designer, a true artist, in a different league than the others."[43] It is not only a question of quality and workmanship.

"The hardest thing is to create something timeless," says Sorokko. "It is a question of style versus fashion. It's easy to be trendy, but it's very difficult to create your own style. Every single time I wear Ralph's clothes, people ask me 'Who made that? Where did you get that?' He's a perfectionist."

The division between client and press is significant. The idea of "timeless" clothes is "not good for a designer," says Cathy Horyn. She talks about going to see the Balenciaga exhibition organized at the Mona Bismarck Foundation in Paris. Although the clothes on display were beautiful, they were "just the client clothes, not the most adventurous clothes" that Balenciaga ever made. No one would deny that Mona Bismarck had exquisite taste, but ultimately Balenciaga's greatest clothes came from his own imagination and from contemporary influences. She implies that the same could be said of Rucci. "You have to open a window! Not just look at pictures of Balenciaga and Mrs. Vreeland! And don't ever let your clients tell you what to do." By going to Paris and expanding his horizons, she says, Rucci was able to make his clothes "lighter" and more modern.

Does Rucci have an outmoded aesthetic? "There is nothing retro about what he does, except the way he does it," argues David Wolfe. "He's taking the great tradition forward, constantly refining the fashion aesthetic. Rucci is not cool and cutting-edge – he's way beyond that. He is immune to trend lunacy. He's really an artist. He's true to his own vision of perfection."[44] Rucci's clothes are completely "modern," insists Joan Kaner, but they also have "an elegance that's missing from our world today."

Rucci exists in "a parallel universe," suggests Bowles; he's creating "hieratic" clothes for "otherworldly beings." On the contrary, argues Amy Fine Collins, Rucci is a "modernist" designer in the "American sportswear" tradition. One of New York's most stylish figures, Collins recently began wearing Rucci after years of wearing exclusively Geoffrey Beene, and she argues that, like Beene, Rucci combines "practicality" with "a will to innovate and purify." Although "sportswear" is probably the last word that most people would associate with Rucci, she argues that he addresses "the anatomy of fashion," going into "the structure of things," rather than laboring over surface effects. His A-line skirts, for example, are "nearly sportswear because of the practicality," although they are much more luxurious.[45]

Rucci himself has said that he feels neither American nor European, but he would appreciate Collins' argument that he has something of an "Asian aesthetic, which is part of what makes him modern," because everything is purified, simplified. Collins is also extremely astute, I believe, in noticing that there is "a little bit of savage grace to his work," exemplified in his use of visible stitching, "like the sutures of a skilled surgeon," or the "whip-like" strings hanging from his ballgowns.

"I remember in one couture collection he did a jacket that looked like an antique Japanese basket made of leather and string," says Deeda Blair. "It was breathtaking. I've never seen anything like it anywhere – and it was totally part of his aesthetic. I think a huge part of Ralph is his appreciation for the work of others. I've visited him wearing an old Chanel suit, for example, and he's fascinated by how the shoulders are done. He's not jealous and competitive with other designers. There's a feeling that he's doing his own thing."

Asked about the living designers who he admires, Rucci enthusiastically describes, in no particular order, an eclectic group of individualists: "Roberto Capucci, because of his mastery of volume, the liberation of color, and the idea of fashion as sculpture . . . Of course, James Galanos brought such integrity and total originality to fashion . . . Azzedine Alaia took hard tailoring and made it more sexual than anyone could possibly imagine . . . There are the two greats of technique, Hubert de Givenchy and Philippe Venet . . . Rei Kawakubo, because she has so much in common with the path of experimentation that Balenciaga took, and because she allows us to see fashion in a different way . . . Josephus Thimister combines a sense of the fragile with hard-edged tailoring. His execution for the couture was so soft and fragile. . . I love the rigor that Narciso Rodriguez brings to fashion . . . Jean-Franco Ferré is like the voice of Maria Callas . . . Karl Lagerfeld is the greatest conductor of an atelier. His encyclopedic breadth of knowledge is astonishing. Chanel couture is inspiring and magnificent!"

Who would have suspected that Rucci admired Rei Kawakubo, the avant-garde Japanese designer behind Comme des Garçons? Or that Rucci would compare her with Balenciaga? But notice how Rucci, unlike his critics, does not see Balenciaga just as a figure from the past, but rather as a designer who relentlessly experimented with cut and construction, creating some of the most extreme shapes that fashion has ever witnessed. Josephus Melchior Thimister designed for the House of Balenciaga before launching his first couture collection in Paris in 1997, seeking to "redefine its perameters, to show that it is possible to be grounded in tradition but still be forward thinking . . . to admire the work of both Yves Saint Laurent and Rei Kawakubo."[46] Unfortunately, he closed his business. The Tunisian-born Azzedine Alaïa, designer of ultra-sexy dresses, would seem to be the antithesis of Rucci, but both have a very clear vision, which they never compromised, and both worked for years with private clients. As Horyn points out, both of them are "outside the mainstream" of fashion.

Perhaps a revisionist view of Rucci is in order. At this time in fashion history, when construction has been radically simplified (and technical deficits masked in part by the omnipresence of stretch materials), appreciating Rucci's rich and complex techniques requires an attentive and knowledgeable eye. In some respects, his work may be more difficult to understand than more obviously avant-garde fashions. It is certainly less accessible than fashions which make a direct appeal to the look of the moment.

Giles Lipovetzky, author of *The Empire of Fashion*, suggests that with the democratization of fashion, "we have shifted from an 'aristocratic aesthetics' so dazzlingly illustrated in the heyday of haute couture, to a 'marketing aesthetics'," which demands that fashion should be hedonistic, light-hearted, provocative, and accessible.[47] There is less and less room for fashion which is serious, intelligent, and, for all its discretion, sometimes difficult. Yet there may be more real originality in Rucci's technical innovations than in a dozen clever "theme" collections by most designers.

Rucci is "like Muhammed Ali in his prime, faced with merely third-rate contenders," writes Iké Udé. Moving from metaphors of boxing to warfare, the Nigerian-born artist and editor argues forcefully that Rucci's work can be construed as "a crusade against the overwhelming vulgarity and gimmickry of contemporary fashion, especially that of the American fashion world." In a fascinating interview with the designer, he asks: "Why does the practice and exaltation of beauty appear so radical a position today?" "If people think like this, it is only out of fear," suggests Rucci. "Because mediocrity is the norm, they accept it. They are angered by beauty, fearful of it, because it is so hard to attain."

Perhaps we could say that Rucci's technical innovations are in the service of a particular "aristocratic" vision of beauty. If so, then it is hardly surprising that his work is a minority taste in a society that produces no more Audrey Hepburns, only Paris Hiltons. But those who appreciate his work really love it. "Ralph Rucci is my favorite designer," says David Wolfe. "It's so wonderful to see beautiful clothes that make women look beautiful."

Since Rucci studied philosophy (Descartes, Thomas Aquinas, Kant, and an obscure Renaissance philosopher Nicolas Causanus who suggested that man is the microcosm through which the rays of the macrocosm shine), perhaps it is appropriate to quote from Schopenhauer, who wrote: "The man of talent is like a marksman who hits the target that others cannot hit, but the man of genius is like a marksman who hits the target others cannot see." Rucci himself modestly identifies his contributions to fashion as "technique and tenacity." He sees himself as someone who "remains steadfast" to a "different way of making clothes that respects the idea of individuality."

"Rucci reminds me of a mad monk in the Inquisition," says journalist Tim Blanks. "He has that kind of fierceness and fanaticism that's unique in fashion. He's like the Dark Prince of Seventh Avenue. He has shown a devotion to the artistry of what he does that is above and beyond the call of duty. It's fanaticism. What he does is not just craft, it's art. And that's a formidable proposition for fashion people. They say 'Where's the humor and sex appeal?' Total mediocrities have great careers in fashion because they play the game. He's like a prophet without honor in his own country. But there is a revisionist streak in history, and he will be reassessed. History will be kind to him."

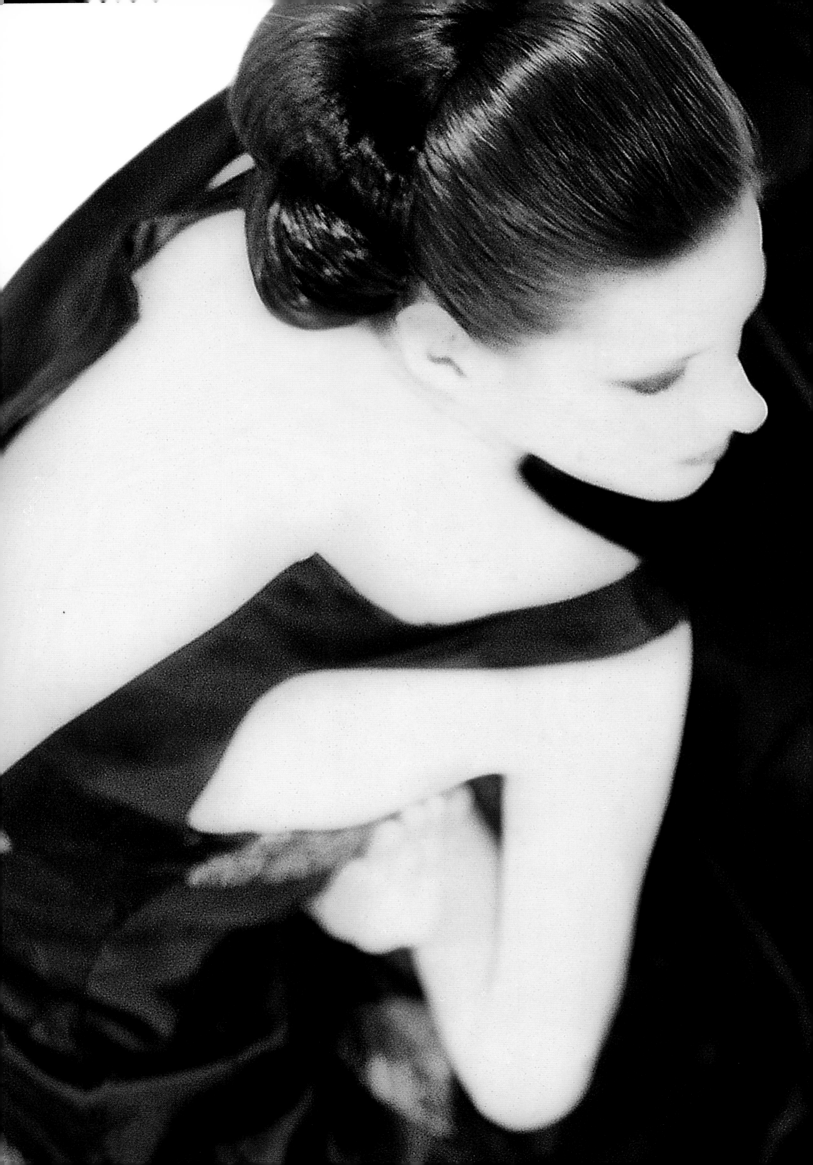

1 Cathy Horyn, "One Day on Welfare, the Next He's Showing in Paris," *New York Times* (May 7, 2002), p. A24.

2 Andre Leon Talley, "StyleFax: An American in Paris," *Vogue* (June 2, 2002).

3 Ralph Rucci, in interview with the author.

4 "Runway Success," CBS Sunday Morning News (October 27, 2002). www.CBS/Style.com.

5 Deeda Blair, in interview with the author.

6 Suzy Menkes, "Season's Nod to American Beauty," *International Herald Tribune* (July 16, 2002).

7 Cathy Horyn, "Fashion Review; In Paris, Discipline, Decadence and the Old Order Changes," *New York Times* (July 14, 2002).

8 "Viva la Couture!" *Women's Wear Daily* (July 12, 2002), p. 5.

9 "Haute Times," *W Magazine* (September, 2002), p. 338.

10 Hamish Bowles, "The Life Fantastic," *Vogue* (October , 2002), p. 314.

11 Godfrey Deeny, "Ralph Rucci: An American in Paris," *Fashion Wire Daily* (July 15, 2002).

12 Janie Samet, "Pour une femme parée d'exception," *Le Figaro* (July 13–14, 2002).

13 Dominique Ageorge and Sarah Shard, "Gaultier Takes Orient Express to Vienna," *Agence France Press* (July 11, 2002).

14 "An American in Paris," *Harper's Bazaar* (August, 2002).

15 Suzy Menkes, "Ralph Rucci, artist as academic," *International Herald Tribune* (September 15, 2005).

16 Vivian Van Natta, in interview with the author.

17 Deeda Blair, in interview with the author.

18 Vivian Van Natta, in interview with the author.

19 Marilyn Kirschner, *American Masters of Fashion*.

20 CBS Sunday Morning News.

21 Joan Kaner, in interview with the author.

22 Linda Gillian Griffoon, "High Fashion, Fine Art," *The Houston Chronicle* (April 8, 2001).

23 Cathy Horyn, "He's Back: Klein Shows His Stuff, and It Struts," *New York Times* (February 20, 2001).

24 Janet Ozzard, "Killing the Buzz," *Women's Wear Daily* (August 29, 2001).

25 Cathy Horyn, in interview with the author.

26 Linda Gillan Griffin, "High Fashion, Fine Art," *The Houston Chronicle* (April 8, 2001).

27 Quoted in Anne Bissonette, *Chado Ralph Rucci* (Kent State Museum, 2005), p. 25.

28 "De Bruxelles à New Delhi, tous à Paris," *Libération* (July 14, 2003).

29 Suzy Menkes, *International Herald Tribune* (Jan 24, 2003).

30 Andre Leon Talley, "Ralph Rucci hits his stride," www.vogue.com (September 2003).

31 *International Herald Tribune* (January 21, 2004).

32 Tim Blanks, "More than Meets the Eye," *Town and Country* (January, 2005), p. 118.

33 Cathy Horyn, "Reports of Couture's Death were Exaggerated," *New York Times* (July 23, 2005).

34 David Wolfe interview with the author.

35 Notebooks, 1987.

36 Cathy Horyn, "Mysteries of Inspiration," *New York Times* (September 4, 2001).

37 Ralph Rucci, in interview with the author.

38 "The Perfect Form," Iké Udé interviews Ralph Rucci, *aRUDE: The Index of Elegance* (The LOOK Issue, no. 21, 2004).

39 Notebooks of Ralph Rucci.

40 Hamish Bowles, in interview with the author.

41 Quoted in Cathy Horyn, "One Day on Welfare, the Next He's Showing in Paris."

42 Varjorie Fisher, in interview with the author.

43 Tatiana Sorokko, in interview with the author.

44 David Wolfe, in interview with the author.

45 Amy Fine Collins, in interview with the author.

46 Stephen Gan and Alix Browne, *Visionaire's Fashion 2001: Designers of the New Avant-Garde* (New York: Universe Publishing, 1999), n.p.

47 Giles Lipovetzky, *The Empire of Fashion*; see also *The Power of Fashion*.

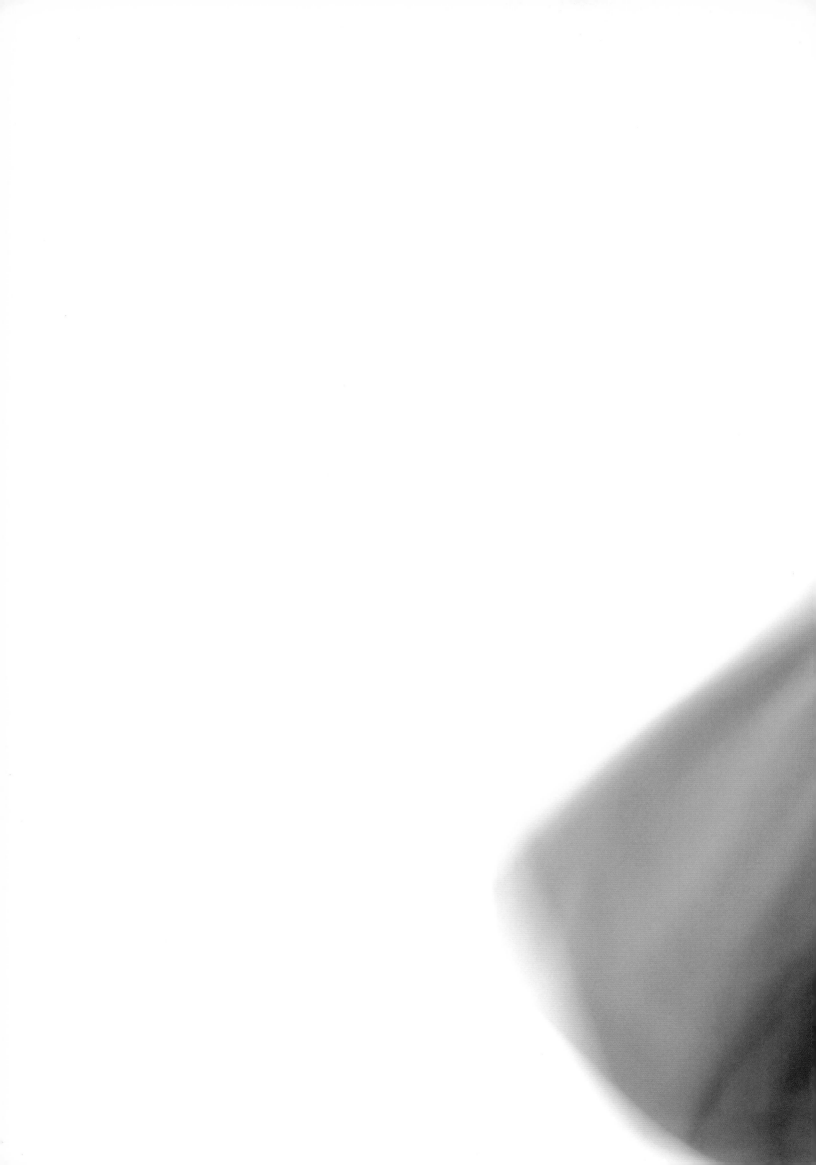

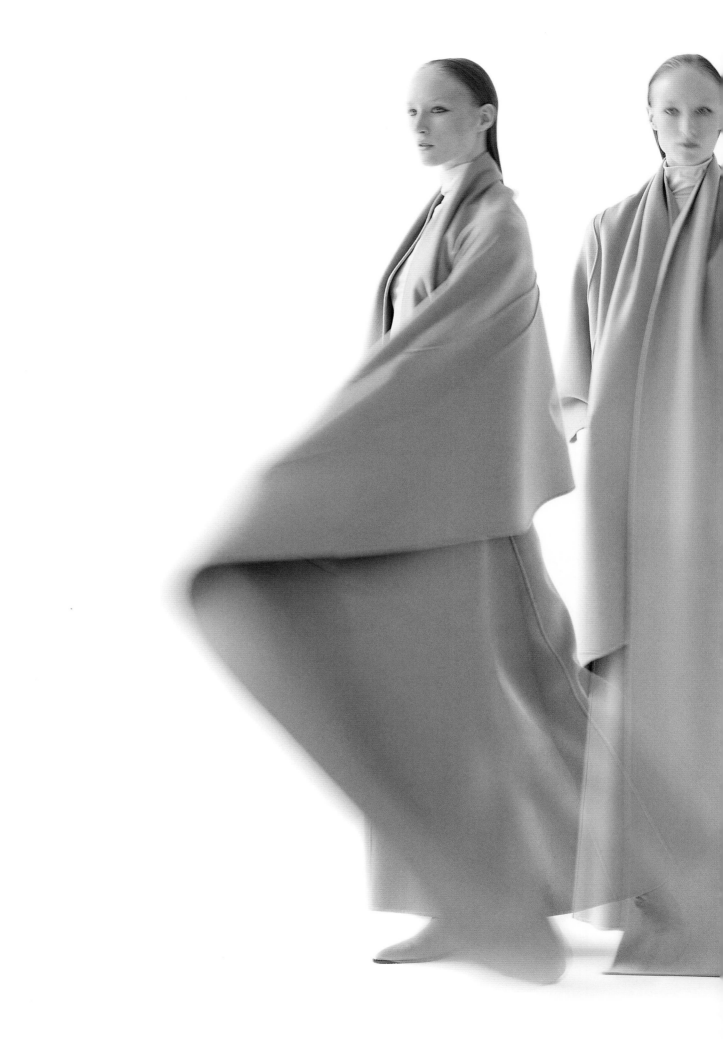

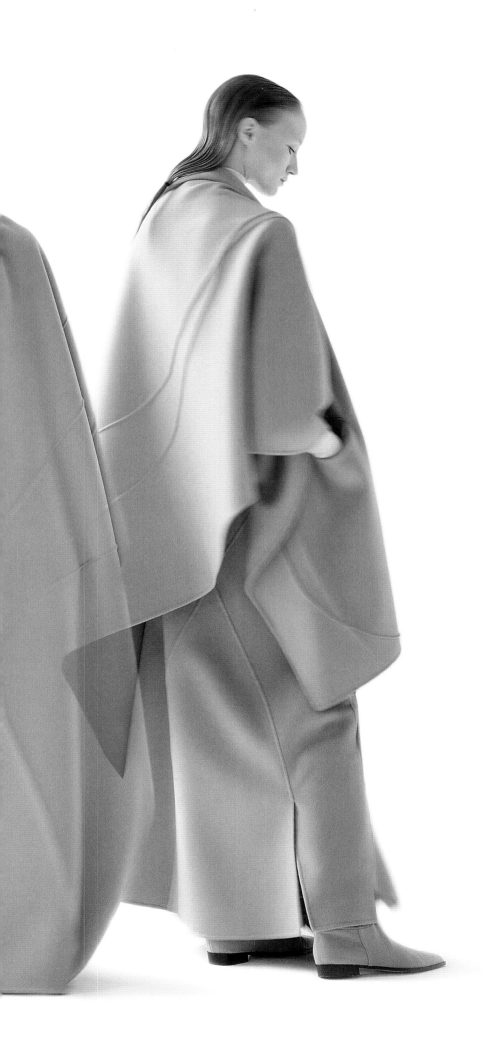

Exquisite details, luxurious fabrics, and expert tailoring are just some of the reasons to covet a Ralph Rucci creation. The clothes are timeless; they are made to be worn and enjoyed not just for a season, but forever. At a time when many fashion editors and stylists were lauding bad taste and extolling that "a little bad taste is a good thing," Ralph Rucci was the exception. His designs possess a tranquility that transcends fashion and trend, and instead exude style and elegance for the discerning, self-assured women who wear them. Indeed, elegance and grace are inherent in everything he does.

I am proud to be his number one fan.

Joan Kaner

fall/winter 2002

Cashmere top and scarf, sable head
scarf and trousers.

Topography map jacket, with
top and pants.

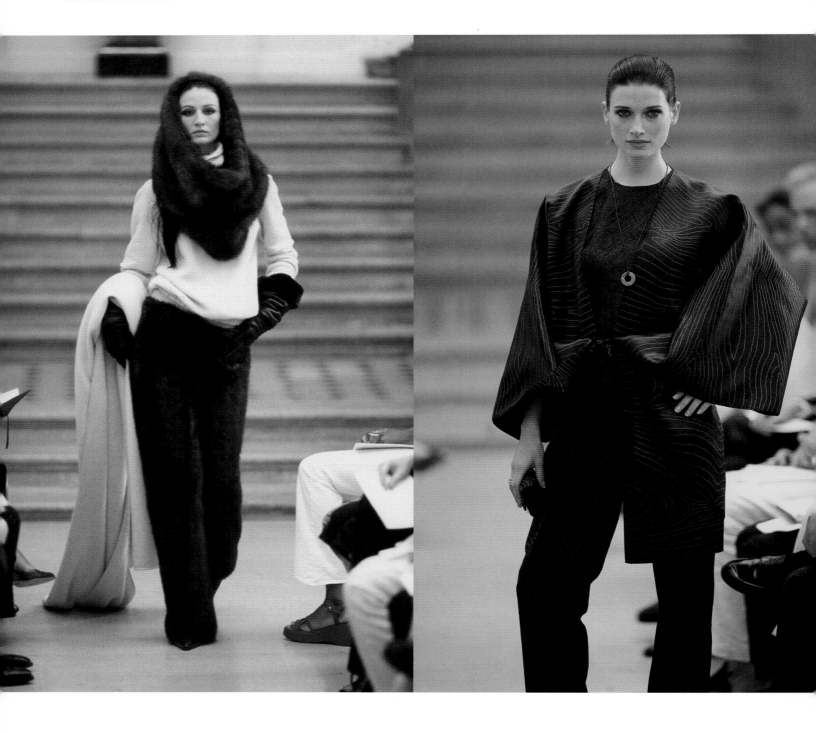

Green feathered jacket and dress
with alligator bodice.

Black cocktail dress and jacket
made of tulle and embroidered with
turquoise stones.

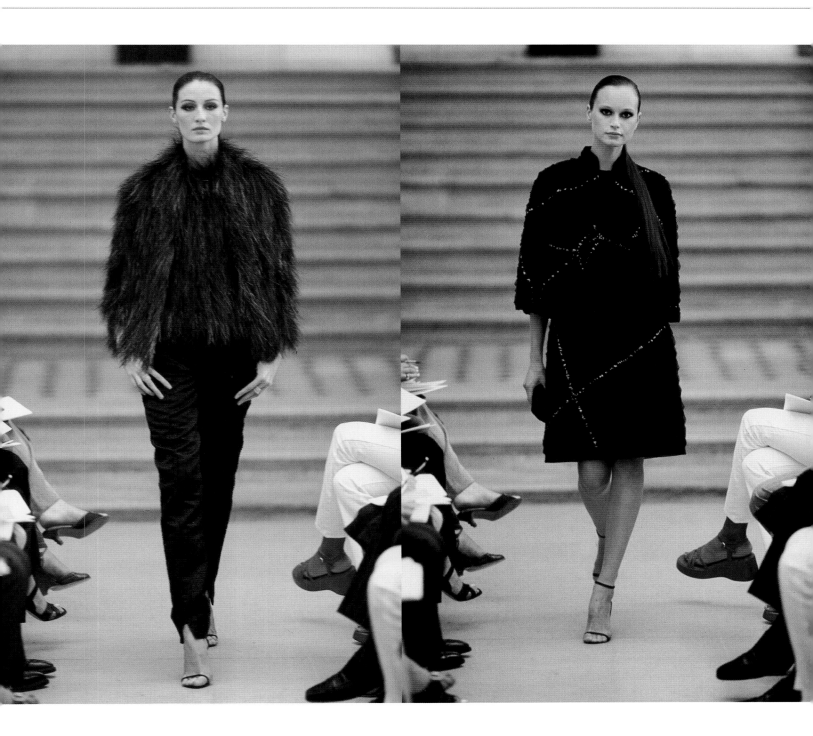

Paprika duchess satin coat, pants,
and matching embroidered top.

Below: printed chiffon shawl,
black evening dress.

Facing page: wool jersey
empire-waist day dress.

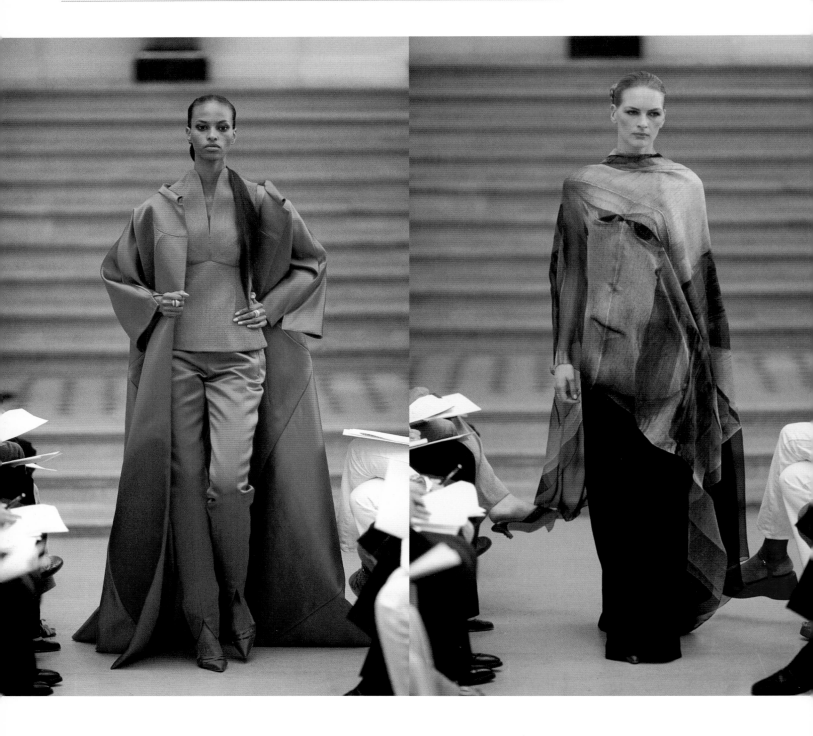

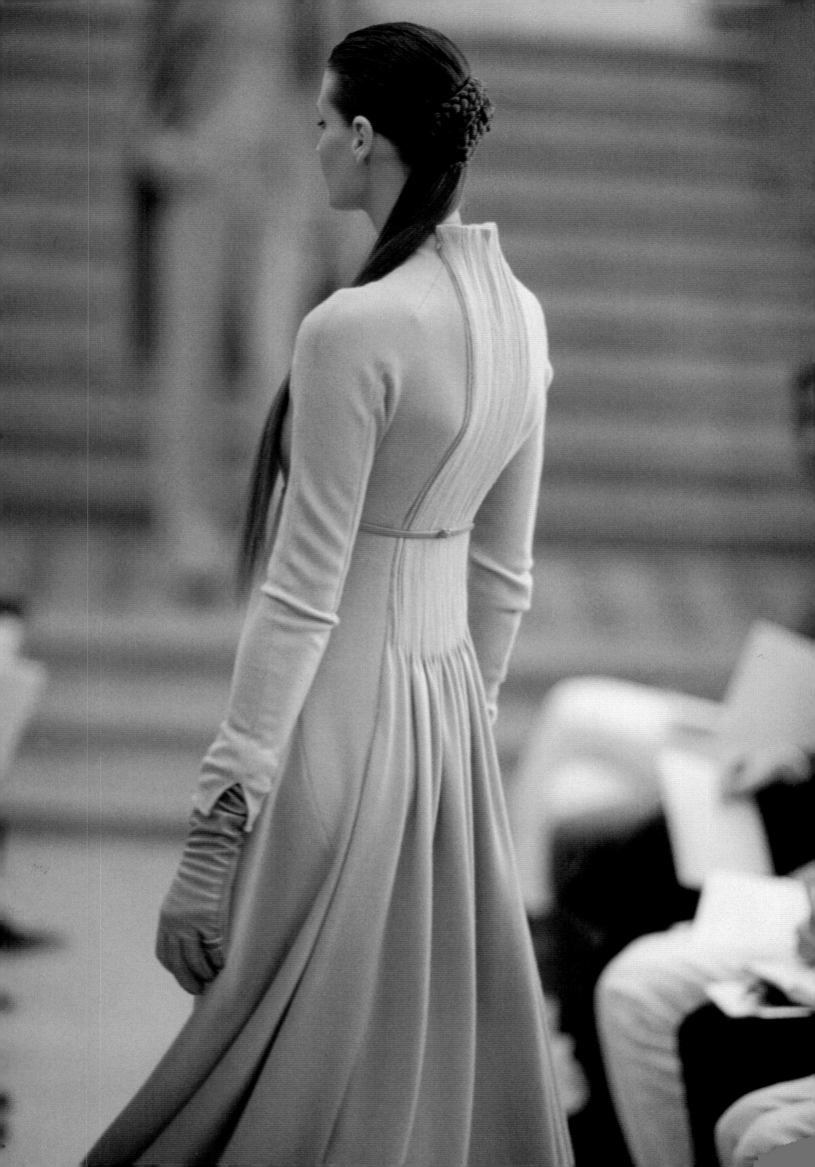

Garnet silk duchess Infanta gown
and stole.

Orange satin Infanta with ostrich
bodice and matching bolero jacket.

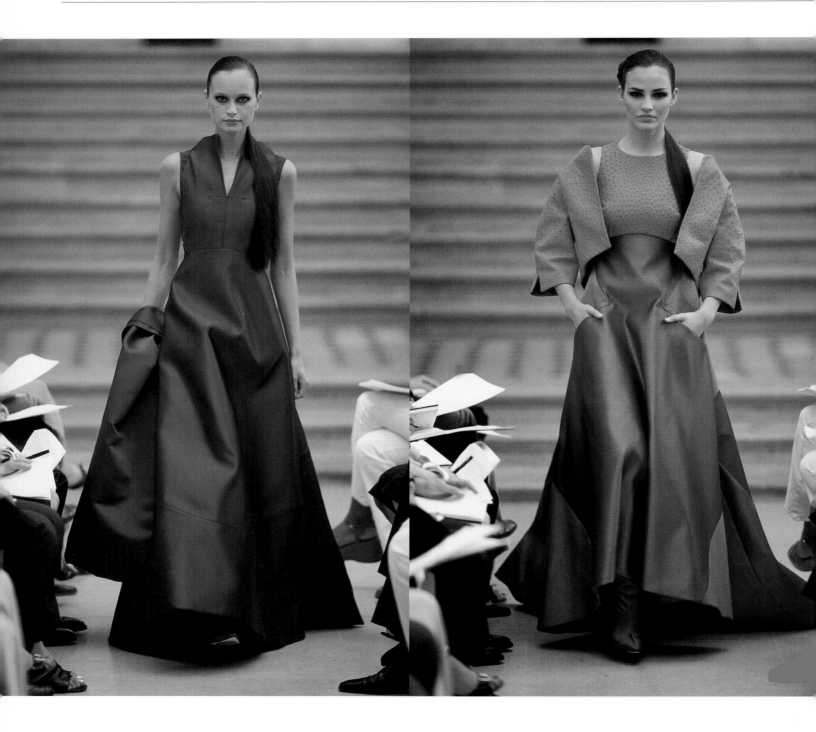

Sleeveless cashmere dress.

Black silk cigalline and gazar
"Pauline" tunic appliquéd with
hand-looped ribbon, black silk
velvet pants.

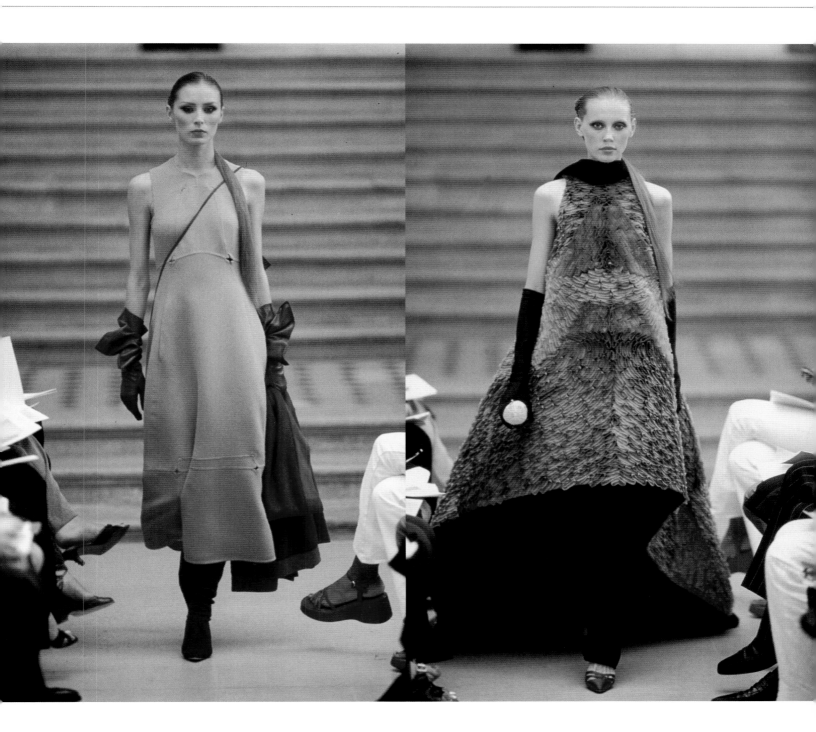

fall/winter 2003

Black silk dress with bleached
brush strokes (detail on facing page).

Black sheer jersey evening bodice,
duchess silk satin skirt with bleached
brush strokes.

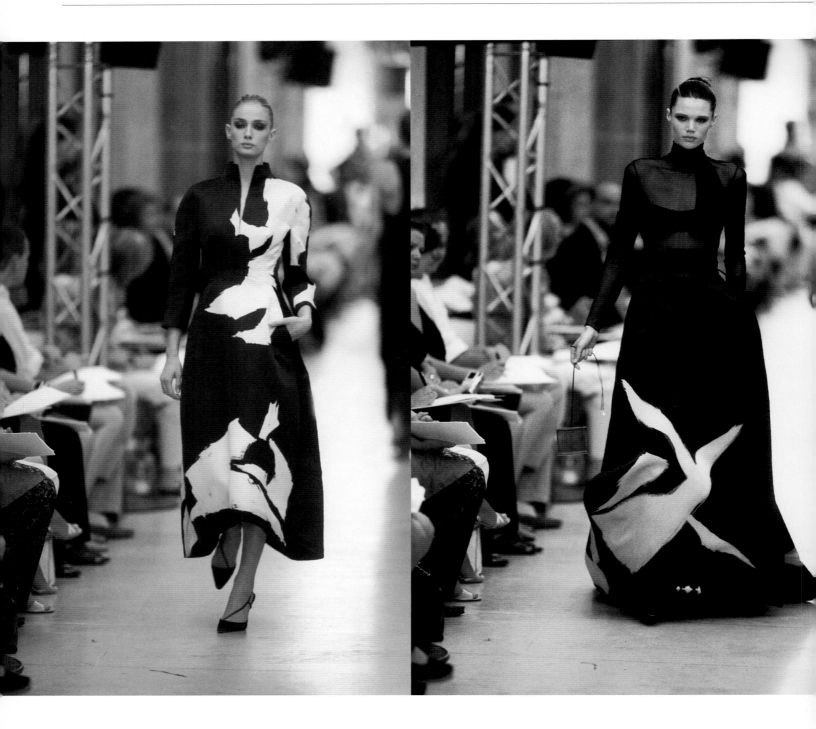

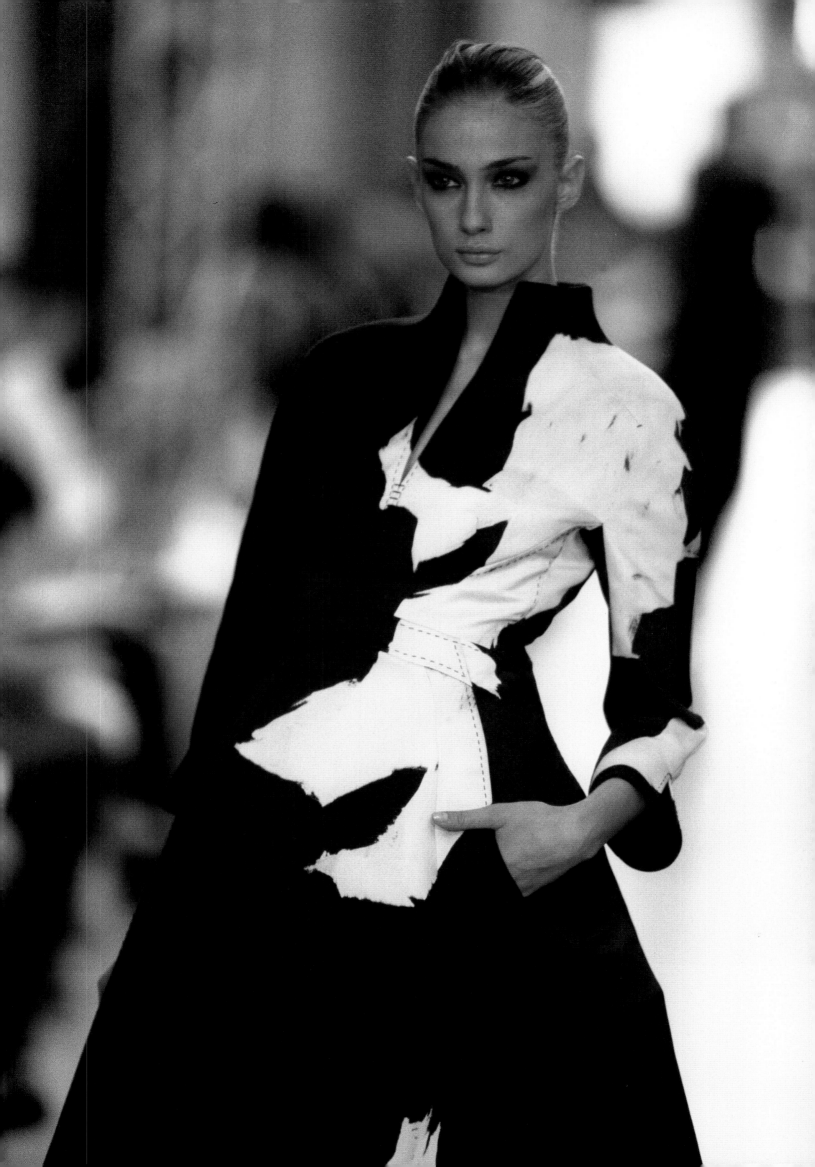

Printed chiffon evening gown.

Black lace, silk faille moiré, organza
and cigalline Infanta gown.

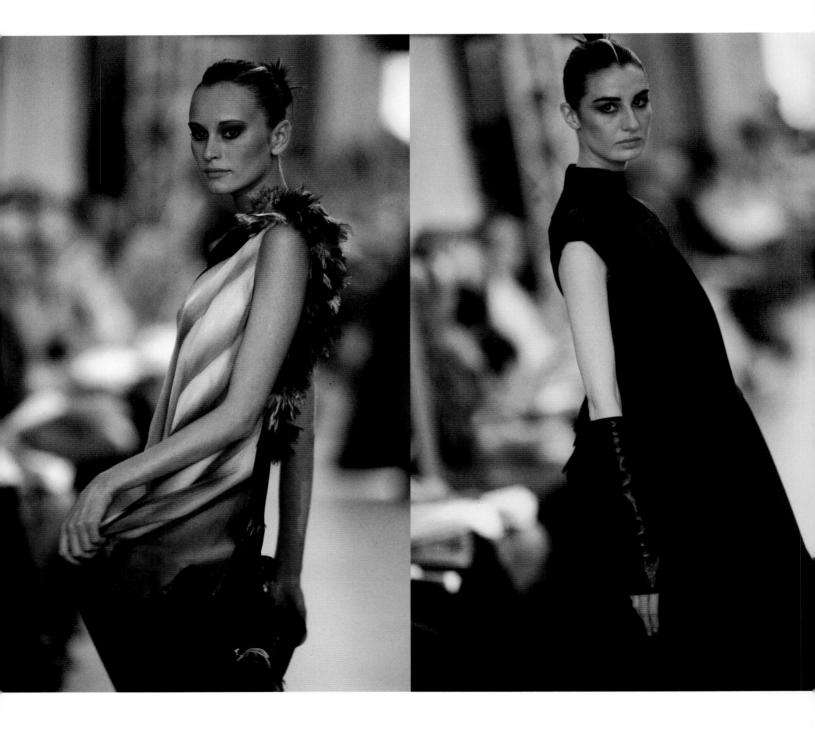

Brown ostrich coat.

Black wool day dress with
leather inserts.

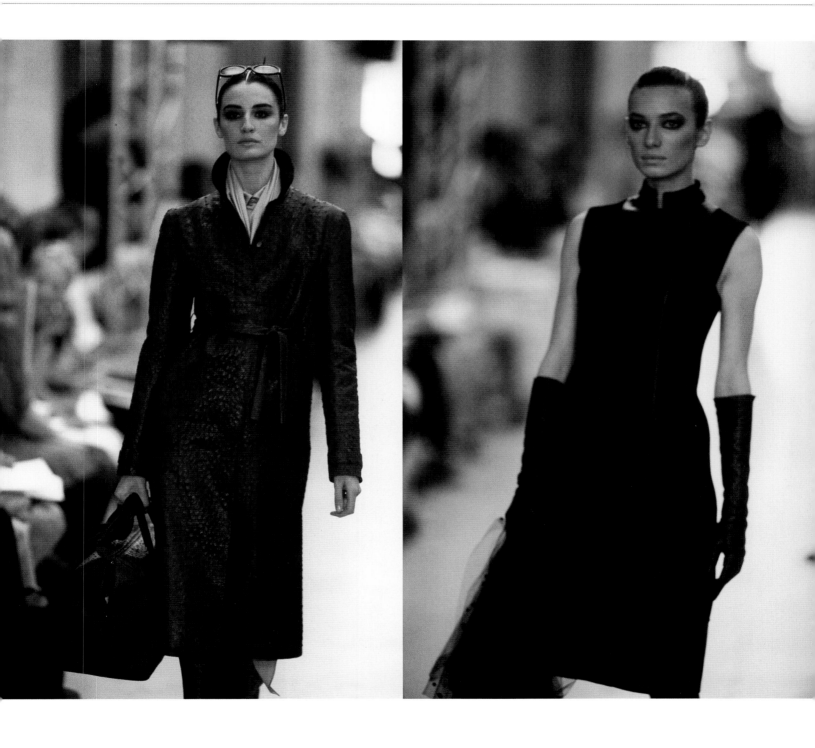

fall/winter 2004

Black silk point d'esprit Infanta
bodice and skirt, trimmed with burnt
ostrich feathers (detail on
facing page).

Embroidered jacket, chiffon bodice,
taffeta skirt.

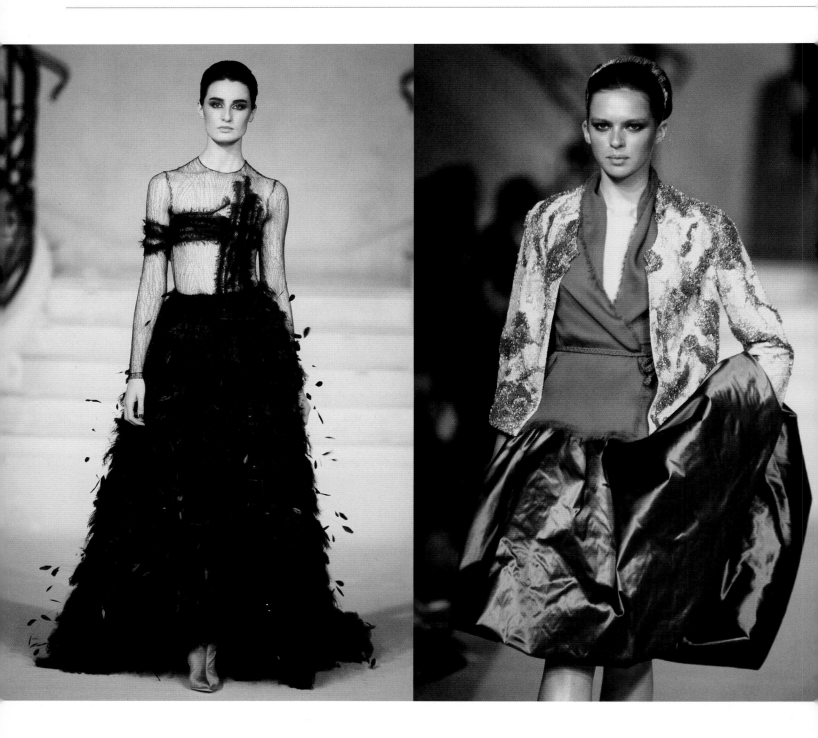

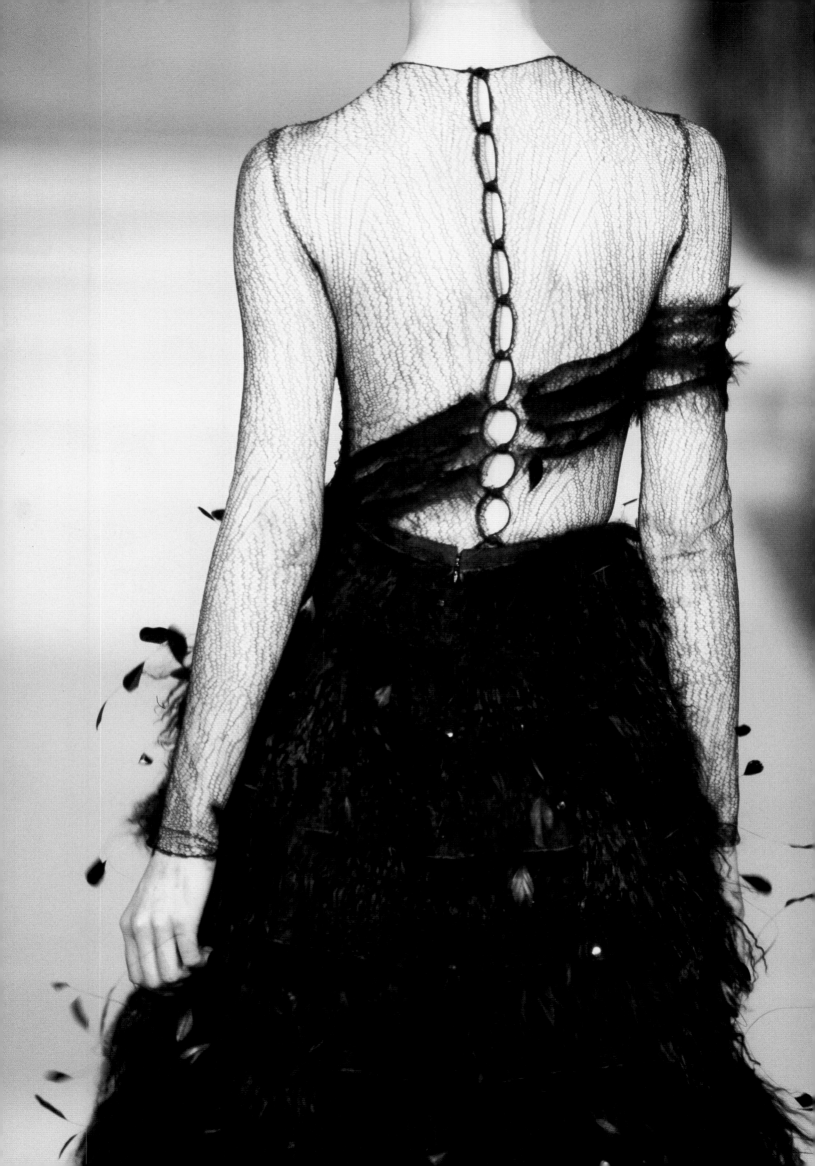

"Stained glass" dress and scarf.

Embroidered evening coat
and dress

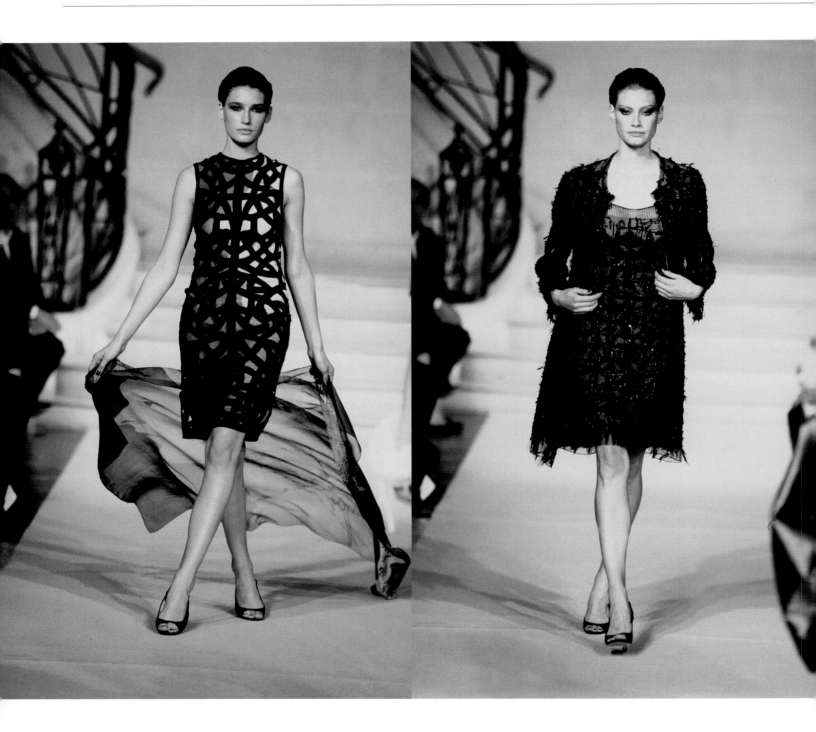

Alligator ensemble and
broadtail suit.

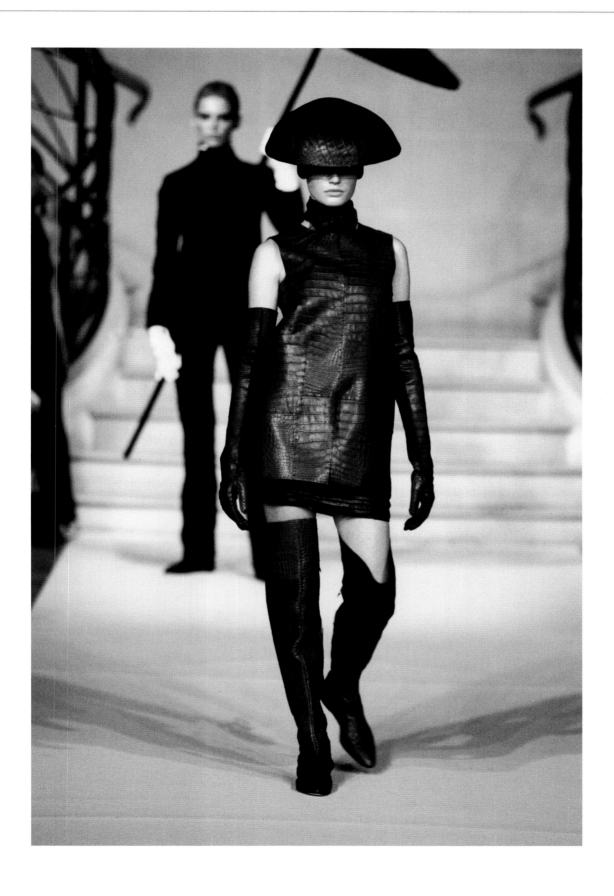

fall/winter 2006

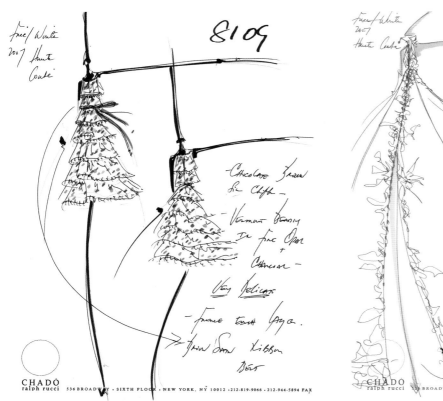
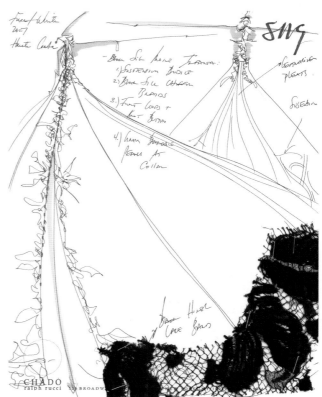

Chocolate brown chiffon dress with
fire opal embroidery.

Black silk moiré suspension infanta.

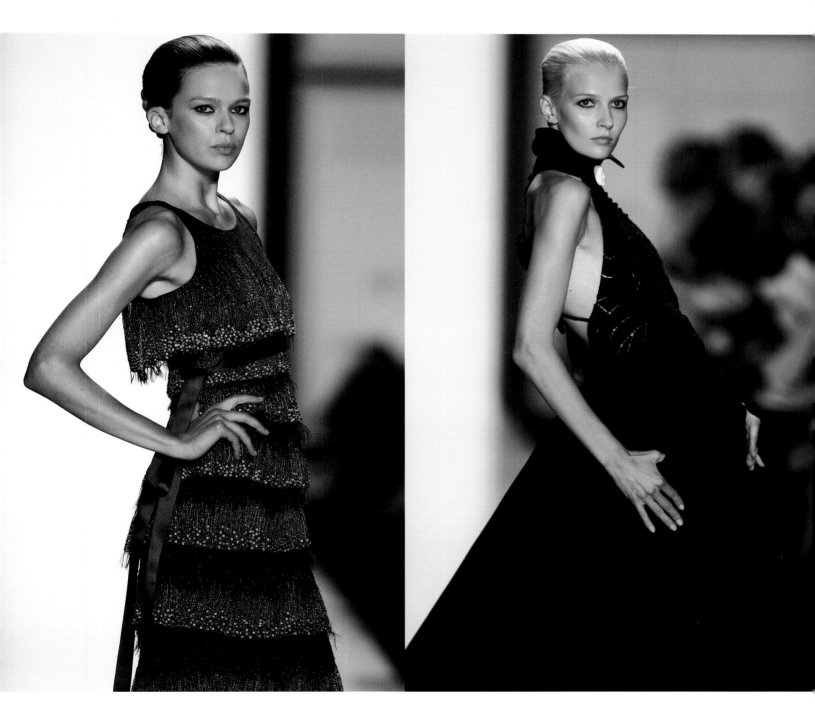

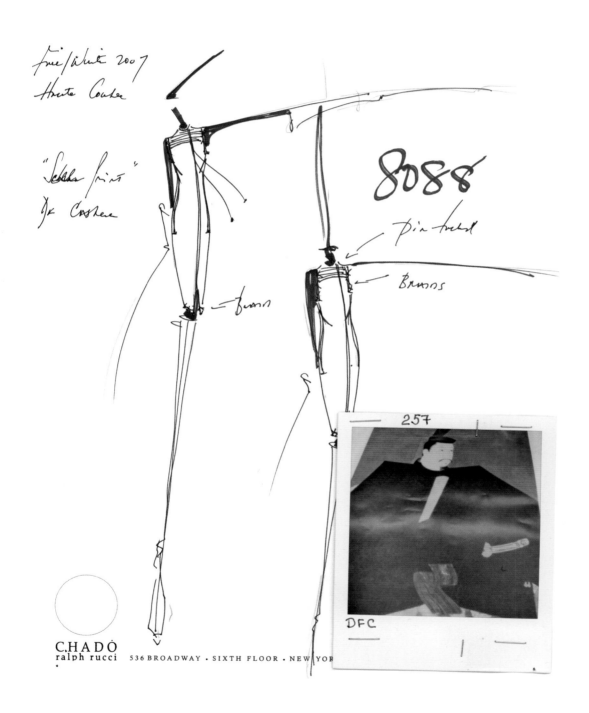

8088

257

DFC

Coat and dress of double-faced
cashmere, screened with Japanese
scholar print.

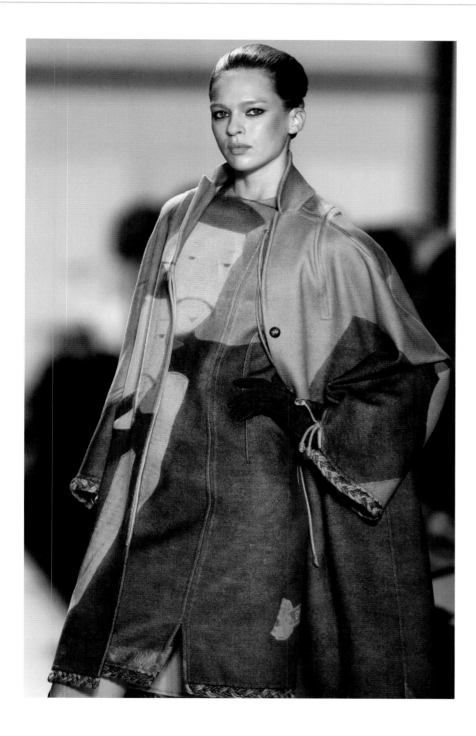

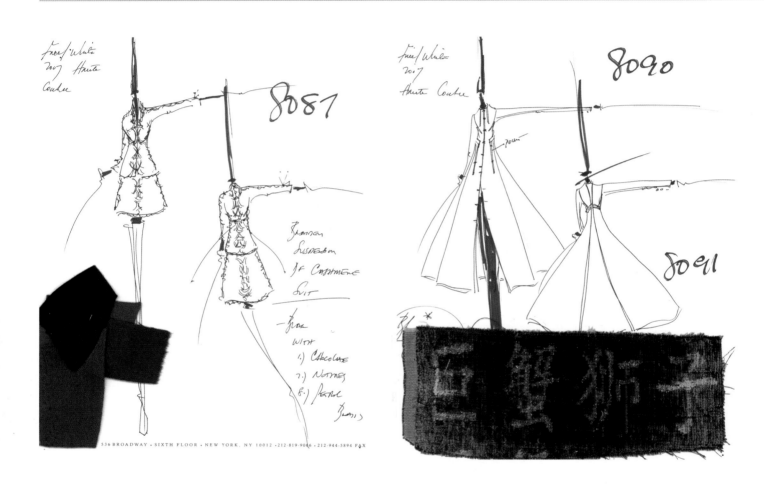

Double-faced cashmere
suspension suit.

Silk velvet calligraphy
morning coat and skirt.

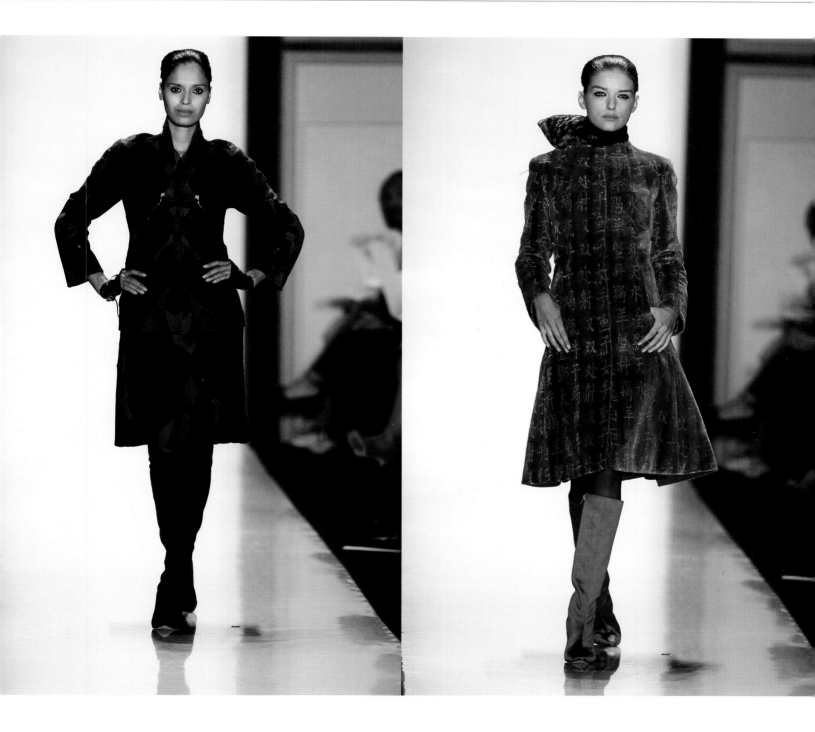

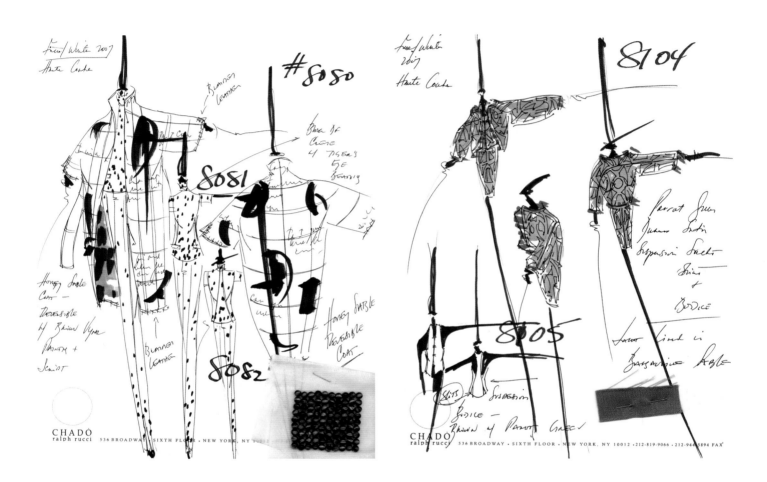

Paper-faced Russian honey sable
coat and serape, black
double-faced wool crepe tunic and
pants with tiger's eye embroidery.

Parrot green silk satin suspension
suit with barguzine sable lining.

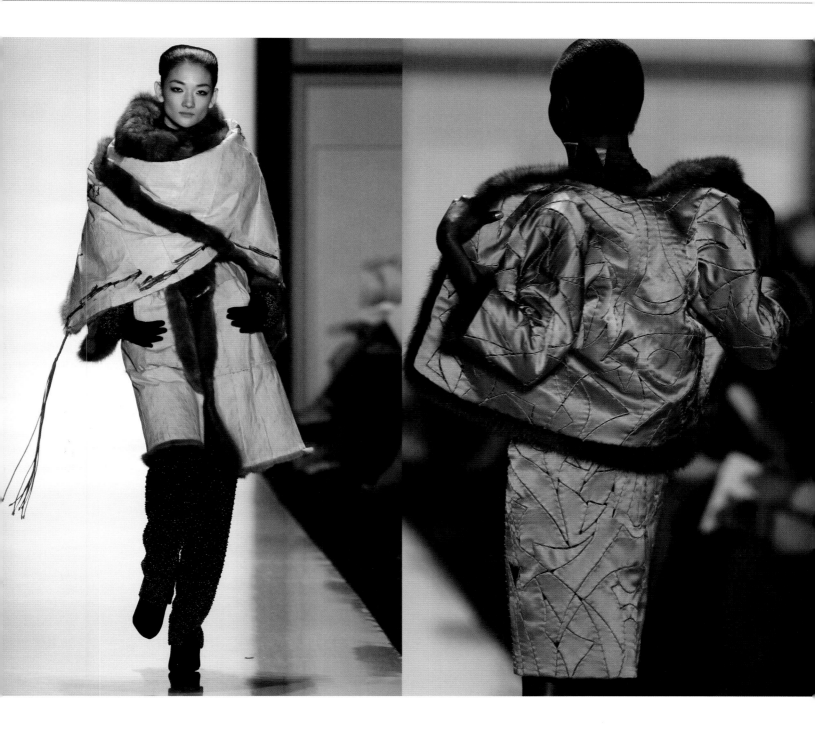

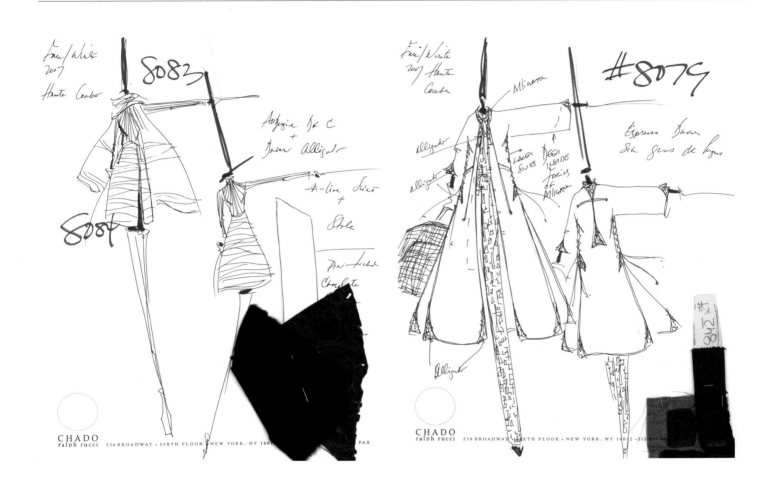

Aubergine double-faced cashmere
skirt and stole with chocolate brown
alligator insets.

Chocolate brown alligator paillette
jogging suit, silk gros de longres
and alligator raincoat.

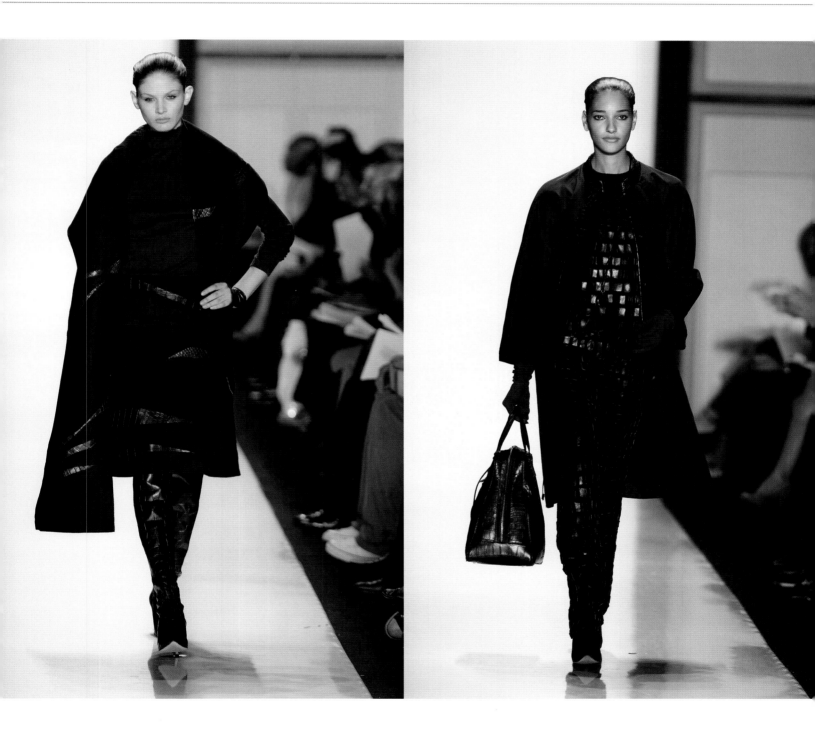

Masai/Goya Infanta.

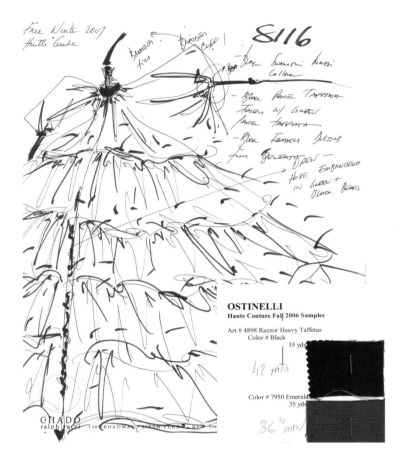

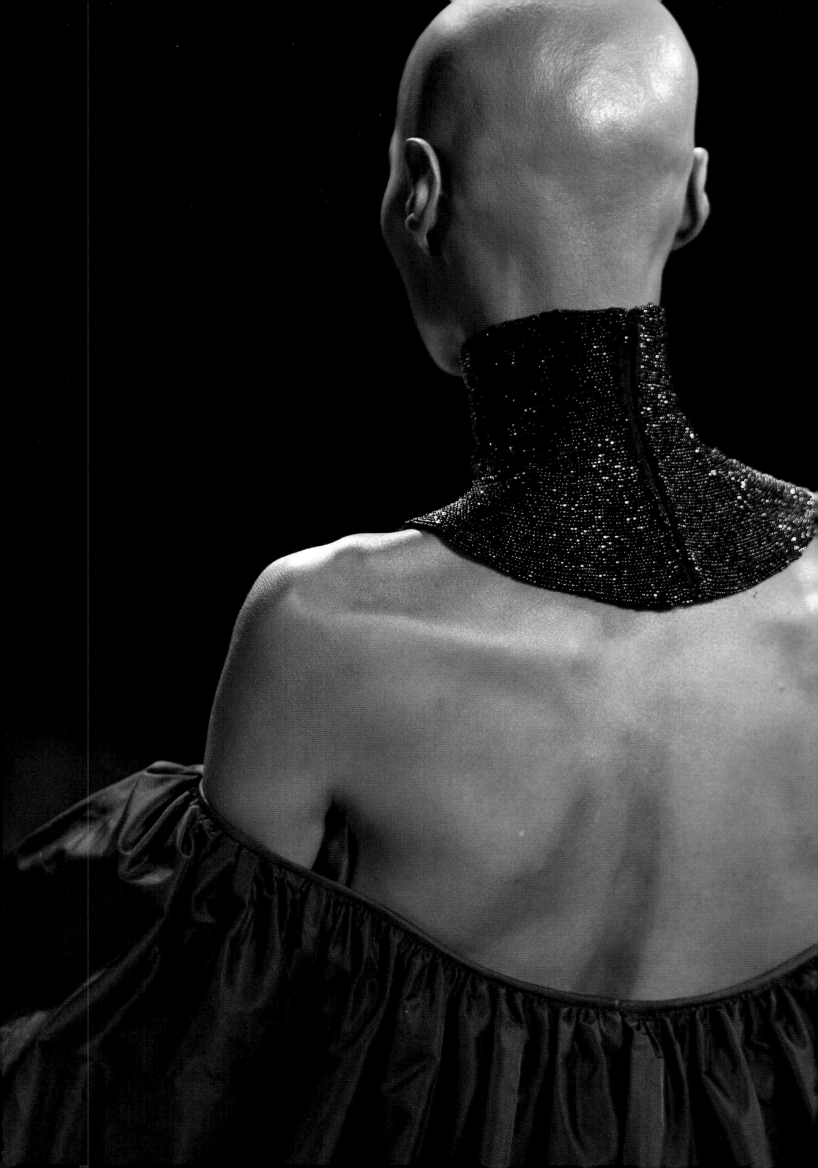

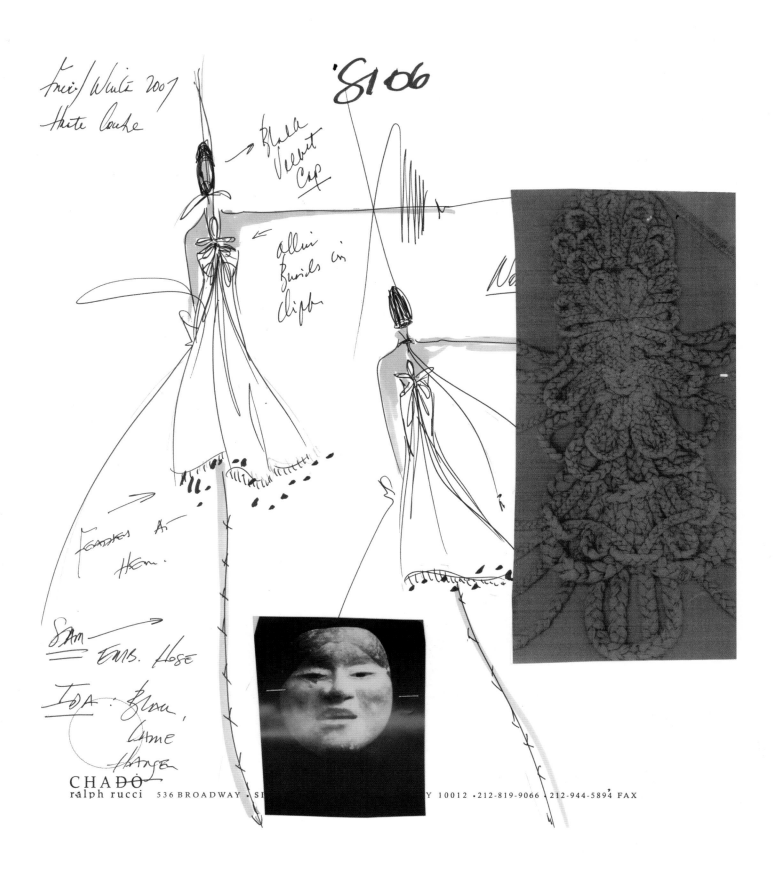

'8106

Fall/Winter 2007
Haute Couche

Black
Velvet
Cap

allni
Burels in
Clip...

Gathers At
Hem.

Sam
Emb. Hose

Ida: Brow,
Cume
Hanger

CHADO
ralph rucci 536 BROADWAY · S.... Y 10012 · 212-819-9066 · 212-944-5894 FAX

Black matte alligator and gazar
gown printed with a Japanese Noh
mask and sable, alligator and
horsehair jacket.

Braided halter chiffon dress printed
with a Japanese Noh mask.

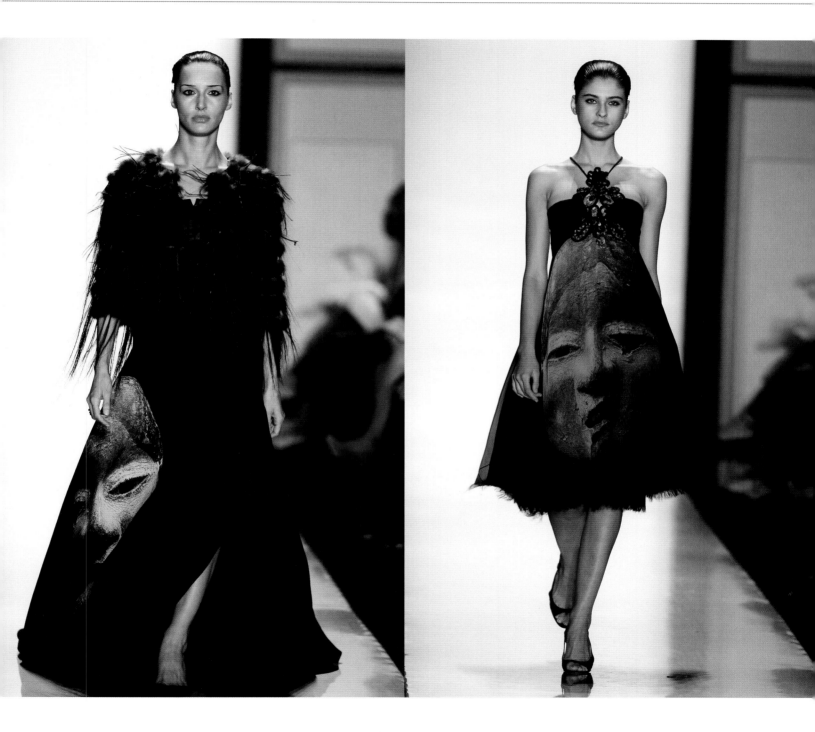

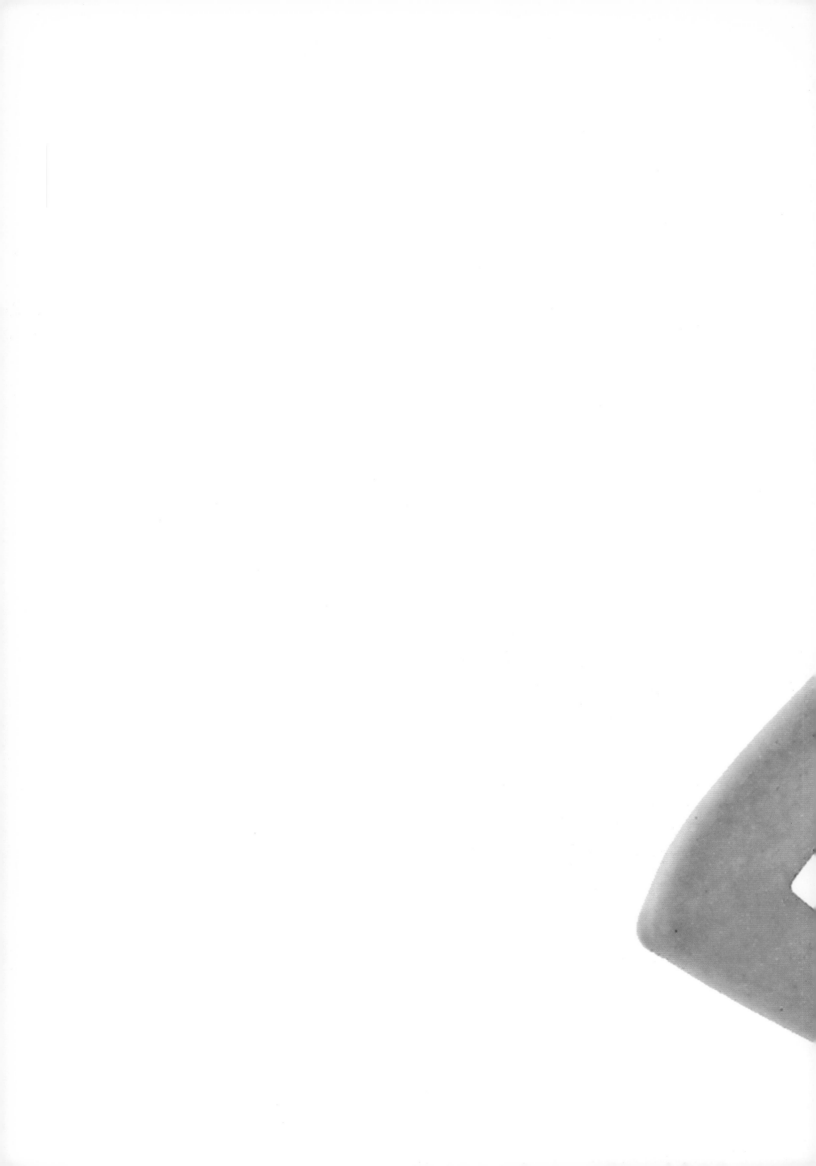

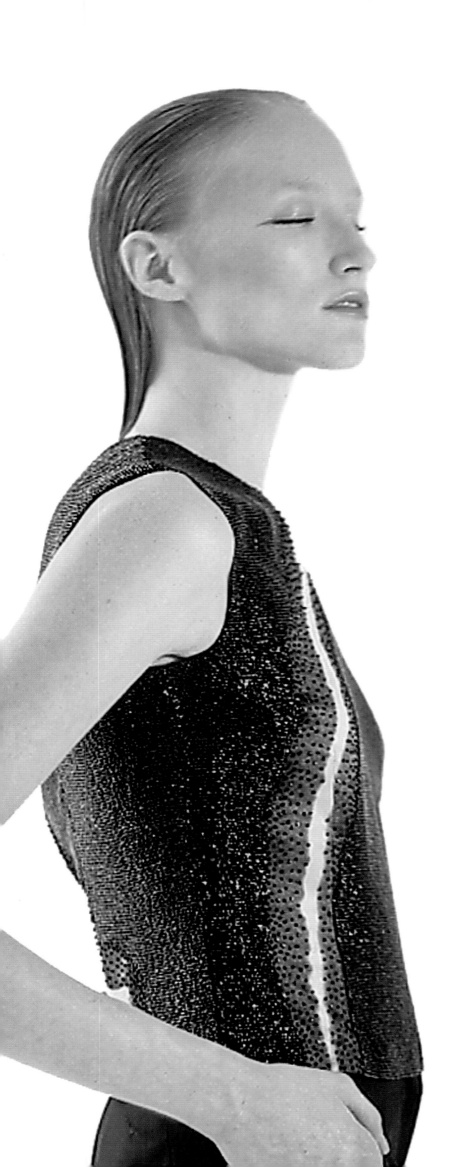

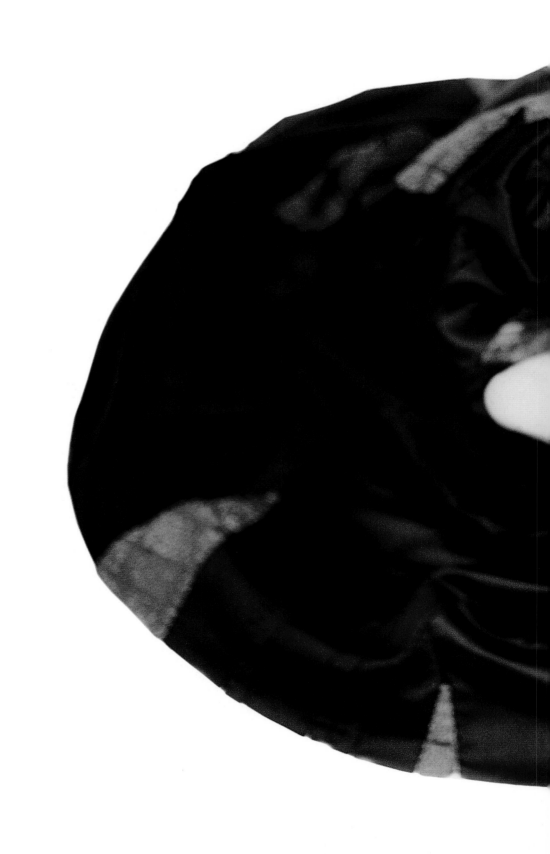

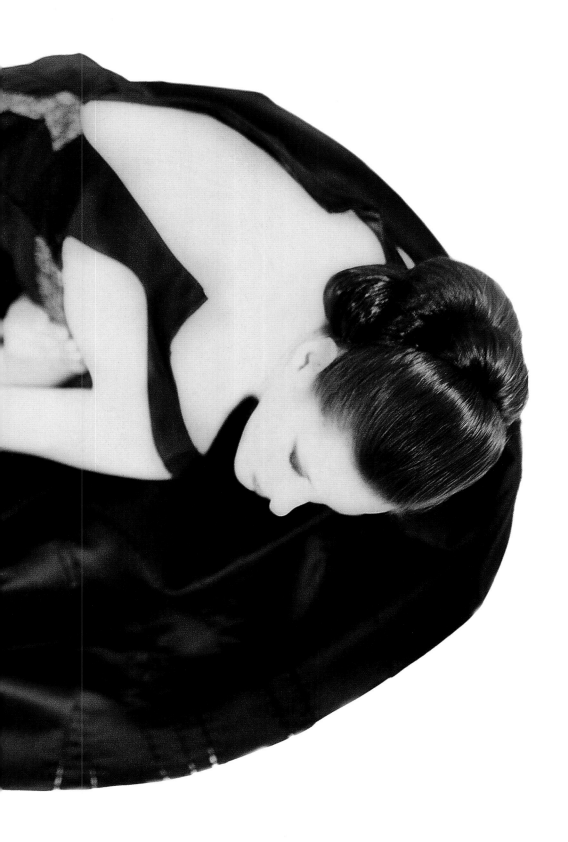

Ralph Rucci: his aesthetic is marvellous. His work expresses at all times an exuberance combined with restraint. It is at once colossal and fragile, a Rucci construction of peerless seams and details. In his passion for "old school" ideals, he refuses compromise. The high standards of classical verities established by the masters of Paris haute couture are essentially the foundation of everything Ralph Rucci achieves. His clothes possess a deft magic. They demand a consciousness of elegance.

André Leon Talley

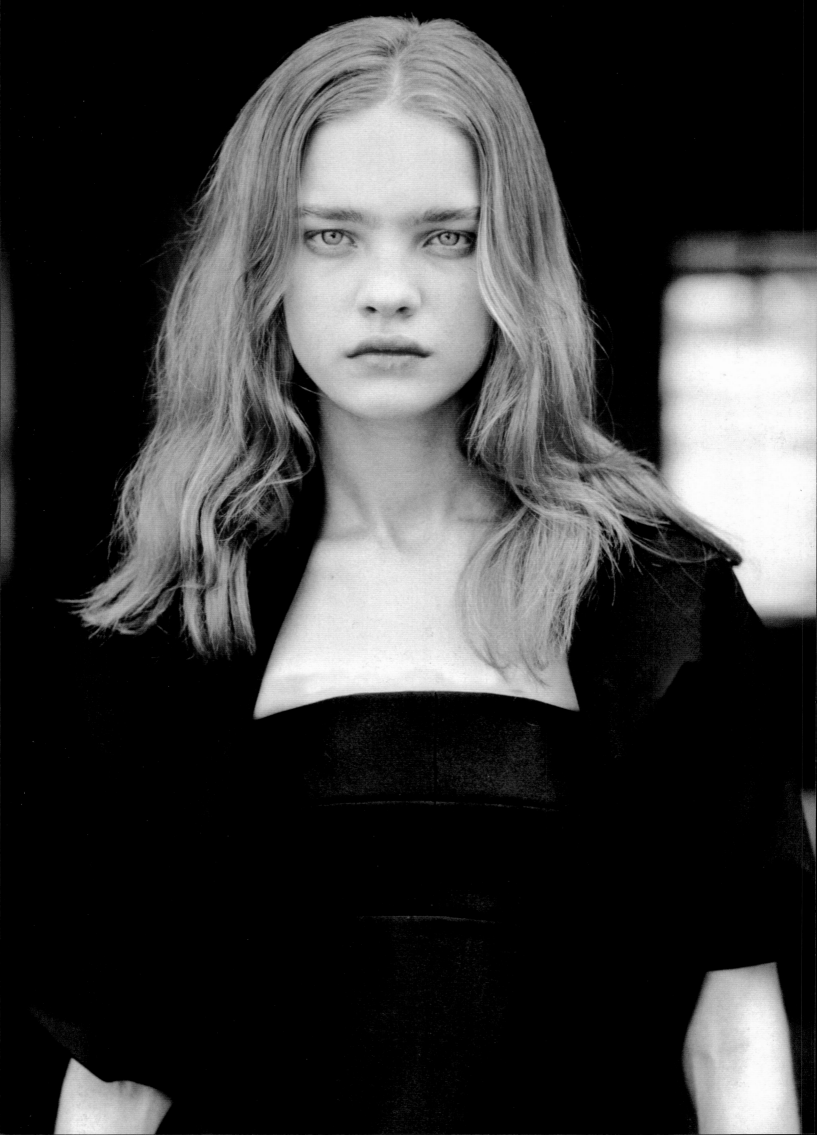

V Magazine, by David Armstrong.
Ripple Effect Infanta,
November/December 2002.

The work of Ralph Rucci is like an exotic island in the vast sea of contemporary fashion – enchanting, but not well known. Even for many people in the fashion world, Rucci seemed to come from nowhere when he presented his first – and highly praised – haute couture collection in Paris in 2002. But at that point Ralph Rucci had already been quietly toiling away as a designer since 1981. His sudden "discovery" by the fashion community twenty years after he began working did not, however, excite much enquiry into the years of vision, dedication, and hard work that brought him to that moment of triumph. Yet it was precisely the background of those two "hidden decades" that made possible the simple-seeming complexity and the profound commitment to perfection inherent in every garment designed by Rucci and executed in his atelier. A Rucci retrospective thus provides an important opportunity to assess his work, not just since Paris 2002, but in the broad context of his entire career. This essay will examine the types of garments that constitute his oeuvre and what makes them so special, and it will explore some of the influences that Rucci has acknowledged to be important in his work, such as past couturiers, contemporary artists, and Asian cultures. It will also attempt to explain why curators and the cognoscenti label Rucci as one of the greatest fashion designers in the world today.

What defines a Rucci creation? The question is simple to ask but not easy to answer. Rucci's work does not fit comfortably into the standard world of seasonal fashion collections and constantly changing lines. His work defies easy labeling. He balances seemingly contradictory elements: he is traditional in his method of working yet progressive in meeting the needs of his clientele; he is inspired by past masters but has (with his devoted staff) developed new dressmaking techniques and accompanying vocabulary; he carves monumental three-dimensional forms and adheres to a strict and somewhat rigid silhouette but is also a great colorist and embellisher of surfaces; and he is both a creator of and collector of fine art. This balance of Apollonian and Dionysian aesthetics has proved hard to confine and define within fashion's simple and tidy generalizations.

But however one approaches his work, one of its defining features is its strong connection to historic methods of creation. As with the greatest couturiers of the modern era, such as Madeleine Vionnet, Cristóbal Balenciaga, and Madame Grès, Rucci's work is the end result of a long evolutionary process. He maintains and extends the traditional, rigorous methods of the Paris couture. He sees his work as a cumulative body created over the course of a lifetime, and has shown little interest in the usual designer's ploy of creating novel seasonal collections with dramatic themes or silhouettes that are attention-getting but rarely long-lasting. His silhouettes and the construction methods have evolved so slowly that the changes are imperceptible to most. He has been criticized by some journalists because, with little dramatic change from season to season, there is no new story to report.

Rucci's unswerving commitment to deep quality rather than surface glitter goes a long way toward explaining why he is illustrious but little known. Rucci's work, in comparison to others who also embrace a strong affinity for artistic couture, is formal in its framework and yet so multi-layered in its aesthetic that he cannot be easily placed within recent fashion developments. Rucci has further distanced himself from his contemporaries by embracing the ideals of the classical past (and subsequent revivals of classicism) and certain schools of Asian philosophy with little regard for current trends. His work builds over time to create a kind of epic narrative – but it is one that sails over the heads of most members of the MTV generation. Like one of his heroes, the artist Cy Twombly, Rucci too "seems to be born out of our time, rather than into it."[1] Fittingly, because Rucci is deeply immersed in the world of painting, his work appeals most strongly to people with a serious knowledge and love of fashion who understand that a great dress is truly a work of art.

Another key reason Rucci remains relatively unknown, or at least misunderstood, is that the extraordinary quality of his garments is not readily apparent from photographs. They do not yield up their secrets very readily on the printed page. Most fashion journalists, caught up in the hectic world of day-to-day reportage, have little time to examine and explain the qualities that form the foundation of Rucci's designs such as: the richness and diversity of his fabric choices, the ingenuity of his surface ornamentation, the broad range of his sophisticated color palette, the artistic sources from which he draws inspiration, and the mathematically complex construction methods he employs in executing his creations.

Nevertheless, if Ralph Rucci is only famous within a very select segment of the fashion world, among those cognoscenti he is not only famous but revered. A Ralph Rucci outfit is instantly recognizable, highly coveted, and a guarantee of its wearer's good taste. That being so, let us turn to a consideration of the elements that have gone into the making of Rucci's career, and into the making of every garment that leaves his atelier.

rucci and the couture tradition

Fashion designers today rarely acknowledge the influence of other creators upon their work. Most emphatically deny what seems readily evident to unbiased observers – that designers of the late twentieth and twenty-first centuries consistently appropriate elements of the past into their work. Rucci is an exception. He readily admits that Cristobal Balenciaga, Alix Grès, Charles James, and Halston, among others, have all inspired him and still resonate in his subconscious. However, Rucci does not mimic historic modes. He has consistently been able to take the techniques of the past and bring them into the present.

In the lectures that he delivers regularly, Rucci points out that it was the work of the Spanish-born Balenciaga (1895–1972) that first galvanized his desire to become a couturier. Rucci was a regular reader of *Vogue* in the 1960s, when that magazine was at the height of its influence under the direction of its legendary editor-in-chief, Diana Vreeland (who later would become the impresario of crowd-pleasing fashion exhibitions at the Metropolitan Museum of Art's Costume Institute). Rucci became entranced by two Balenciaga silk gazar gowns created and photographed from the back by David Bailey for the July 1967 issue.[2]

Created near the end of his career, Balenciaga's ivory bridal gown with matching headdress and "flag-blue" evening cape and dinner dress were the ultimate distillations of construction and form based purely on the inherent quality of gazar, a slightly stiff open weave fabric. At rest, these gowns were "a graceful series of soft bias undulations. They achieved their conical shape by the wearer in motion." The dramatically canted hemline of these evening dresses would, in

Falcon-printed silk chiffon evening
dress, collection of Tatiana Sorokko.
Photograph: William Palmer.

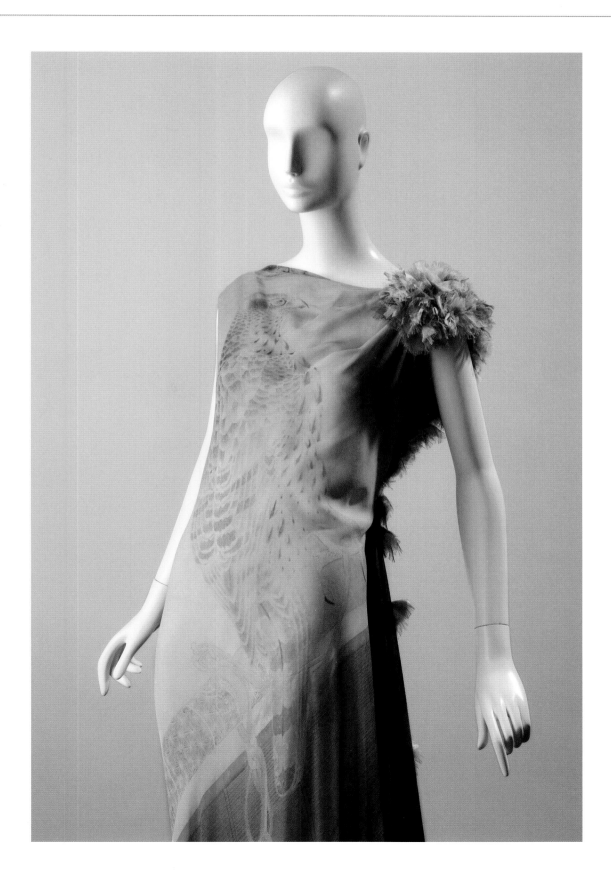

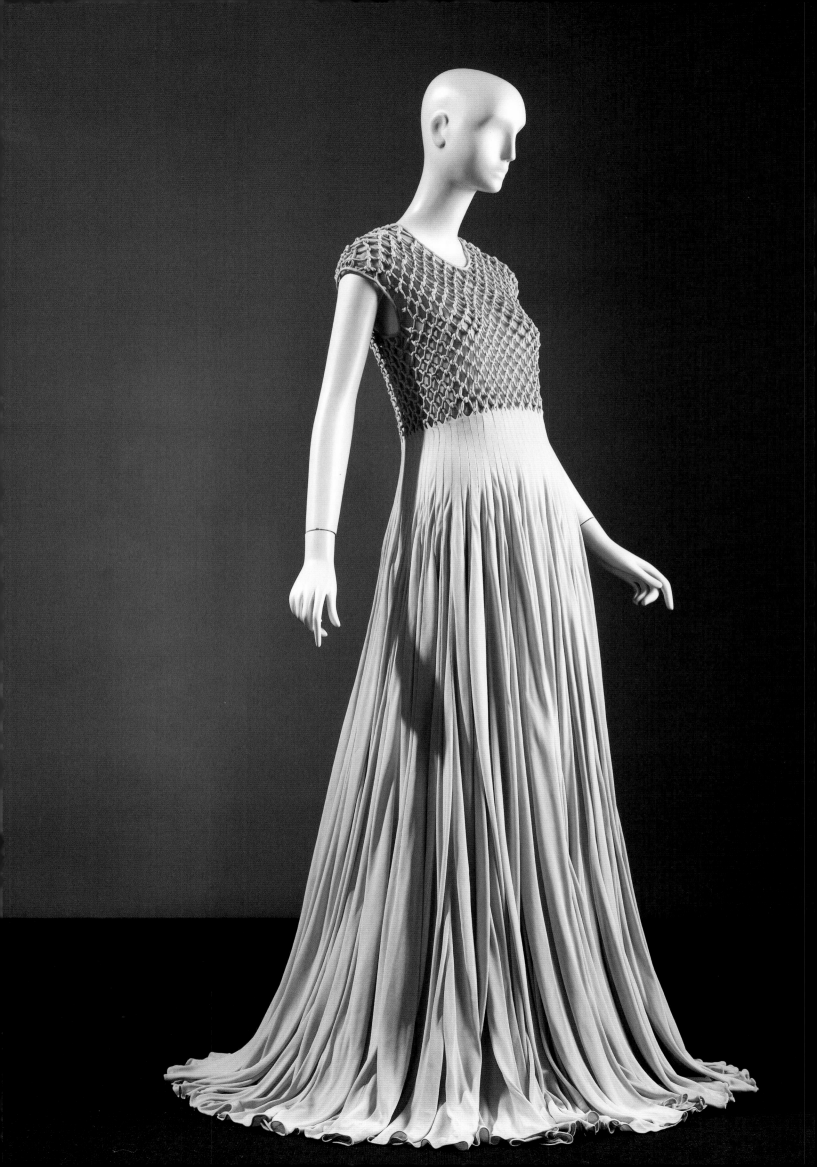

Alabaster-colored silk jersey evening
dress with hand-knotted bodice,
spring summer 2003 haute couture
collection.
Photograph: William Palmer.

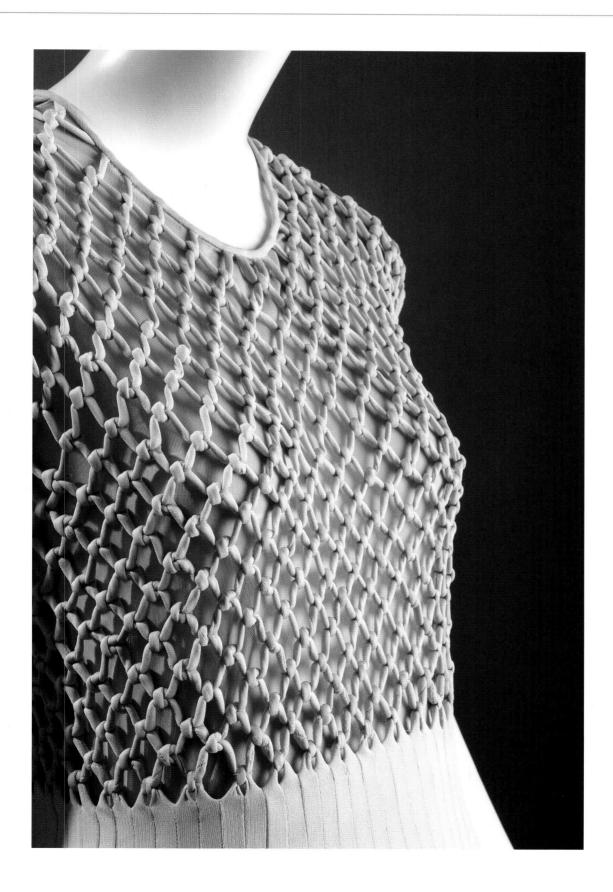

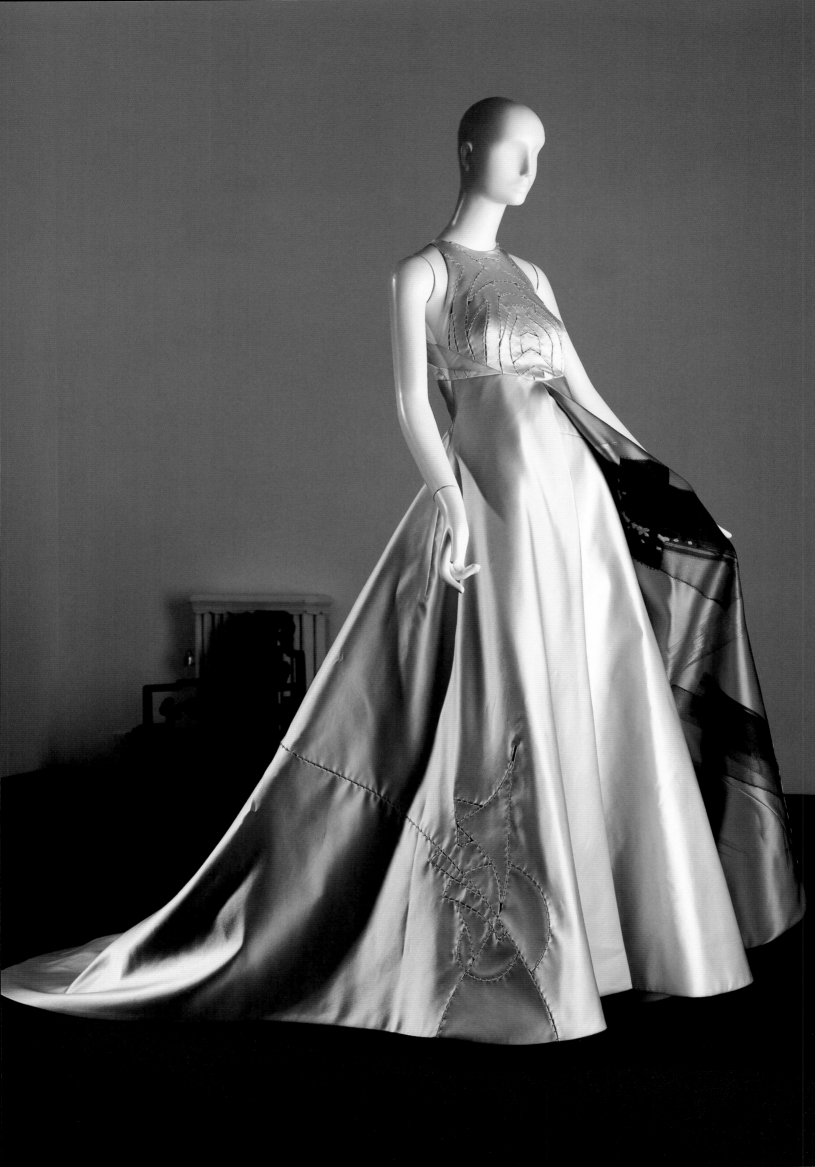

Infanta evening gown, duchess silk
satin, spring/summer 2006
haute couture collection.
Photograph: William Palmer.

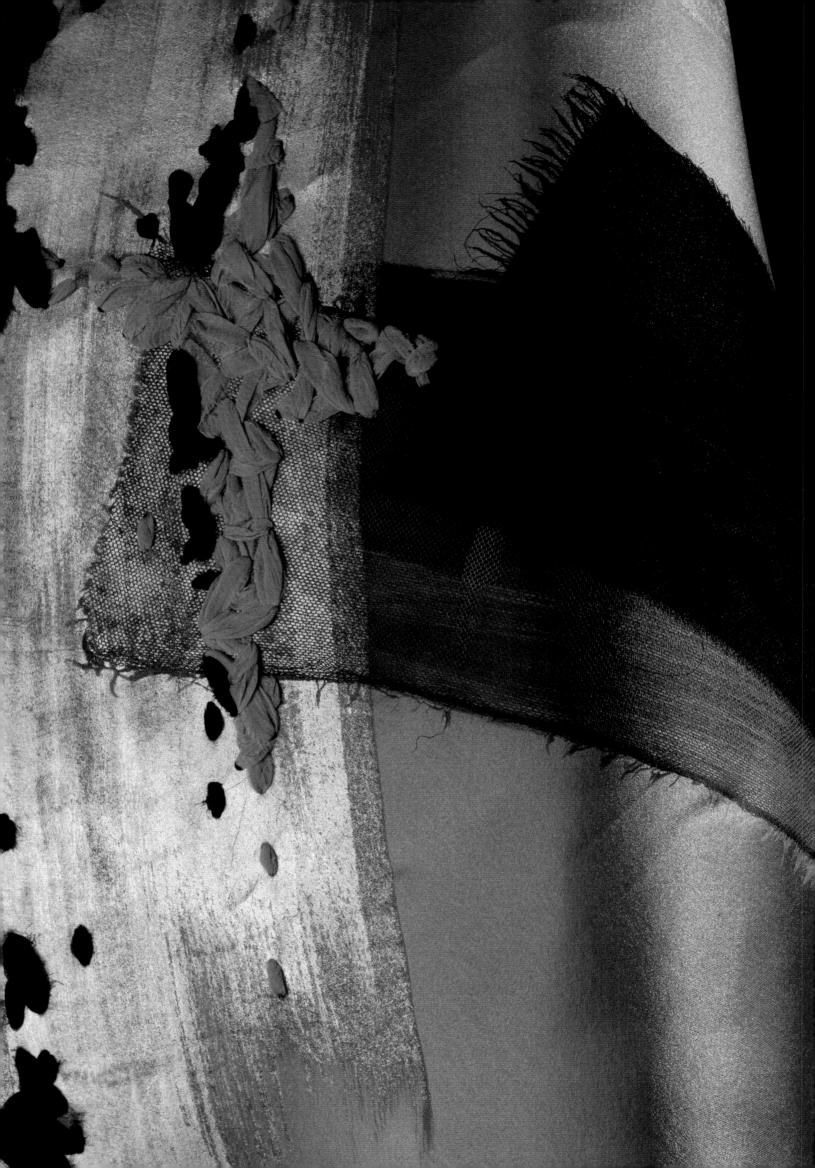

Below: upturned skirt of Infanta
evening gown, duchess silk satin,
spring/summer 2006
haute couture collection.

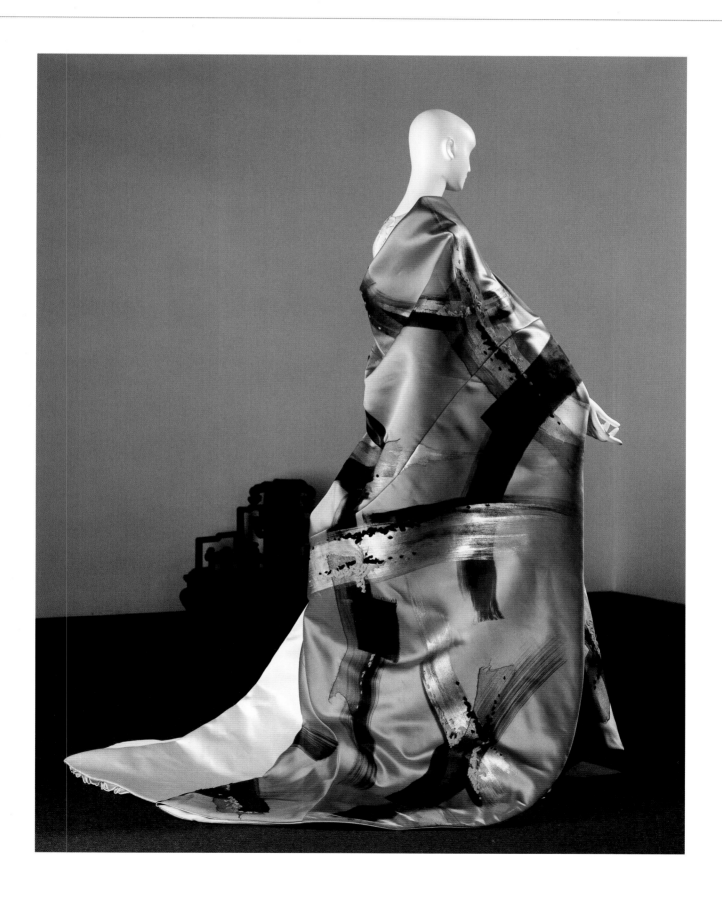

the words of Balenciaga's great client, Baroness Pauline de Rothschild, "displace the air so that her skirt would billow out just so much; front, back, and sides would round out each in turn imperceptivity, like a sea swell."[3] The volume of a Balenciaga comes from the structure of the stiffened but nearly weightless cloth and the reinforcement of grain through judicious seaming. While Rucci understood this method of construction, he did not wholly embrace this type of absolute minimalism.

Nor has Rucci advocated the creation of garments like those of another inspirational figure, Charles James (1903–1972). Widely regarded as America's greatest couturier, James is one of the few designers from the United States who is widely respected overseas. But, unlike Balenciaga, James did not pare down his methods of construction. Beginning his foray into fashion as a milliner, only later did James become a couturier. His remarkable body of work is astonishingly small, due in part to his meticulous working and reworking of ideas and in part because he accepted few commissions and failed to complete even some of those.

While James's magnum opus, the famed four-leaf-clover gown of 1953, demonstrates how beautiful his engineered garments could be, it also reveals his disdain for standard dressmaking techniques and lack of concern for his client's comfort and mobility. The bodice of this dress, made from ivory duchess satin, is asymmetrical and very complex in its cut. Along with its rigid understructure made of millinery materials such as buckram, as well as interfacing and a custom interior corset, it is meant to partially support the vast lobes of the undulating and extremely voluminous skirt, also made from layers of buckram, horsehair, and covered wire. The skirt is deftly balanced on the wearer's hips to carry and distribute most of its great weight but not enough to offset the stress to the bodice. Two versions of the four-leaf-clover now in the collection of the Brooklyn Museum of Art, with their torn and badly worn bodices, illustrate the problems of a brilliant concept that is overruled by the improper application of craft.

Also of note is the fact that the four-leaf-clover and other similarly constructed garments by James disallowed the wearer a full range of movement. A great James client, Mrs. William Randolph "Austine" Hearst, noted that she was unable to sit down or to dance with her husband at a formal party when wearing one of his gowns. Though he openly lauds James, Rucci never places aesthetics over function as he crafts his most dramatic and sculptural gowns.

Perhaps this is why Rucci feels that James's best designs date to the end of his career. A bodice and skirt ensemble, referred to as the figure-eight and made for the jewelry designer Elsa Peretti in 1978, retain the Jamesian penchant for brain-teasing complexity but with no rigidity. Fluid and body-revealing, the garment more closely aligns itself with the techniques of another designer very important to Rucci: Halston.

Halston remains one of the most important figures in American fashion history. His dramatic rise and fall in the corporate realm have unfortunately tended to obscure his artistic legacy. Along with his languid personal style and infamous drug-suffused evenings spent at Studio 54, Halston was also an excellent designer and innovative dressmaker. His finesse in handling featherweight chiffons, for example, resulted in designs that were anything but the frothy and ruffled garments most typically associated with this fabric. Halston's spare evening columns and flowing caftans are faintly echoed in recent Chado collections.

Another key couturiere who consistently informs the Rucci aesthetic is Madame Alix Grès. Nicknamed both the "Sculptress" and the "Sphinx" of fashion, Grès, of all the couturiers Rucci references, has perhaps had the most direct influence on his early experiments. According to Rucci, his first collection in 1981 paid homage to her as all the garments were cut on the bias and some were constructed using a pleating technique called fluting, one the hallmarks of Madame Grès's work. Rucci draped, cut, and fit all the garments himself, often working for hours while wearing basketball-player kneepads, immersing himself in her working methods.

Rucci has, over the duration of his career, come to understand that Grès was more than just a classicist whose style, as inaccurately recorded by many, never changed. In fact, her work was a constant evolutionary process and she designed far more than the Grecian-inspired gowns made from matte silk jersey. Grès excelled at creating caftans and pajamas cut from large geometric pattern pieces that were loosely based on ethnic costume as well as three-dimensional, sculptural woolen coats and dresses made from stiff silks like taffeta and faille. She was able to hold onto and expand upon the techniques learned in the early phase of her career and apply them to make her unique fashions in the decades after her contemporaries, such as Balenciaga who closed his house in 1968, were no longer working. During the last twenty years of her career, which ended with her retirement in 1988, Grès was the last couturiere from the golden age of French fashion design. Rucci made a point of meeting his idol while she was in New York in the early 1980s and noted it as one of the highlights of his career.

rucci and the world of art

Couturiers are by no means the only important influences in the evolution of the Rucci style. Designers from other disciplines, such as the American-born and Parisian-based jeweler extraordinaire, Joel A. Rosenthal (better known by his initial JAR), have expanded Rucci's fashion vocabulary. Like Rucci, Rosenthal, who hails from the Bronx, studied liberal arts at Harvard and fell into designing. Called the "Fabergé of our time" by some of his clients, Rosenthal is an artist who knew nothing about the technical side of jewelry-making when he began designing in the 1970s. He was unfettered by convention and crafted forms unlike any other jeweler of the late twentieth century.

Nature and fantasy are inherent in all JAR creations. His pea brooch, for example, consists of a large pod glimmering with a variety of green stones – ranging from grassy green jade drops to chartreuse-colored tourmalines and garnets – that dangle from a microscopically fine strand of gold and silver covered with pavéd diamonds. JAR is also capable of crafting a poppy brooch bursting forth with hot fire opals, rubies, pink, violet and blue sapphires, and black and white diamonds. Rucci has appropriated the essence of JAR's unorthodox use of brilliant color palettes, diverse and contrasting materials, unusual three dimensional forms and hidden supports and structures.

The arts of East Asia have also been fundamental sources of inspiration throughout Rucci's career. For example, detailed photographs of Indian architectural elements were printed onto a range of silk fabrics; they cover the length of chiffon used to make a flowing evening dress or small pieces of organza that are cut then inset into a black crepe cardigan. A vase and chair from China were printed onto the back of a black gazar skirt (which was ornamented with a free-flowing tasseled cord cut and looped onto the fabric), and a chiffon evening dress respectively. Not only do Khmer Buddhist sculptures adorn Rucci's home, but the muted color palette of the stone and the sinuous, deeply carved pleats of their robes can be found in many examples his of daywear and evening clothes.

Though Rucci draws from many cultures throughout Asia, none has had more impact on his work than that of Japan. Perhaps this fact is not surprising for a designer who named his company Chado, after that nation's rigorous and contemplative tea ceremony famous for its requisite 331 steps. Everything – from knotted silk cords that ornament swords and quivers, basketry both functional and artistic, and the imagery of falcons painted onto seventeenth-century screens – appear consistently on Rucci's designs. Japanese motifs and details are printed on textiles or inspire the braided leather belts and textured surface treatments of many types of clothing.

Rucci has also been inspired by the more cerebral and spiritual elements of Japanese art and design. For example, his organza caftan and matching trousers embroidered with tiny matchstick sized twigs are similar to artwork that depicts floral petals, such as cherry blossoms and chrysanthemums, cascading down the length of a pictorial surface. Rucci captured the Japanese view of nature's fleeting beauty, though few in the fashion arena would have understood the symbolism.

For all the beauty found throughout Asia, the greatest source of inspiration for Rucci comes from the world of western fine art. Whether they are renaissance portraits of young Italian beauties depicted in profile or the vibrant paintings of the abstract expressionists, Rucci's taste for art is both far-ranging and somewhat unpredictable.

The connection between fine art and fashion has become a popular topic for contemporary critics in recent years but the reality is that the two disciplines rarely intersect and only on occasion directly influence one another. Even when designers are able to cite specific works of art or artists that form the basis of their seasonal collections, few are able to articulate those connections convincingly. One of the few exceptions is Ralph Rucci. He is able to clear this hurdle due to his lifelong study of art and the fact that he also paints.

Rucci is the product of a rigorous academic training, having attended a Jesuit preparatory school before earning a bachelor's degree in literature and a minor in philosophy at Temple University. He also studied aesthetics under one of the great art historians of that time, Irwin Panofsky, and was able upon seeing the first images of Balenciaga to make direct comparisons to Robert Motherwell. The images of Balenciaga's bride and attendant from 1967 mentioned above were, for Rucci, pure geometric shapes that evoked the painter's seminal work, *Elegy to the Spanish Republic*.

While the connection between Balenciaga and Motherwell is not immediately evident to most viewers, it does give a clue as to how Rucci perceives and appropriates art into his garments. Another example of his expansive but discerning taste is the fact that two of Rucci's favorite artists are Francis Bacon (1909–1992) and Cy Twombly (born 1928). It is indeed an odd pairing. Bacon is viewed by some to be the greatest British artist since Joseph Mallord William Turner

(1775–1851). His preoccupation with the melodramatic and psychological impact of terror in his early career continued to resonate in the curved and blurred bands of color that marked his later works. Twombly, an American who immigrated to Rome as a young man, employed abstraction in his spare graffiti-like pencil scribbles that found root in the art and literature of antiquity.

In one evening ensemble from his spring/summer 2002 collection, Rucci took his cue from a lithograph he owns – one part of a Bacon triptych dating to 1972. The figurative elements are ignored completely in the gown. Rucci isolates tiny slivers of the color palette: only the acidic green, aqua blue, and a coal black background. Despite this selective choice of elements, the artistic sensibility of Bacon can be felt in the drama, theatricality and darkness of the gown and matching stole. The strong, curved bands of color seem to vibrate as they swirl around the ovoid shaped train. The color forms serve to confuse the shape from some angles yet underscore its monumentality at others. Still, one would be hard pressed to note the connection to Bacon without prompting.

If the connection to Bacon is abstruse, another dress from the same collection much more clearly reveals its artistic roots: the "Twombly Swan." Made of white silk gazar, it is embroidered in tumultuous swirls of black, gray, red and ivory silk floss, and beads not unlike the 1955 Cy Twombly works entitled *The Greeks*, *Criticism*, *Free Wheeler*, and *Academy*. The dense and variegated white canvases by the artist were covered with multiple layers of paint while "pencil and crayon lines and colorless scumbling with a blunt stylus are worked into and against the viscosity of the cream field. These thickets of marks have a congested, 'hot' frenzy"[4]

Rucci was able to capture that sparseness of line and vibrating intensity for the "Twombly Swan" because of Francois Lesage. Proprietor of the world's most prestigious embroidery house, Lesage, according to Rucci, "called and asked if I wanted the brush strokes to be angry or calm." It is why, stated the couturier, "I go to Europe."[5] What is unusual about Rucci's gown is the fact that it is so sculptural and dramatic in shape. Most fashion designers who create garments with bold or graphic imagery opt for simple, tubular silhouettes. The obvious reason is that the artwork is more legible against a form that more closely resembles a canvas.

The ultimate tribute to Twombly was Rucci's creation of four gowns entitled *Le Quattro Staggione* for the spring/summer 2006 haute couture collection. Based on the artist's 1993–94 series of four enormous canvases (each one measuring over ten feet high and more than six feet across) and now owed by the Tate Modern in London, they and the inspirational dresses are emblazoned with color and movement. The embroidery, executed by the firm of Jean Luca Bernardi of Lyon, France, combines imagery and the writing from the Twombly paintings.

Rucci not only channels the work of specific artists onto the surface of his garments, but also recreates the pageantry of the old masters using thoroughly modern clothing, specifically for his runway presentations. One outstanding example of this was the opening two looks presented at his fall/winter 2004 haute couture show. Poised in shadow, the first model on the runway was dressed in a short tunic, domed hat and thigh-high boots, all made of brown alligator. She was immediately followed by her "page," clad in a fitted jacket and narrow trousers made of black Russian broadtail embroidered with a sprinkling of black caviar beads. Fittingly, the latter model carried a parasol for her predecessor. The overall effect evoked grand baroque pictures such as

Silk satin and gazar dress inspired
by Francis Bacon, spring/summer
2002, collection of Tatiana
Sorokko, Bacon lithograph in
background.
Photograph: William Palmer.

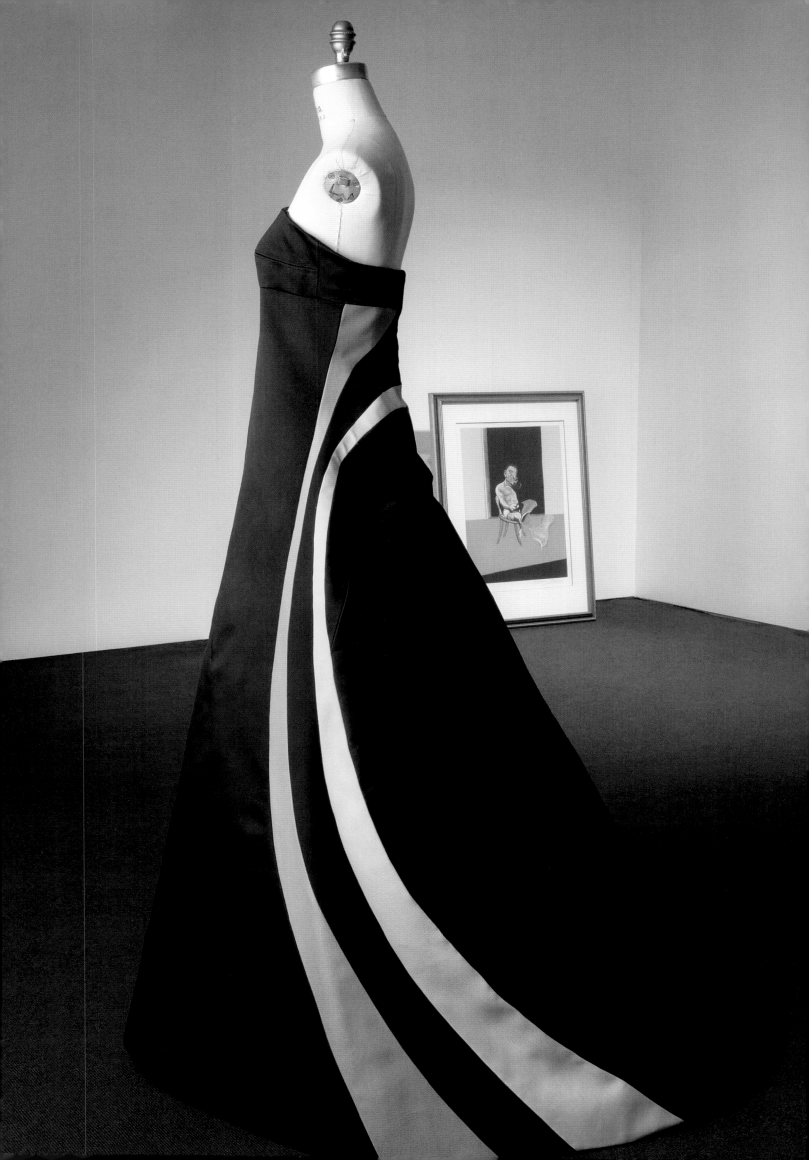

"The Four Seasons" gowns inspired
by Cy Twombly's *Quattro Stagioni*,
spring/summer 2006 haute couture
collection.
Photograph: William Palmer.

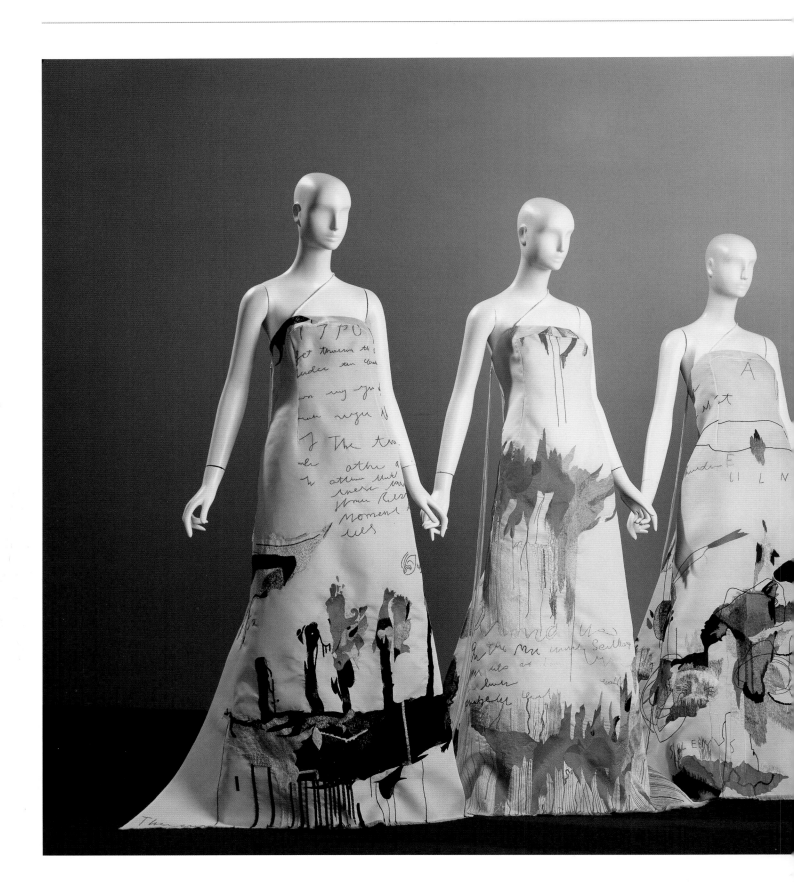

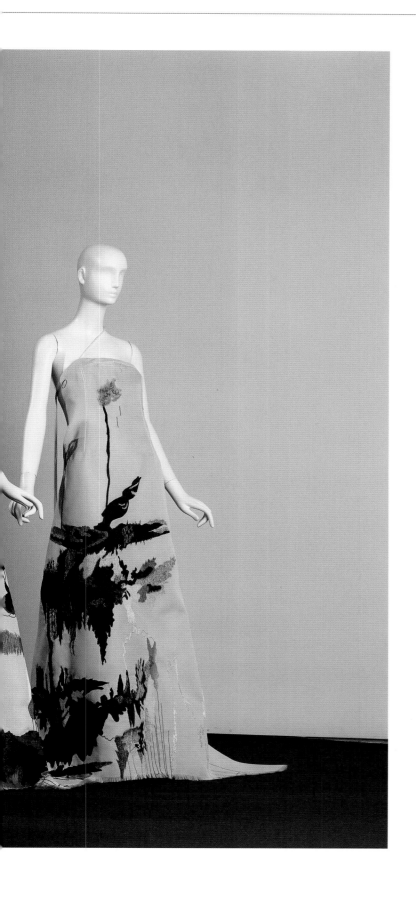

Detail, "The Four Seasons" gowns
inspired by Cy Twombly's *Quattro
Stagioni*, spring/summer 2006
haute couture collection.
Photograph: William Palmer.

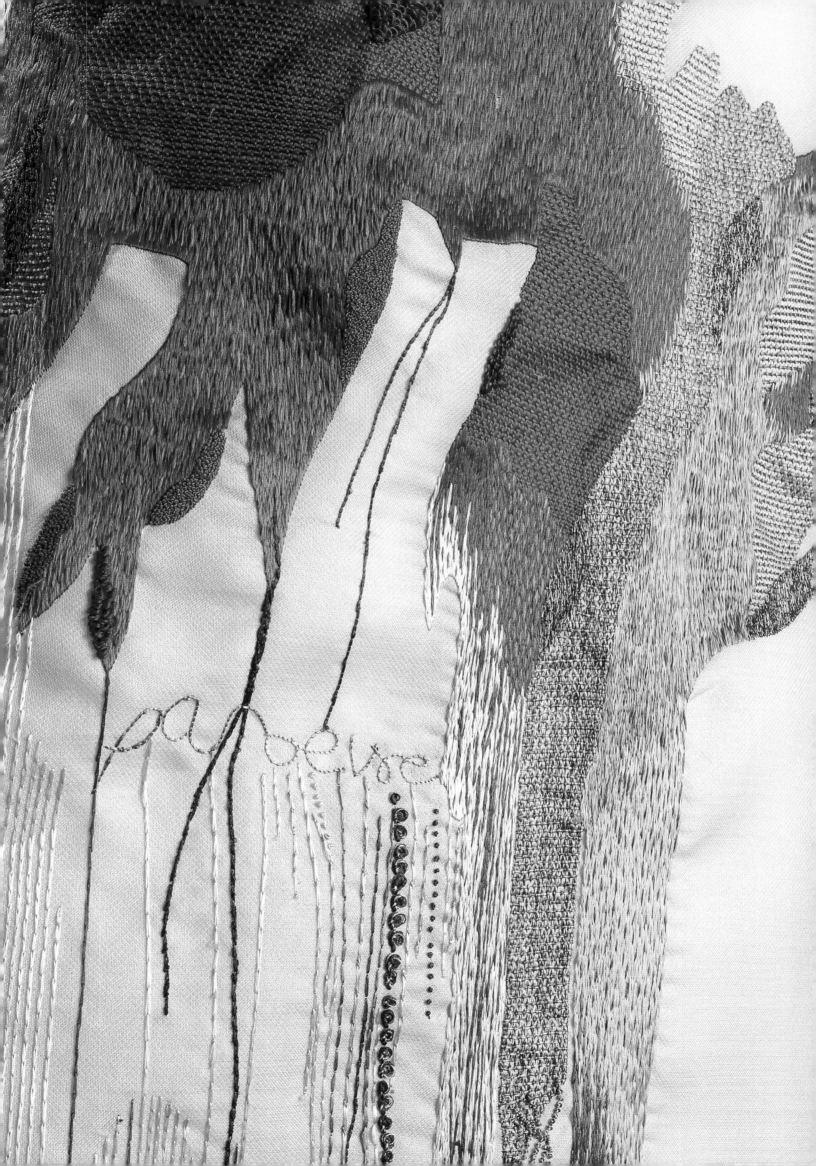

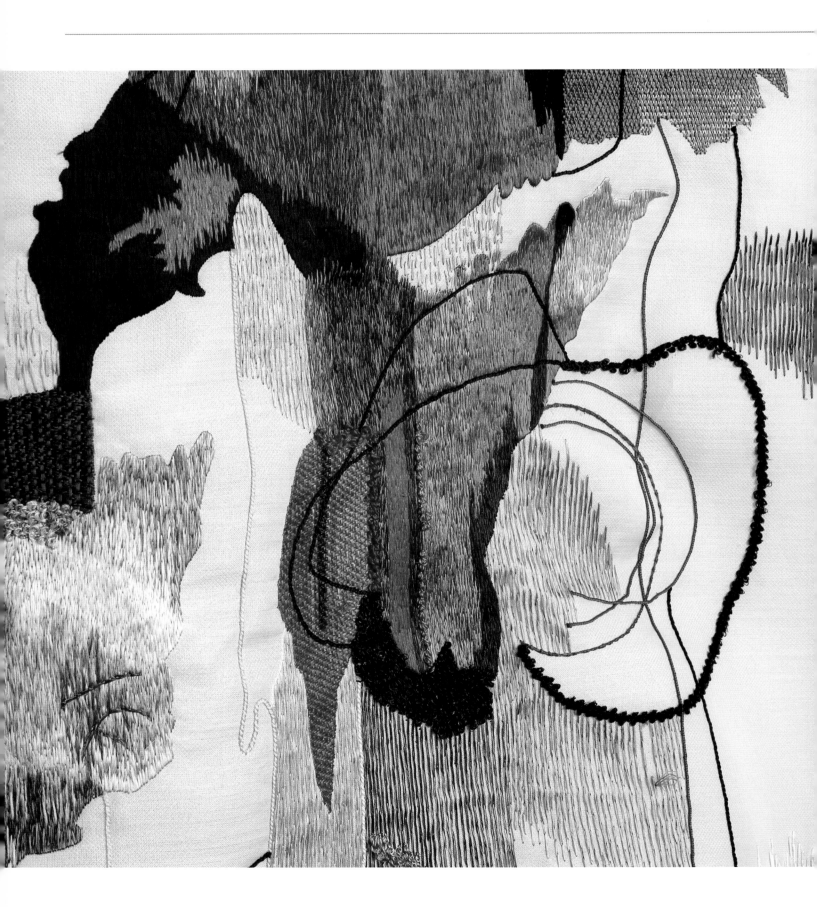

Detail, "The Four Seasons" gowns
inspired by Cy Twombly's *Quattro
Stagioni*, spring/summer 2006
haute couture collection.
Photograph: William Palmer.

Charles Le Brun's *Equestrian Portrait of the Chancellor Seguier* (1661) or the masterpiece of 1622 by Peter Paul Rubens entitled *The Debarkation of Marie (de Medici) at Marseilles*, as well as later rococo Chinoiserie-inspired paintings, textiles, and ceramics.

rucci's art

When first presented with Rucci's own canvases, it is clear that he is looking to a range of sources in the realm of abstract expressionism. In addition to Francis Bacon and Cy Twombly, other painters, such as Robert Motherwell, Antonio Tapies, Joseph Beuys, and Richard Serra, have imprinted themselves on Rucci. But he also finds connection to the Classical past and to art from non-western cultures.

Yet, for all of his interest and participation in the realm of fine art, Rucci never considered himself an artist. When questioned about this issue, he agreed that there exists a superficial assessment that, in the west, paintings and sculpture reign supreme over the minor or decorative arts. (In turn, there is a similar hierarchy in which furniture, ceramics and metal work outrank other applied arts such as textiles and, finally, fashion). Therefore, Rucci feels that as a designer he cannot call himself an artist if making garments is his main emphasis.

But he also concedes that one of the reasons he respects many other non-western civilizations is that they have traditionally understood that seemingly insignificant objects can be imbued with high levels of intellectual and spiritual importance. For the Japanese, ceramics, textiles, and paper, for example, are still viewed as crafts worthy of respect and devotion. Even the packaging of produce and other foods become works of art in the hands of the Japanese, as vibrantly illustrated in Hideyuki Oka's publication, *How to Wrap Five More Eggs*.

One of the key reasons Rucci paints and is "so drawn to art" is that he feels a strong pull to contemporary artists like Twombly. There is a "visceral reaction that, like it or not, presents the viewer with a psychic drama." Both the work of art and the environment in which the work is presented reach out to Rucci in a way that "pure design cannot."[6]

Rucci's strong emotional response to art and his varied sources of inspiration may account for the diversity of his paintings. His canvases range in size. The small pictures are reminiscent of Mughal miniatures or medieval illuminated manuscripts in their intimacy and, like these historic works, are often covered with swaths of gold leaf. Larger works are more akin to those used by many contemporary artists, often are sparse, and are made with a multitude of materials: paint, paper and textiles. Each of them conveys contemplation and serenity despite the large variation in scale. It is interesting that the emotional rawness of Bacon and the frenetic energy of Twombly are not present in Rucci's own artwork.

Because much of Rucci's artwork is so clear and pure, it can translate well into his fashion. One the most literal appropriations of his paintings can be found in a day coat made for the spring/summer 2005 ready-to-wear collection. A simple black cashmere coat is slashed with a streak of white that cuts down the front of the garment. It is based on a large, mixed media work entitled *Passage Way*, that is now in a private collection. According to Rucci's gallerist, Serge

Sorokko, "If you believe as I do, that some fashion can be art, then there is nothing wrong with someone becoming an artist/ fashion designer and going into another genre."[7]

rucci's approach to fashion design

While the font of inspirational for Rucci is vast and multidimensional, the initial steps of his working methodology are relatively straightforward and not vastly different from other designers. He begins his creative process in much the way other designers do, through the assemblage of inspiration boards, the selection of fabrics from many samples, and the illustration of dozens of ideas. But once concepts become more concrete, the creation of each garment takes on a heightened intensity beyond the kind of refined styling normally associated with fashion creators. For Rucci, great garments are more than an exercise in making attractive clothing. Methods of construction are constantly being refined and new ones explored.

Rucci begins by creating inspiration boards. The genesis of a seasonal collection might be found in a single object or design image such as a Japanese woven basket or an Indian butah (paisley) motif. From there, images culled from art books, photography archives and vintage magazines are gradually accumulated and affixed to oversized boards that are prominently hung in Rucci's office and other workspaces, or they may be stored in small notebooks that he keeps with him.

Fabric samples are added as they begin to come in from the finest mills and workrooms in Europe, primarily those in Italy and France. Many of the samples are modified according to the needs of Rucci and his staff. Colors can be muted or intensified or changed altogether; feather embroideries might be deplumed and lightened, while beading might be enriched and made denser. Rucci will often ask specific firms to create one-of-a-kind prints or bleach textiles to match his own art work or the brushstrokes of a Chinese calligraphy master.

Garments then begin to take shape on paper. Rucci draws the preliminary designs in a sharp, angular and somewhat abstracted style with the cloth he has chosen by his side. These images are then presented to his key staff members so they can begin to create the working patterns. The demands of his business preclude Rucci from working directly with cloth as much as he would like, and most of the draping, cutting, and sewing is now performed by his atelier specialists.

Patterns are first executed on paper, pinned together, draped on a form, and refined. Working samples of the garments are then cut in muslin and fitted on a model. Through a series of discussions with the staff about fabrication, ornamentation and overall fit, Rucci often modifies and refines the muslin several times. Once the muslin meets the designer's criteria, the base fabric is cut and basted together. This preliminary garment is fitted, finished and, if necessary, sent off to be embroidered or otherwise ornamented. When the embellished garment returns, it is again fitted on a model. Minute alterations are made and a final determination about the overall patterning is either approved or again modified according to Rucci's instructions. Custom-fitted to each model, a single garment may be cut, refitted and modified over a dozen times. His more complex designs might require upwards of forty hours to develop a single pattern. Another forty to sixty hours are needed for cutting and sewing, not including the surface embellishments.

Though the problem-solving and execution of garments is done by craftspeople, it is Rucci alone who is the creator from inception to finished product. Annarita Cavallini, who is arguably the most important technical worker on Rucci's team, emphatically states that only Rucci designs each and every garment that the house produces. No exception.[8]

his staff: skills, organization, key personnel

The most important element in executing the Rucci style is the technical knowledge both he and his staff possess. Though based in New York City, the epicenter of ready-to-wear fashion, the Chado workrooms are organized like a traditional Parisian haute couture house. Each garment, be it custom-made for a single client or made for sale in a department store, is designed and executed on the premises in one of his two workrooms. The front (or west-facing) atelier houses Rucci's elite team of patternmakers and drapers. They are responsible for turning the conceptual illustrations into finished products as well as overseeing custom-made garments for couture clients. The back (or east-facing) workroom is the production area that makes clothes primarily from the ready-to-wear line. While some couture garments are made in the production area, they rarely handle the softer garments and never make chiffon dresses and caftans, either for ready-to-wear or for couture.

Not all elements of each garment can be made in the Rucci ateliers. Every fabric is imported, mainly from Italy, and certain surface embellishments are embroidered in France or Asia. His custom-made furs and accessories are designed by Rucci but are outsourced and executed by specialists beyond the borders of his atelier.

Chief amongst Rucci's team of more than fifty employees are Annarita Cavallini, the *première du flou* (head of soft draping), Christine VonAesch, *première du tailleur* (head of tailoring), Gail Gondek, the mastermind behind the grand *Infanta* ballgowns, Larisa Ryzhova, who provides technical assistance but is most valuable as the atelier's in-house artist, and Mr. Joo Yeon Kim, the company's production manager. Each is expertly trained in the fields of pattern making, dressmaking and tailoring. Rucci consistently states that while he studied pattern making and draping and that some of his designs have been cut and sewn by his own hand, the more sophisticated garments could never have been created without the engineering skills of people like Cavallini.

Though his staff is specialized, the top members of the atelier are not bound by rigid job descriptions. VonAesch, a native of Switzerland, works on garments that are not strictly tailored or rigid; softer and voluminous pieces are also part of her vocabulary and output. Ryzhova, from Russia, executes many of the art and design elements for Rucci but is also a gifted pattern maker. While Gondek works almost exclusively on the *Infanta*, her mathematical approach to construction is absorbed into the design elements of other garments.

Most importantly, Cavallini, a Midwesterner who earned her B.A. at Washington University in St. Louis and was raised by her Italian immigrant father and Italian-American mother who were highly discerning about the quality of clothing, is involved with the development of nearly every new garment and concept devised by Rucci. She is also the unofficial point person for the other technicians in the couture atelier.

Cavallini notes that each design begins with Rucci, who brings a sketch and fabric choices to the workroom. The method of construction is determined by the style of the garment and the inherent nature of the fabric. The collaborative relationship between Rucci and Cavallini, for example, involves an ongoing series of discussions about what he wants the garment to look like and how she can execute the final product. Because so many garments have unique, new construction requirements, she often offers him alternative solutions should the initial concept not be viable.

The first consideration is often the overall silhouette. Once the shape of the garment is set, a member of the team breaks up the body into a series of geometric shapes. Those shapes then determine the size of the pattern pieces that are, in turn, mathematically rendered to create a working sample. The sample evolves in one of two ways.

One method is what Cavallini describes as a kind of "controlled construction,"[9] meaning that the starting point begins at either the center front or center back. The placement of fabric along specific grain lines (straight, cross or bias) is then determined. From the starting point, the locus evolves into a series of radiating cuts and seams that follow the line of the body and the silhouette determined by Rucci. Most of the coats, jackets, skirts, and trousers are made using this method of controlled construction. The other, Cavallini explains, includes couture chiffon dresses that are draped in a more intuitive manner, in much the way Madame Grès made her famous Grecian-inspired gowns with little regard for symmetrical patterns.

Whether making garments in the more controlled manner or intuitively, many of the closures, especially zippers, are hidden. Like most couturiers, Rucci and his team opt for the slot zipper (sometimes called the centered or double welt zipper) because it is flatter than a welt zipper and can be more easily hidden from view. These closures, often snaking sinuously along the back, are rarely placed in the center front or back seam, as they are in most other contemporary garments. Like the zipper closure, elements that improve fit, such as darts, are sometimes hidden, are asymmetrical and might be decorative.

All of these methods (and others to be described later) allow Rucci the flexibility to design clothing that cleaves to the body (especially the torso and back), highlights its most attractive attributes, and gives the wearer the best fit and range of movement. Allowing his clientele, composed primarily of working women, the freedom to work all day and travel comfortably is one of Rucci's chief goals. It proves that these couture quality garments are indeed modern. Each item is also made so as to allow the wearer the opportunity to have it altered, no matter how complicated the cut may be.

Rucci relies on Cavallini, VonAesch, Gondek, and Ryzona, and they, in turn, rely on the cutters, sample-makers, and hand-sewers who, in the words of Cavallini "know how to breathe life into Ralph's work." Along with their collective skills is a library where their "internal case studies" have been "accumulated."[10] This wealth of information about the craft of dressmaking can be extracted by the team to find solutions to an ever-changing set of new challenges.

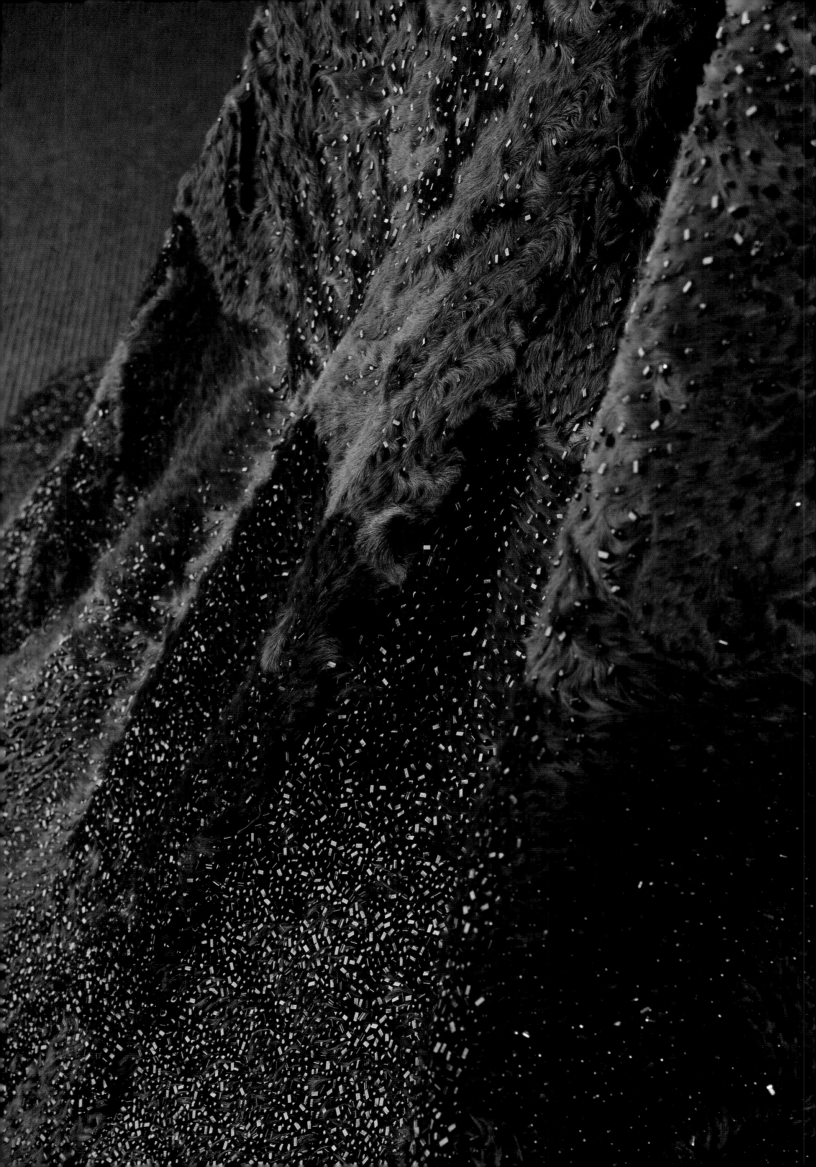

Understanding the working methodologies of any fashion designer also requires an analysis of his oeuvre's building blocks – textiles. Rucci has continued to evolve as a couturier and become ever more sophisticated in his output but has also adhered to a more or less consistent style throughout his career. What has changed are the materials he uses; there was a drastic jump in quality that began in the late 1990s as his business grew and expanded. By the time he entered the world of haute couture in 2002, Rucci was able to reach the stratosphere by choosing the most expensive and exclusive textiles and embellishments in the world.

Long before he was able to buy the best textiles, Rucci yearned for deeply dimensional damasks, silk velvets woven on baroque-era looms, novelty weaves that appear to be embroidered, or petersham, a stiffly sized quadruple-weight gazar. He knew that gazar, for example, was a material first developed by the Swiss textile firm of Abraham for Cristobal Balenciaga in 1958. Today, Rucci is credited with reviving interest in this costly and unforgiving material. When covering the spring/summer 2001 collections for the *New York Times*, journalist Cathy Horyn described using quadruple-weight cotton gazar and asked how a person would even know about such a thing.[11]

While Rucci occasionally laments the loss of access to textiles no longer made, he has made great efforts to work with the world's leading mills and to track down weavers who still create luxurious textiles on centuries-old looms. Of great assistance to the couturier is Jean François Ricat. A Parisian who began working for French textile firms and then the couture house of Balmain before moving to New York more than a decade ago, Ricat has been instrumental in acquiring and overseeing the acquisition and production of textile and surface treatments for Rucci since 2005.

Rucci chooses historically accurate fabrics, like the black silk damask used for the skirt of a cocktail dress dating to the fall 2006 haute couture collection, that are woven in small quantities by companies like Old World Weavers. Founded by interior designer and fashion maven Iris Apfel and her husband in the 1950s, the company was created because historic materials were already not readily available in quantity by the mid-twentieth century.

While on a trip to Venice in 2004, Rucci discovered a mottled green silk velvet fabric woven in a tortoise shell pattern that was still being made by a firm called Antica Tessitura Serica Luigi Bevilacqua. Headed by the founder's descendents, Mario Bevilacqua and his wife Paola, the firm still makes textiles as it has for more than two centuries on wooden, manually-operated auroserici looms. Their master weavers work these machines (some dating to the seventeenth century) that can only produce 30 centimeters, or just over 10 inches, of cloth per day. While the process is excruciatingly slow, the fabric is also far narrower (at 65 centimeters or about 26 inches) than the standard 45- and 60-inch wide materials made today. The challenge for Rucci and his staff is to create contemporary garments from historically made materials. The solution for the fall 2006 haute couture collection was to craft a narrow day coat using the maximum width of the velvet in front and in back and to join them with wide bands of black trapunto-stitched satin inset down each side of the coat.

Although the art of weaving such rarified textiles has been on the wane for decades, Rucci and other couturiers still have outstanding resources for luxurious materials. Arguably, the designer's most important textile creator is Roberto Columbo of Luigi Colombo in Borgosesia, Italy. It is Rucci's sole source for double-faced cashmere, a dense but luxuriantly pliable fabric. Sharply cut jackets and coats, slender trousers and dresses for both day and evening were no longer being made exclusively in wool as they had been since Rucci began to design under his own name. Columbo cashmere has become Rucci's favorite for haute couture and ready-to-wear and for both day and evening. Rucci, in turn, is one of Mr. Columbo's biggest clients. In fact, nearly two-thousand yards of the firm's cashmere are bought by Rucci each year. Most often, the firm dyes the fabric in saturated or neutral monochromatic colors that range from garnet red to beige. On occasion, Columbo will produce the most subtle of patterns, such as the faint chalk stripe woven into a charcoal-colored ground that Rucci used to make an haute couture, floor length day coat and matching trousers accented with patent leather insets. In this case, the fiber was vicuna and not cashmere.

One of Rucci's long-time suppliers of fabrics, mainly woolens and silks, has been Gandini. Located in Milan, Italy, and headed by Suzy Gandini, it is the source for a small number of his printed chiffons, silk shantungs, wool gabardines and serges, and especially the double-faced wool crepes that have been a Chado staple for many years.

At Taroni in Como, Italy, Michael Capena and Marcel Bonzinger work with Rucci to provide a broad range of crisp and lightweight silks like gazars, failles and moirés. Taroni is also the primary source for the heavily woven duchess satins that are used to make many of the dramatic evening gowns known as *Infantas*. The firm has also begun to make special novelty fabrics for Rucci like sfumato, a silk velvet with a prominent *gros de londres* ground in either a muted forest green or deep taupe with a black pile so sparse and short that it resembles flocked wallpaper. The overall effect, as its name in Italian implies, is the blurring or softening of sharp outlines through the subtle and gradual blending of one tone into another, and is similar to the word for smoke.

From early on in his career, Rucci has used knitted jerseys to make everything from his empire-waisted dresses (with a high waistline positioned directly under the bust), to his sinuous evening columns. Like one of his favorite couturiers, Madame Grès, renowned for her pleated Grecian gowns, Rucci bought his silk knitted jersey from the French firm of Racine. When they went out of business, he turned to the New York company, Jasco. After its doors were closed in 2005, Rucci began to buy both silk and wool jersey from Roberto Columbo of Italy.

Another important firm that Rucci has consistently relied upon is Bucol. Headed by Olivier Fornier, Bucol is responsible for the creation of many of the specialized inkjet prints that are found on Rucci's large-scale silk chiffon scarves, such as the ones that featured details from Renaissance paintings. A new Bucol fabric made for Rucci for his fall 2006 ready-to-wear collection is a duchess satin coat printed with the writings of the designer himself.

The firm that has been used most frequently for unique printed fabrics is Luigi Verga. Images of rock formations, planets and paintings chosen by Rucci are sent to Italy where they are digitally printed onto a range of silk fabrics. Equally sophisticated are the digital prints of Asian furniture on silk chiffon for evening dresses that are both body conscious and flowing. Perhaps

Cocktail dress detail, black silk
damask, spring/summer 2005
haute couture collection.
Photograph: William Palmer.

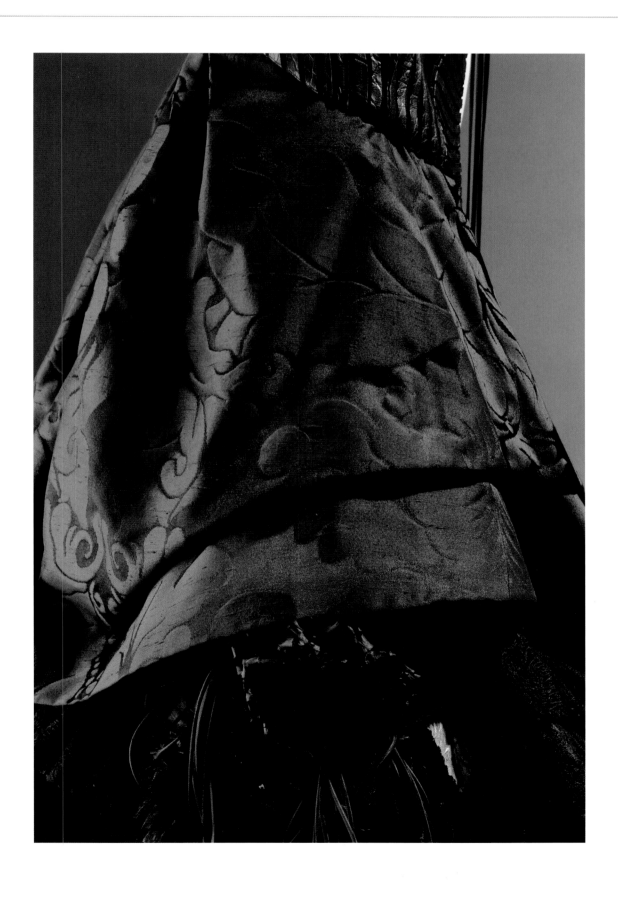

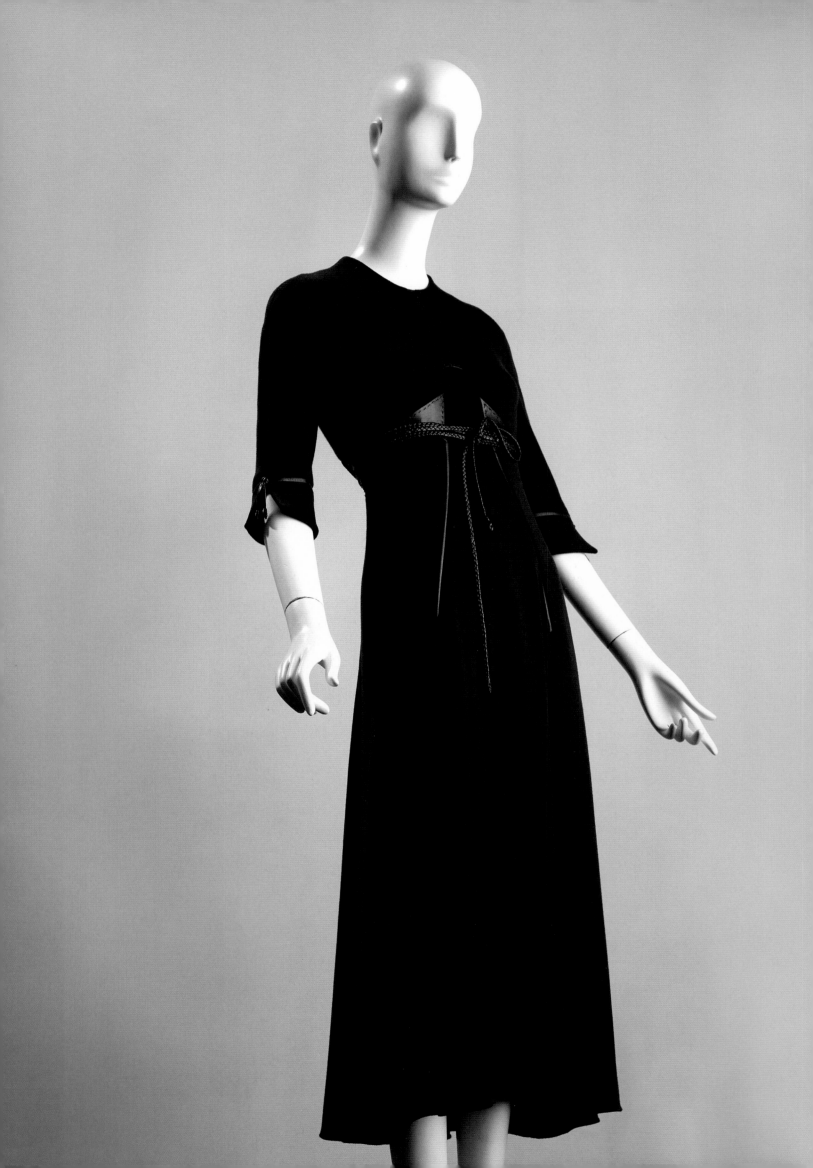

Facing page: wool jersey
empire-waisted dress,
fall/winter 2006.
Photograph: William Palmer.

Below: braided leather belt detail.

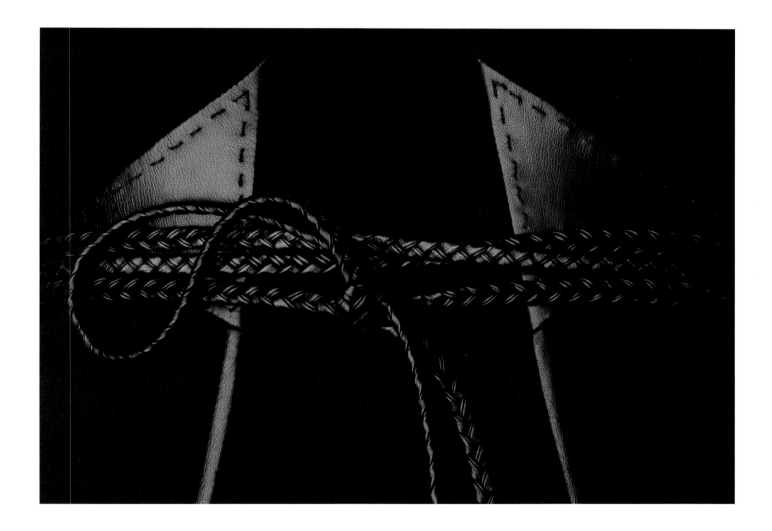

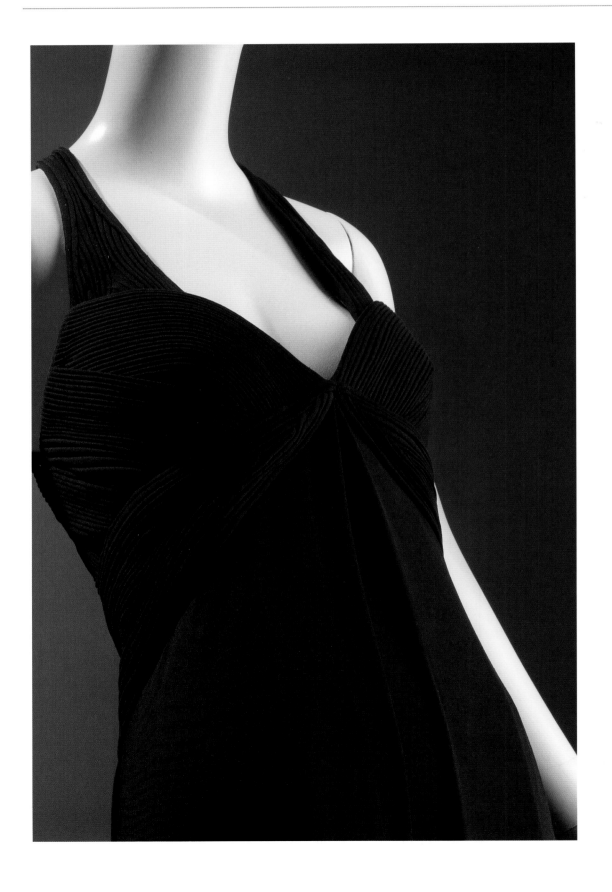

Detail, black silk jersey evening
dress with fluted bodice,
fall/winter 2005 ready-to-wear
collection.
Photograph: William Palmer.

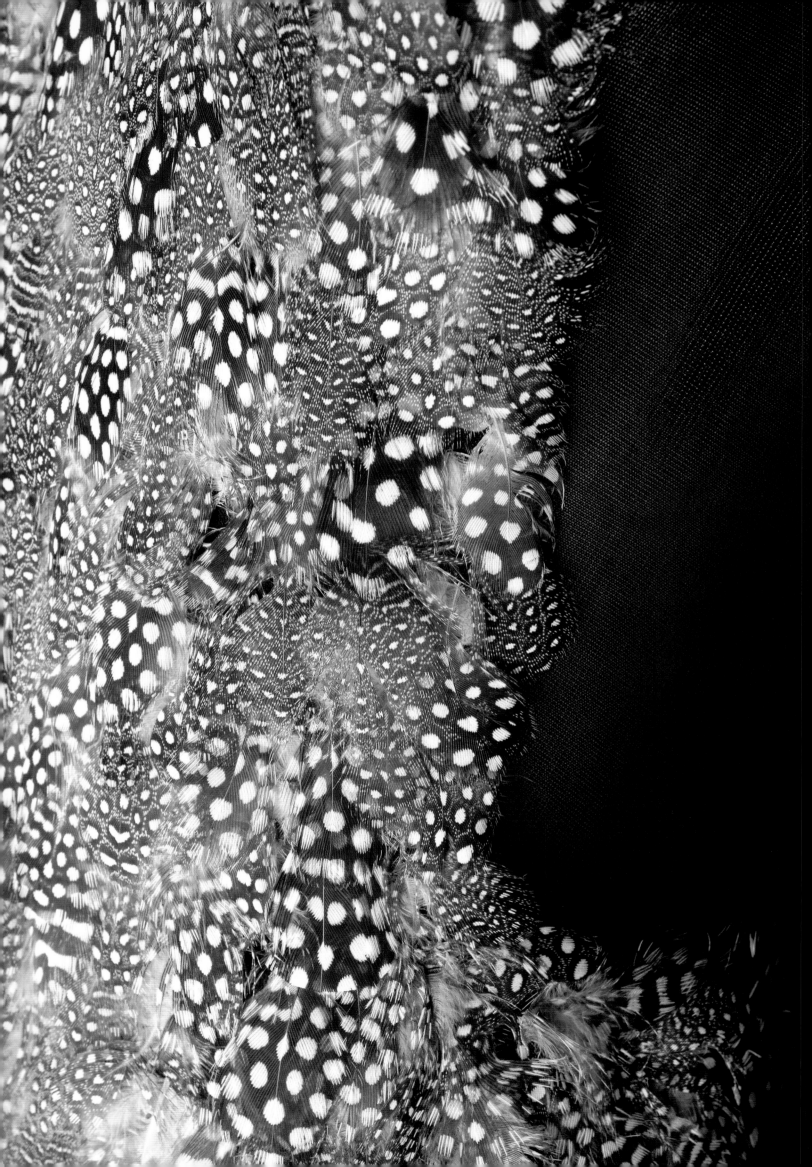

Guinea feather evening dress,
fall/winter 2002,
haute couture collection.
Photograph: William Palmer.

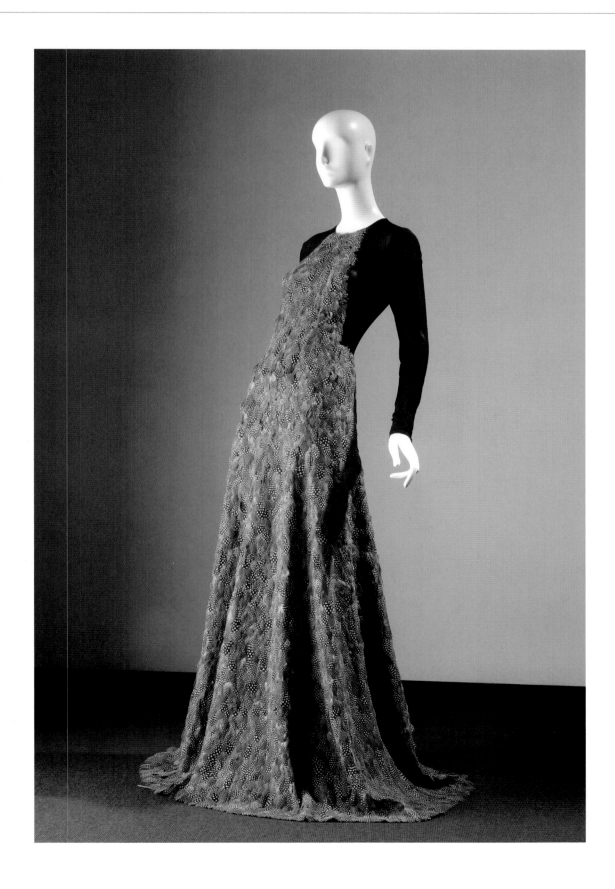

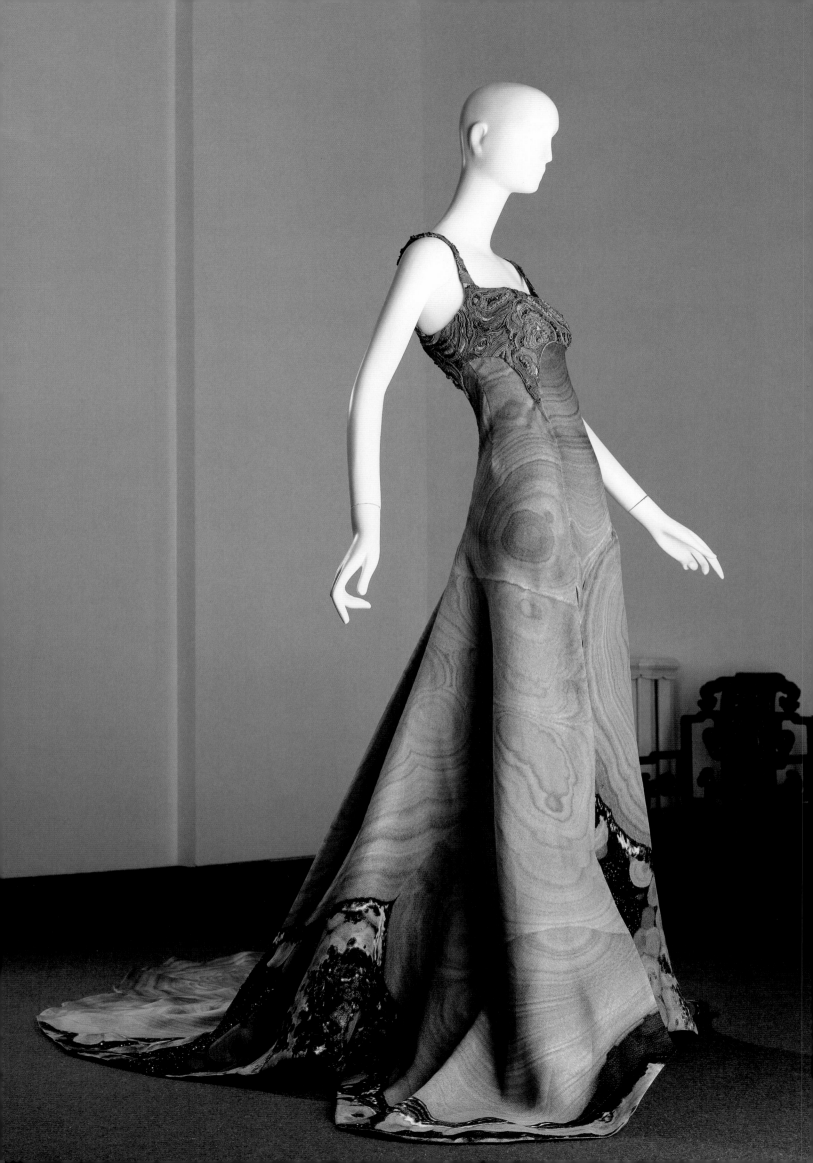

"Malachite" evening dress,
spring/summer 2006 haute
couture collection.
Photograph: William Palmer.

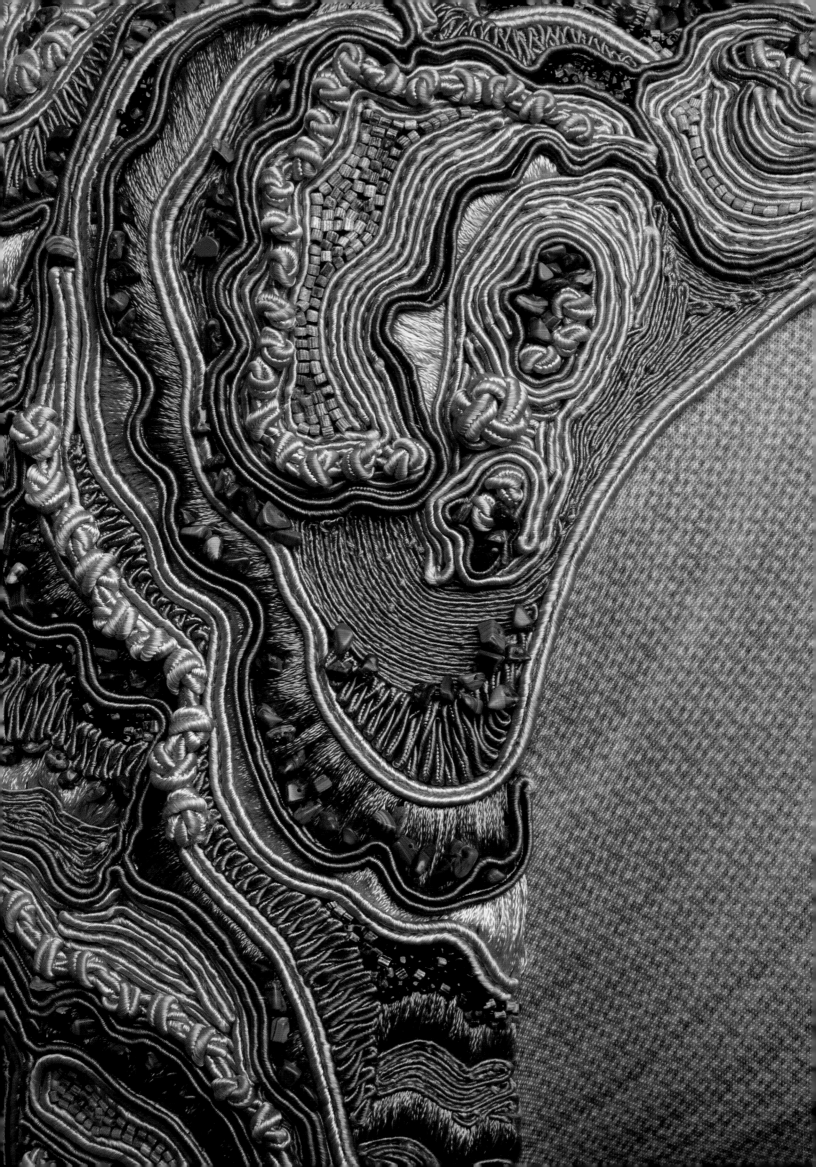

"Malachite" evening dress,
spring/summer 2006
haute couture collection.
Photograph: William Palmer.

Facing page: bodice detail of
"Malachite" evening dress,
embroidery by Lesage.

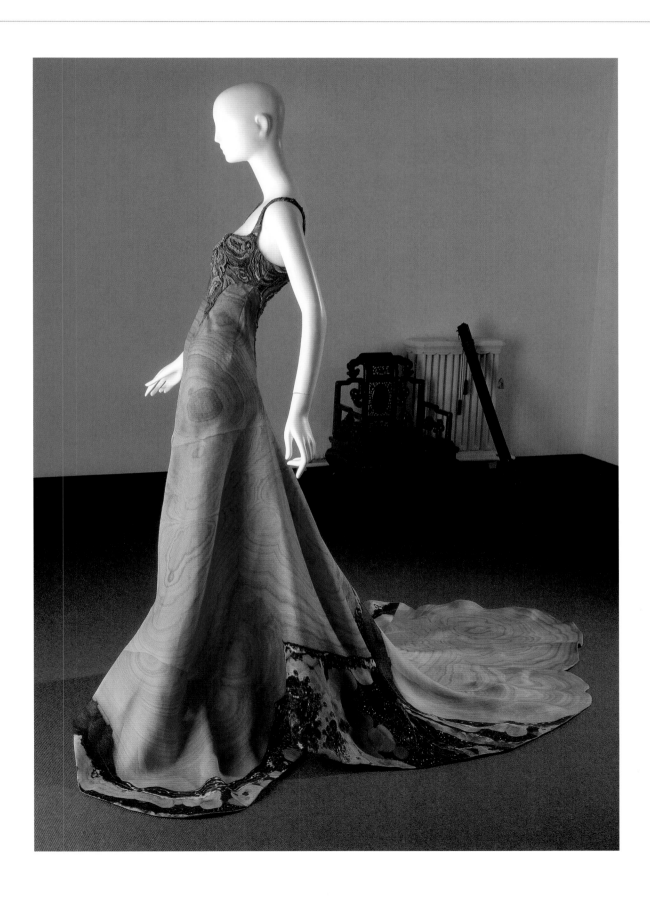

Rucci is at his best when these high tech textiles are combined with other materials and surface treatments. A great example is an evening dress made for the fall 2006 haute couture collection: its skirt is made of feather-weight silk chiffon digitally printed with amber and brown agate stone that has been magnified many times. It is topped with a small bodice of brown leather that has been perforated with countless "polka-dot" holes.

Even more exemplary is the malachite evening dress from the same collection. Both fitted on top and amply flared below, this vibrant green dress is made from silk organza also digitally printed by Luigi Verga from an oversized photograph of this stone. The bodice is ornamented with rich embroidery of thick silk threads that mimic the pattern of the stone and was executed by the venerated Parisian firm of Lesage. The bottom of the skirt is cut to match the scalloped edges of the agate's rippling and undulating layers; the many black patches in the stone are further enriched with tiny black sequins and glass caviar beads that were applied by artisans working for Shagufta of India.

surface treatments

The surface treatments mentioned above represent only a fraction of the surprisingly wide range employed by Rucci. The reason for this breadth of creative options is that a small number of highly specialized firms in France are still able to design individualized techniques and effects based on Rucci's aesthetic demands. Embroidery by the houses of Lesage in Paris (headed by François Lesage and run with the support of Etienne Liets – the "Spine of Lesage" as Rucci calls him), Ollier of Paris (owned by Jean Pierre Ollier), Jean Luca Bernardi of Lyon, France, and Lemarié, the ultimate firm for feather work based in Paris, allow the couturier to embellish, paint, bleach, and ornament both the outside and inside of garments with decorative details seen only in the most rarified and exquisitely rendered clothing.

The great couturiers of the twentieth century, such as Balenciaga and Grès as well as Madeleine Vionnet, were masters of the art of dressmaking and tailoring. Their most successful designs, garments made from flat geometric pieces of cloth transformed into mobile pieces of sculpture, were most often monochromatic and devoid of any ornamentation. While it is true that they used embroidery and printed fabrics, ornamented garments are not generally viewed as the best examples of their work. The purity of cut and form were far more important than color and embellishment to these couturiers. This is not the case for Ralph Rucci. Unlike all but a few of his predecessors, Rucci is able to create garments that are beautiful as both pure forms and as vessels rich in color and resplendent in texture.

For example, one of the most labor intensive pieces Rucci commissioned from Lesage is a cardigan and matching shell dating to 2001. While the cut of the garment is relatively simple, its surface, completely encrusted with stone-like beads in varying sizes, had the mottled effect of sharkskin or shagreen but with a three-dimensional quality that resembles an aerial view of a beach covered in shells and sand.

Ollier, on the other hand, creates embroideries that have a deconstructed quality to them. "Deconstructed" garments are often unfinished-looking, with loose, frayed hems and edges;

Detail, embroidered evening
cardigan and shell, 2001.
Photograph: William Palmer.

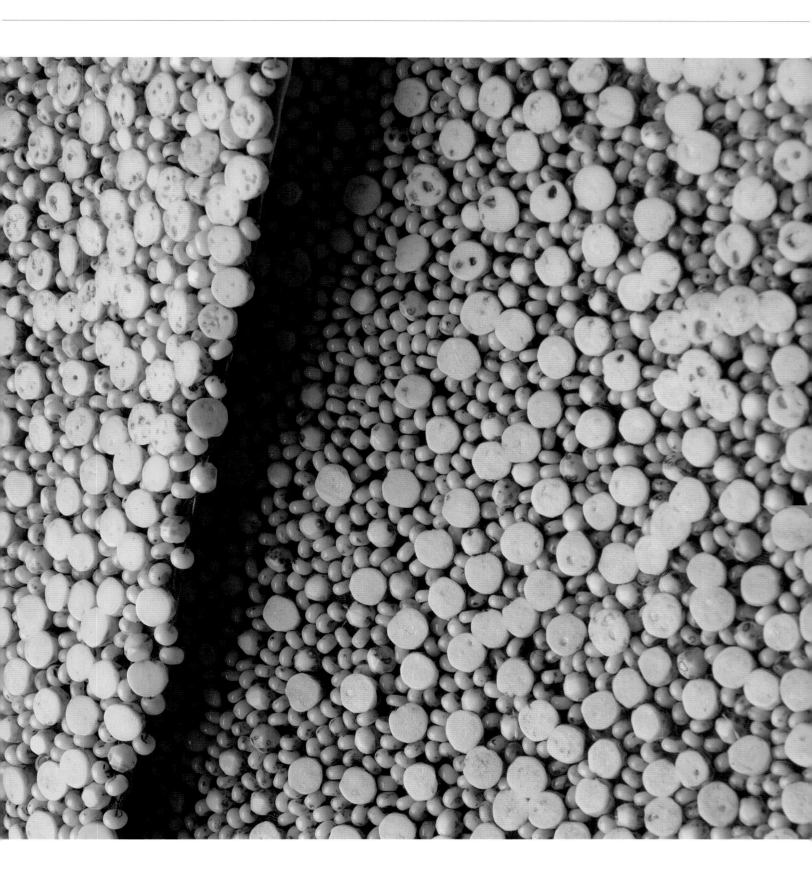

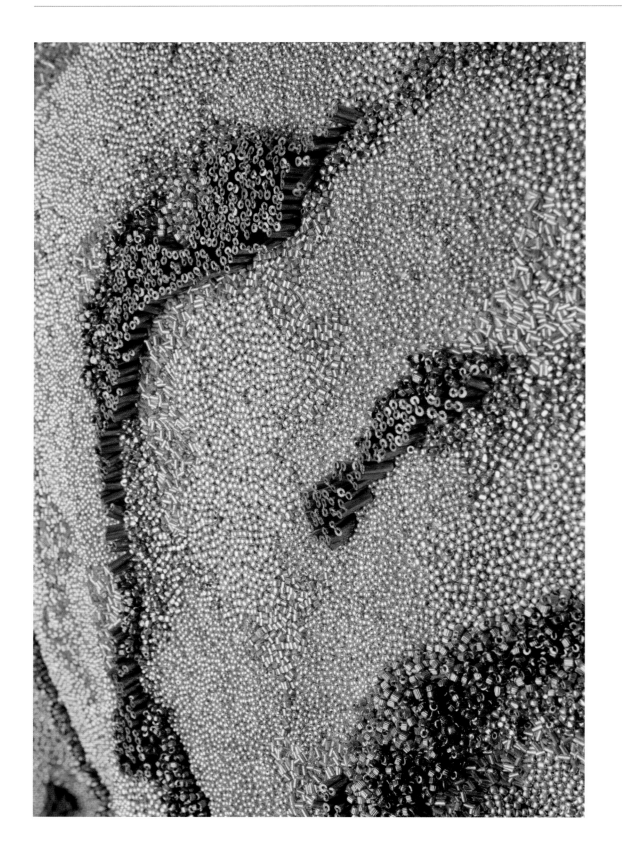

Detail, evening jacket, embroidery
by Shagufta, fall/winter 2004
haute couture collection.
Photograph: William Palmer.

they sometimes appear to be coming apart or look as if they were recycled or made from composite parts. For a champagne-colored *Infanta* gown from the fall 2006 haute couture collection, Rucci commissioned Ollier to embellish the interior of the grand garment's copper-colored satin overskirt. But rather than apply the broad strokes of black and gold paint to the outside surface, the interior was decorated instead. The design was further enhanced by the meticulous application of wide, ripped bands of silk netting throughout and was further embellished with gathered bands of chiffon that were woven into the satin ground. It should be noted that all of this work would scarcely be seen by others because it would require the wearer to open and turn back the overskirt like the pages of a book.

Even more rarified is the feather work that is executed for Rucci by the firm of Lemarié. Founded more than a century ago in 1894 and now owned by the house of Chanel, Lemarié is the last of the grand plumassieres, or feather-working houses, which numbered nearly one dozen strong at the end of World War II. Though the Parisian couture houses such as Chanel and Dior account for most of its business, they create equally lavish pieces for Ralph Rucci such as an ostrich and peacock cape and evening dress covered with spotted guinea feathers for his first haute couture collection, fall/winter 2002. Later collections featured gowns of coq and burnt ostrich plumes applied to point d'esprit or lace.

Because of the great cost, not all of the firm's feather work can be executed by Lemarié. Therefore, Rucci also relies on an American firm based in New York called Dulkin and Derrick. Depending on the technique or materials, outsourcing feather work from Dulkin and Derrick can appear on an haute couture garment but is used almost exclusively for the ready-to-wear designs. On occasion, feathers are also applied by specific Rucci staff, such as Samantha Storto, who made the short white cocktail dress for the spring/summer 2006 haute couture collection.

Feathers are not the only animal products regularly used by Rucci. Leathers, ranging from calfskin to ostrich to alligator to shagreen (the skin of rays and deep sea dogfish), are materials that are featured in every collection. The sources for these skins include leathers from the French firm of Bodin-Joyeux and ostrich skins imported directly from South Africa. Controversial today, animal skins were the oldest fabrics used for clothing and were a crucial resource in the survival of humans during the Ice Age. For centuries they have also been a staple in the world of high fashion. Leather and furs have characteristics very different from those of woven textiles, and must be worked by specialists.

While exotic skins like alligator and shagreen are limited in the ways in which they can be manipulated (they are so tough and impenetrable that even heavy gauge sewing needles frequently break when sewn into the latter), leather is used both as a ground cloth and as ornamentation. So creative are Rucci's designs with leather that, on some occasions, only upon close inspection is this material revealed. Sometimes the leathers are cut into thin strips, rolled into tiny tubes then sewn together in open lattice-work patterns that result in garments such as his "capillary" jackets.

The most luxurious and costly of these skins used by Rucci are furs, primarily broadtail, chinchilla, and sable. Rucci's main collaborator and source for his furs is Nick Pologeorgis, head of

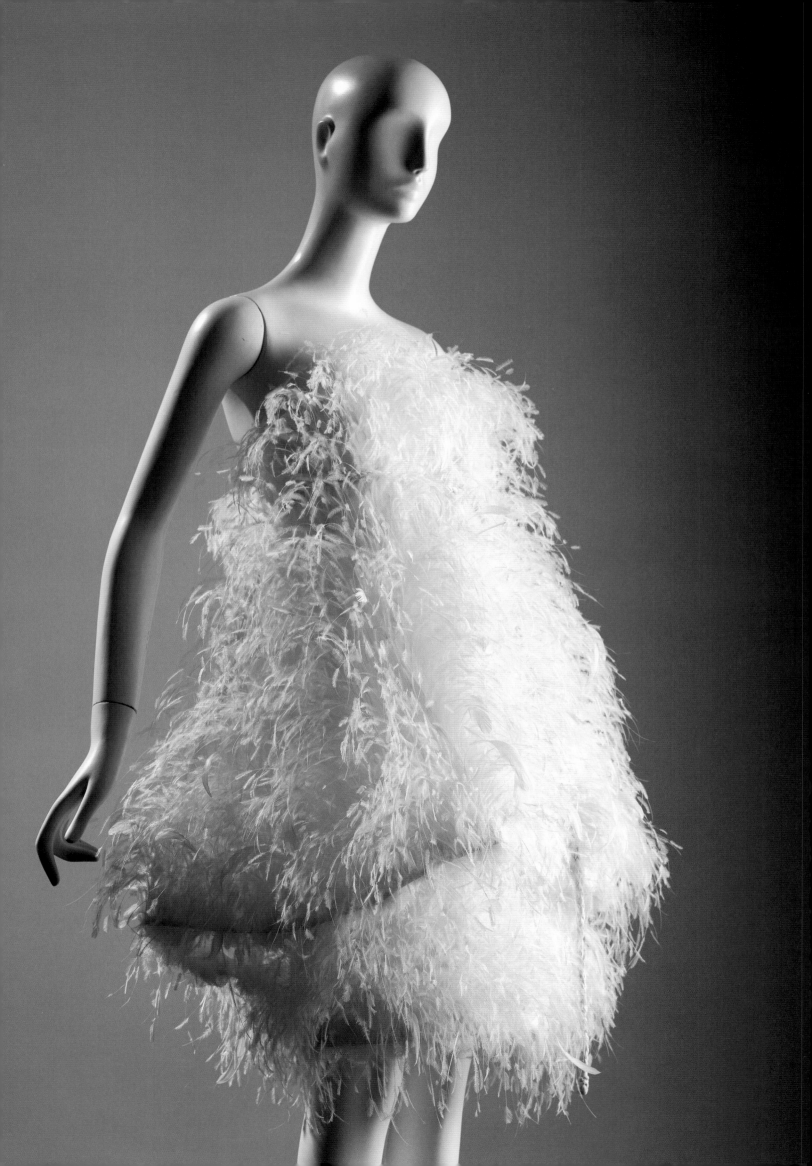

White ostrich plumed evening
dress, spring/summer 2006,
haute couture collection.
Photograph: William Palmer.

the family firm based in New York City. Each of these three furs is treated differently in terms of design and ornamentation.

The most flexible in terms of construction and surface embellishment is broadtail. Though the term is often confused, broadtail comes from the lambs of the Karakul sheep, a breed native to Central Asia that are prematurely born, stillborn, or harvested very young. The benefit of taking the pelts of such a young or premature animal is the skin's pliability and texture of the fur, which is relatively flat and light weight but has a distinctive moiré (or watery effect) pattern.

The creation of a broadtail garment is made in several stages. First, the Rucci team drafts the pattern of the desired garment, such as an haute couture evening skirt. Next, they rely on the Pologeorgis team to create a kind of base fabric out of the fur. This technique of assembling then joining or sewing assorted fur pelts is called plating. The plated skins are returned to Rucci so the placement of the artwork (in this case embroidery) can be determined and a small border can be marked. Then the skirt is sent to an embroiderer to have, for example, a sprinkling of black glass caviar beads sewn in. Finally, the skirt is returned to the Rucci workroom where it is lined and the hem finished.

For the furs with denser piles, very little is done to the surface other than dying. A brilliant example of this can be seen in the "tuxedo" jacket made of chinchilla. This small rodent from the Andes Mountain range of South America is known for its long, dense, extremely soft fur. A farmed animal, chinchilla fur is usually pale gray with a black streak running the length of the tail. For his fall/winter 2004 haute couture collection, Rucci chose to have the tuxedo jacket dyed a bright magenta pink. Nick Pologeorgis achieved the color based on the woven textile standard in duchesse silk satin. After the fur was dyed and plated to fit the pattern made by Rucci's team, the jacket was then ornamented with matching duchesse satin discs dangling from the surface.

Of all the materials used by Rucci, none matches the luxury of sable. One of the most rare and expensive furs in the world, the finest sable is found exclusively in Russia. Even today the sale of pelts is limited and the export of live animals is forbidden. Each pelt is extremely light, long and narrow. Rucci has used both crown and golden sable; the former is brown with a blue cast and the latter has an amber tone. The hallmark of both is the soft, deep fur in dark lustrous brown with silky dark hairs. The finest examples have a tinge of silvery hair dispersed throughout. His favorite is barguzine sable with a coat noted for its dark brown fur highlighted with silvery blue guard hairs.

Pologeorgis crafts sable in a variety of ways for Rucci: narrow bands trim the edges of coats and suits; silk raincoats are fully lined with the fur; sable is used to make his short hooded pullovers; undulating sweeps of fur fall from the patched leather yokes of his capes; and full-length coats swath the wearer. Rucci even designs accessories, such as Russian-style hats, using sable.

Rucci chooses, whenever possible, to work with the finest pelts. Most frequently, his furs are made using the "skin-on-skin" method: trimmed pelts are laid out and sewn together in large blocks. The advantage is that the fur has as few breaks in the pattern as possible. It is visually superior to the "let out" method, in which narrow strips of fur are sliced along a diagonal then sewn back together to make large pieces.

Detail, white cotton shirt *c*.2001,
Museum at FIT. Gift of
Mrs William McCormick
"Deeda" Blair.
Photograph: Jennifer Park.

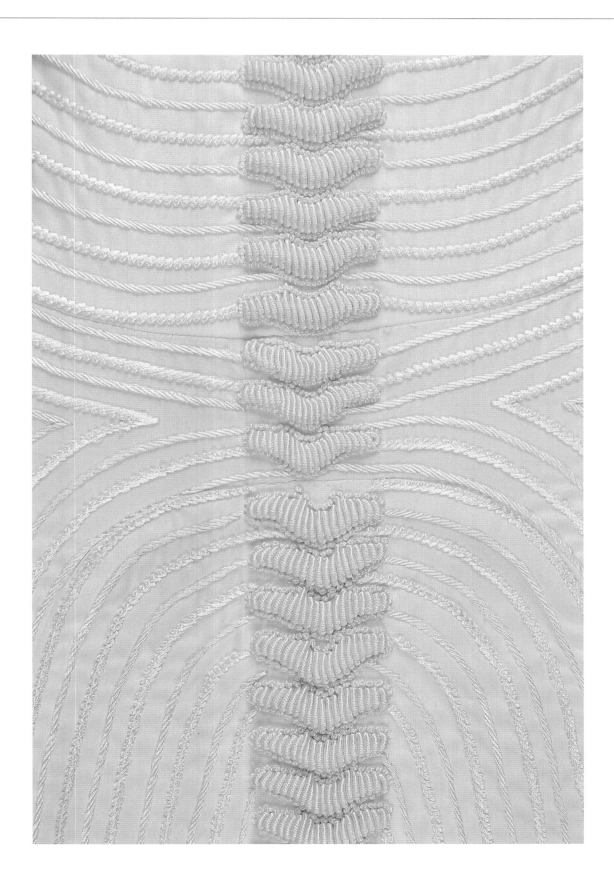

It should be noted that the farming and harvesting of furs from the former Soviet Union and other central Asian countries is less reliable than in past decades. The fall of the subsided farming system since the overthrow of the communist government in 1989 led to mass foreclosures of fur farms. Nick Pologeorgis estimates that at least fifty percent no longer survive. This drop in production, coupled with the instability in that region of the world, make the cost of raw pelts at auction increasingly high.

day wear: cutting and tailoring

Rucci often notes that while his evening gowns, particularly, his *Infantas* and swans, garner the most press coverage, it is his daywear that he feels have made the greatest contribution to fashion. It also forms the foundation of his thriving business. The main reason for this is that while many women buy his suits and dresses, few indulge in the purchase of a major ballgown.

Rucci's daywear might not have the drama of an evening dress but it is equally complex in design and execution. His clothes for day also dispel the oversimplified conclusion by some that Rucci's work is too rigid and architectonic. Three images photographed by Sandi Fellman in 2001 clearly illustrate how fluid and pliant Rucci's woolen trousers, coats and jackets can be. It is also clear to see, especially in the beige cape and matching skirt, that Rucci's unique use of seaming departs from standard methods of construction. Raised seams appear to slither down the shoulder and wrap around the back of the legs as they enhance the wrap of the cape and the fall of the skirt.

In a statement about his spring/summer 1987 collection, Rucci wrote: "seams no longer decorate; they are there for cause and subliminal effect. Seams become relief and cut echoes thought."[12] Many of his most important designs benefit from his break from conventional tailoring and its singular reliance on straight and vertically placed seams. Rucci's jackets, for example, often combine standard methods of construction perfected in ready-to-wear – such as set-in sleeves and vertical side seams that join the front and back panels – with arcs and curves that run along a more horizontal plane to provide the wearer with a better fit from behind.

Sleeves, however, are rarely made using standard constructions, such as set-in or dolman; Rucci never makes garments with a raglan sleeve. Unique cuts sometimes supplemented with gussets allow Rucci, depending on the rigidity of the fabrics and their placement, to create volume and unexpected shapes. Fullness in the sleeves does not come from pleating or gathering fabric and setting it into a fitted bodice; a single arced cut can determine the shape of a billowy sleeve that has volume, control, and grace.

Empire-waist dresses made of woven silks and wool jersey are another important staple in the Rucci daywear arena. Comfortable and made for movement, the dresses are flattering on most women due to the fact that they accentuate the shoulders and bust and mask the abdomen and hips. They are made with simple, raglan sleeves and skim the upper torso before gently flaring out to a relatively long, A-line skirt. Most are minimally embellished with a simple, knotted leather belt and a judicious smattering of suspensions or welted insets of self-fabric, using contrasting materials in the same color palette.

The most compelling of Rucci's daywear garments are those called "suspensions." The process evolved from the insertion of small, free-floating pieces of fabric set into a more standard cut garment. Made from thick, double-faced fabrics, each one of these pieces is individually cut, then "opened" or sliced into along the sides. The sides are then "cleaned" (Rucci and his staff refer to this process by their own term "cleaned double-faced") or turned in on itself and finished off by hand to prevent unraveling and to allow the fabric to be as bulk-free as possible. Each suspension piece is then lined by hand, usually in silk. These amoeboid-shaped pieces are then secured to the larger base fabric of a garment using thread connectors made from modified French knots called "worms." The worms are spaced approximately between half and one inch from one another and are purposely visible.

Rucci and his team have progressed to using the suspension method far beyond just inserts. Increasingly, whole garments were constructed using more and more suspensions. At first, on a single garment, suspensions occupied space on one shoulder and a section of the torso. Gradually, entire garments and suits were made of suspensions. The day ensemble consisting of a white tunic and pants in double-faced wool crepe and an *Infanta* made of black duchess satin are stunning in their complexity. Often, Rucci will break up the solid color with a judicious peppering of contrasting pieces, as seen in both day suits and evening gowns.

Suspensions are more than just a technical exercise or decorative element; they are also functional and serve a very important purpose: they improve the fit of a garment. Annarita Cavallini noted that the process of construction begins with a standard pattern made of muslin. Then, the suspensions are mapped on the pattern and numbered. The size and placement of each is precisely calculated in order to gracefully enhance the shape of the wearer. As a result, garments made entirely with suspensions are rarely symmetrical and are most often reserved for the haute couture.

The suspension idea is developed further in garments such as the "Stained Glass" dress for the haute couture collection of fall/winter 2004. A fretwork of rounded and connected serpentine pieces of black wool was created using techniques similar to the "opening" and "cleaning" of suspensions described above. The double-faced pieces were sewn into each other, notched at every curve, descending from the top with the ends inserted into the next curved piece. One hundred and thirty-four pieces were mapped onto a pattern, individually numbered, and placed symmetrically on the right or left of center front. This black, openwork dress was placed over an underdress of silk chiffon printed with the face of a young renaissance beauty who appeared to be peeking out through elaborate fretwork.

the *infanta* and *swan*

Though not representative of his typical business output (few clients buy it), the Rucci *Swan* and *Infanta* are his most spectacular and notable garments. One of the first specially commissioned photographs of Rucci's voluminous evening gowns was the Watteau swan. As the image by pho-

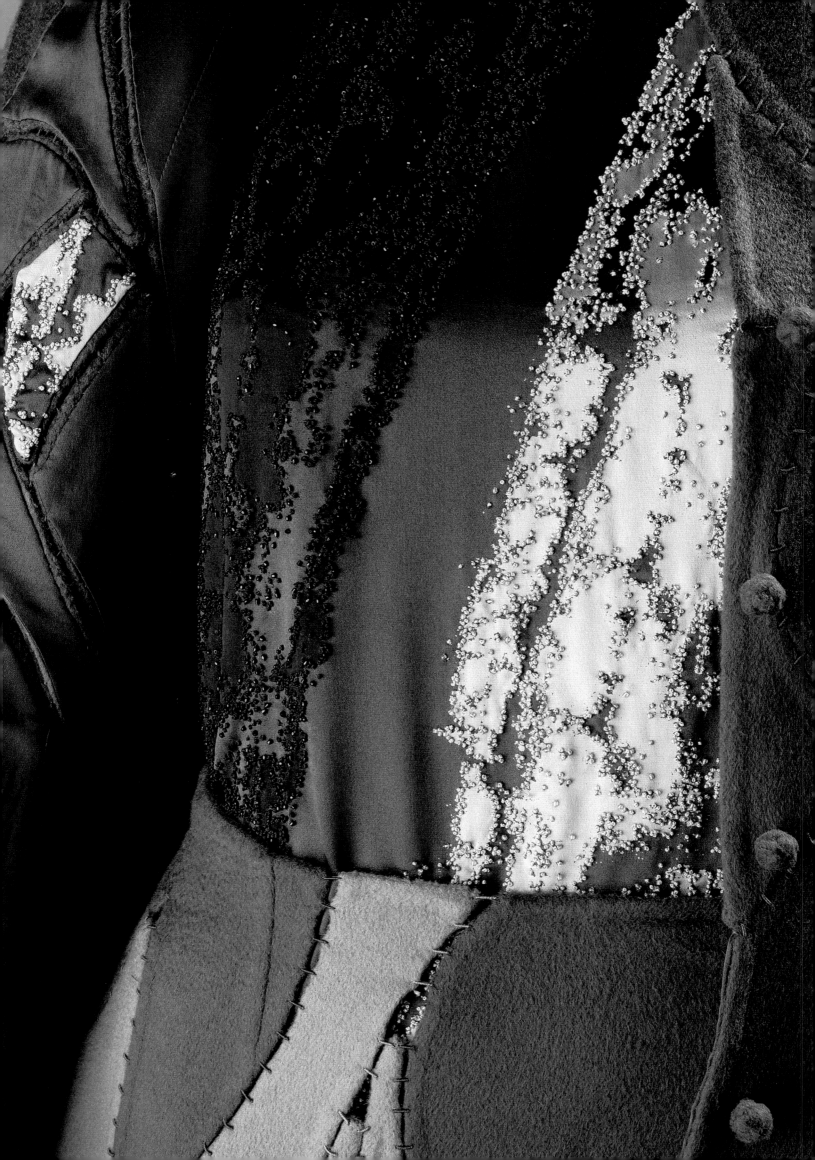

Detail, beaded bodice and
interior of olive green
suspension suit, fall/winter 2005
haute couture collection.
Photograph: William Palmer.

tographer Sandi Fellman illustrates, the garment is a modern reminiscence of the great rococo Franco-Flemish painter, Antoine Watteau, and the willowy water bird, the swan.

The fact that Rucci himself labeled his grand gowns *Infanta* shows not only the designer's affinity for art history but also for fashion history. Infantas, or the daughters of the Spanish kings, were most famously painted by old masters such as Diego Velasquez in the mid-seventeenth century. The greatest artist of Spain's golden age, Velazquez immortalized the young princesses and their magnificent panniered gowns in such works as *Las Meniñas* (1656) and the portrait of the *Infanta Margarita* (1664). The grandeur of the infanta's dress, with enormously wide skirts that reached beyond the fingertips of its wearer's outstretched arms, in the hands of Velazquez, endowed his sitter with a "mood of harsh disenchantment" and strict religious stoicism.[13]

The *Infanta* gown would be revived in modern times by couturieres like Jeanne Lanvin in the early twentieth century. Her leitmotif, the *robe de style de dix-huitieme siècle* (or dress in the style of the eighteenth century) sought its inspiration from the French court gowns of the eighteenth century that were born a century earlier on the Iberian peninsula, but her voluminous dresses possessed not the severity of the official Spanish court costume.

That somber aesthetic and the term *Infanta* were revived later in the twentieth century by Cristobal Balenciaga. In 1939, Balenciaga created the *Infanta* gown as it is understood today. Though references note a series of Balenciaga gowns labeled "Infanta," only one is clearly identified in both primary and secondary sources. It is an arrestingly severe creation made of ivory duchess satin and trimmed around the neckline, down the center front, around the dropped waistline and edge of the three quarter length sleeves with a thick undulating scroll of appliquéd black velvet. Photographed by George Hoyningen-Huene, the model stands in a full frontal pose so that the sharply padded shoulders and wide, panniered hips are clearly emphasized.[14]

The Rucci *Infanta* is constructed somewhat like the early Balenciaga gowns in the use of heavy satin and hidden supports such as horsehair and interfacing. They also, on occasion, borrow from the color vocabulary of Charles James. Like Rucci, James was an unusual couturier in that his three-dimensional gowns were varied and rich in hue due to his unusual blending of colors. In some cases, James looked to rococo combinations (such as pale water blue and rose pink) or those from the Victorian era, such as tobacco brown and black. Rucci's slightly stiffened structure and the use of colors, the combination of brown and purple, are evocative of past masters but not literal translations.

The process of making an *Infanta* gown for Rucci is very much a collaborative effort with master pattern maker Gail Gondek. After working with him for a decade, she embraces his aesthetic, such as the penchant for a high jewel neckline, small and high armholes,[15] raised and canted waistline and hemline, and a skirt that forms a shape somewhere between that of a right and a scalene triangle, with greater volume in the back. There is also a clear choice of silk fabrics, either duchess satin or gazar. On occasion, Rucci opts to inset small amounts of faille or brocaded silk for contrast.

One of Gondek's chief challenges is the creation of the voluminous *Infanta* skirt. Rucci, ever the modernist, insists that there be no heavy or rigid understructure. His dislike of petticoats comes from the understanding that they are cumbersome, heavy, and prevent the garment from moving fluidly and gracefully. To support the skirt, "each part [or individual pattern piece] is underlined with organza and Filogil," notes Gondek, "a brand name for the French version of marquisette," (the latter being unavailable in the United States since 1990). It is a preferred material because "it is very lightweight, very stiff and tightly woven."[16]

The use of Filogil is judicious and exacting and "cannot be enclosed in the seam because it is too stiff to be bent back on itself." Each piece of Filogil is cut one-eighth of an inch smaller than the seam of the base fabric and the organza lining. It is then applied to the organza using a cross stitch (machine stitches cannot be used because they can be seen through the taffeta lining when pressed). The organza is then "framed to self layer [or base fabric] by machine."[17] The hems often need more support and are reinforced with a bias strip of "hymo canvas" and wide nylon bands of faux horsehair are applied in the same manner as the Filogil.

The strapless versions of the *Infanta* require an additional set of steps to construct an inner corset or bustier. This underpinning is constructed with silk taffeta and has its own separate zipper closure and fitted grosgrain waist stay. Taffeta is an ideal choice for such underpinnings, notes Gondek, because it is a tightly woven fabric that does not lose its shape over time. The plastic stays are cut and melted with candle flames in order to mold them to the desired shape. When the bustier is finished, it is attached to the outer layer of *Infanta* along the top edge. Gondek notes that the "strapless gown is actually suspended from the boning that is anchored at the waist" and relies on the "same construction principle seen in the suspension bridge."

Perhaps the most astounding element used by Gondek to construct the *Infanta* is her use, like that of Annarita Cavallini, of mathematical formulae. A favored model is the "Golden Mean," a classical "Greek equation derived from the Fibonacci sequence . . . that is considered pleasing in Western cultures" and suggests a "natural balance between symmetry and asymmetry."[18] Shapes based on its proportion are derived by multiplying "X" by 34 and dividing the result by 55. Gondek takes this equation one step further when considering how best to translate Rucci's designs into a working model. In the *Ripple Effect Infanta* of 2002 for example, she created an algebraic equation to determine the exact size of the graduated, concentric squares that dominate the back of the skirt. Gondek chose "Y" as the total length of the skirt and the dimensions of each square was calibrated using the formula "$y = x + (x+2) + (x+4) + (x+6) \ldots$"[19] Like Cavallini and VonAesch, Gondek prefers to apply a mathematical model rather than rely solely on intuition and experience.

Though few fashion journals ever detail the construction of Rucci's great garments such as the *Infanta*, when they do the impact is sharp and immediate. For example, in an issue of *V Magazine*, the young model, Natalia Vodianova, is pictured from the hip upward in a deceptively simple Ralph Rucci gown and matching bolero featured in his first haute couture collection for the fall/winter 2002 season. The image, though beautiful and arresting, is overexposed and not very much of the ensemble can be seen. But the caption is compelling; it reads "'Ripple Effect Infantas': 22 yards of black Taroni double-faced silk-duchesse-satin faille; 20 yards of silk-taffeta lining; 16 yards of hand-overlapped inner structure of gazar; organza, and filogil; 70 yards of horsehair."[20] Though Gondek disagrees with the use of so much horsehair (she estimates something closer to 20 yards), the sheer volume of materials, both visible and hidden, is extraordinary.

Detail, black satin
suspension Infanta gown with
olive green embroidered insets,
fall/winter 2006 haute couture
collection.
Photograph: William Palmer.

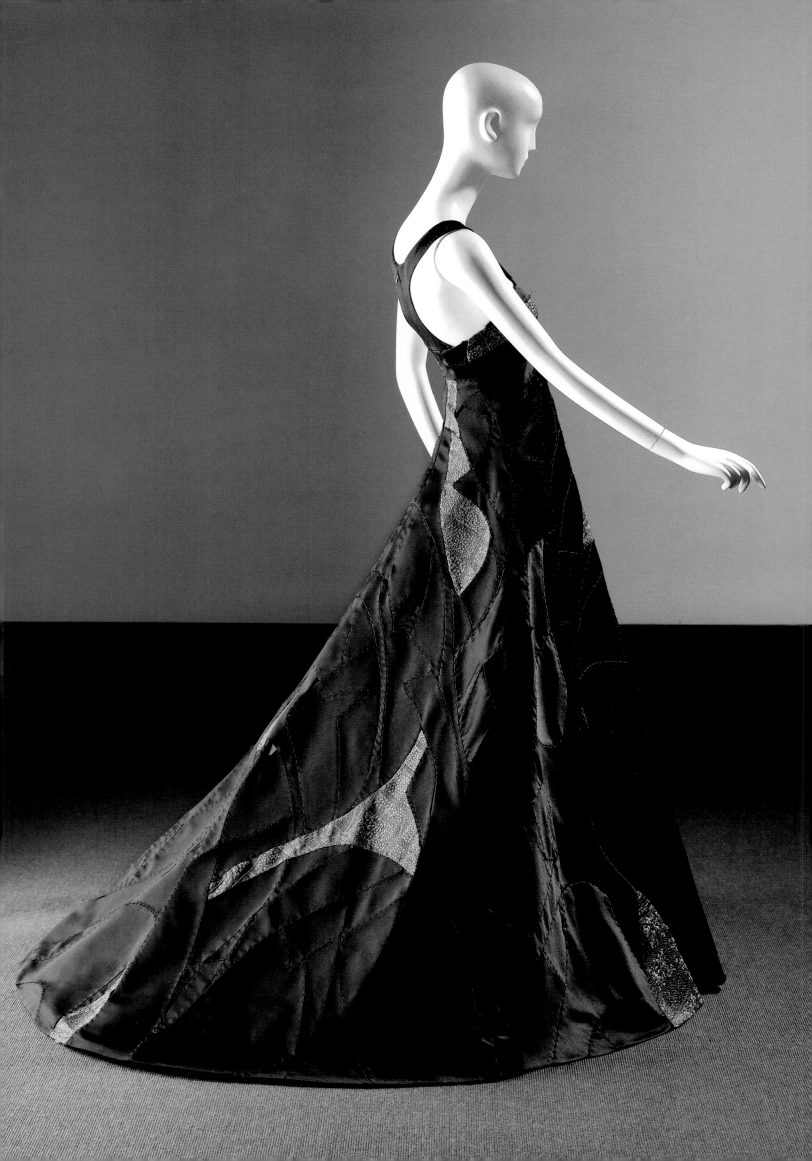

Black satin suspension
Infanta gown with olive green
embroidered insets, fall/winter
2006 haute couture collection.
Photograph: William Palmer.

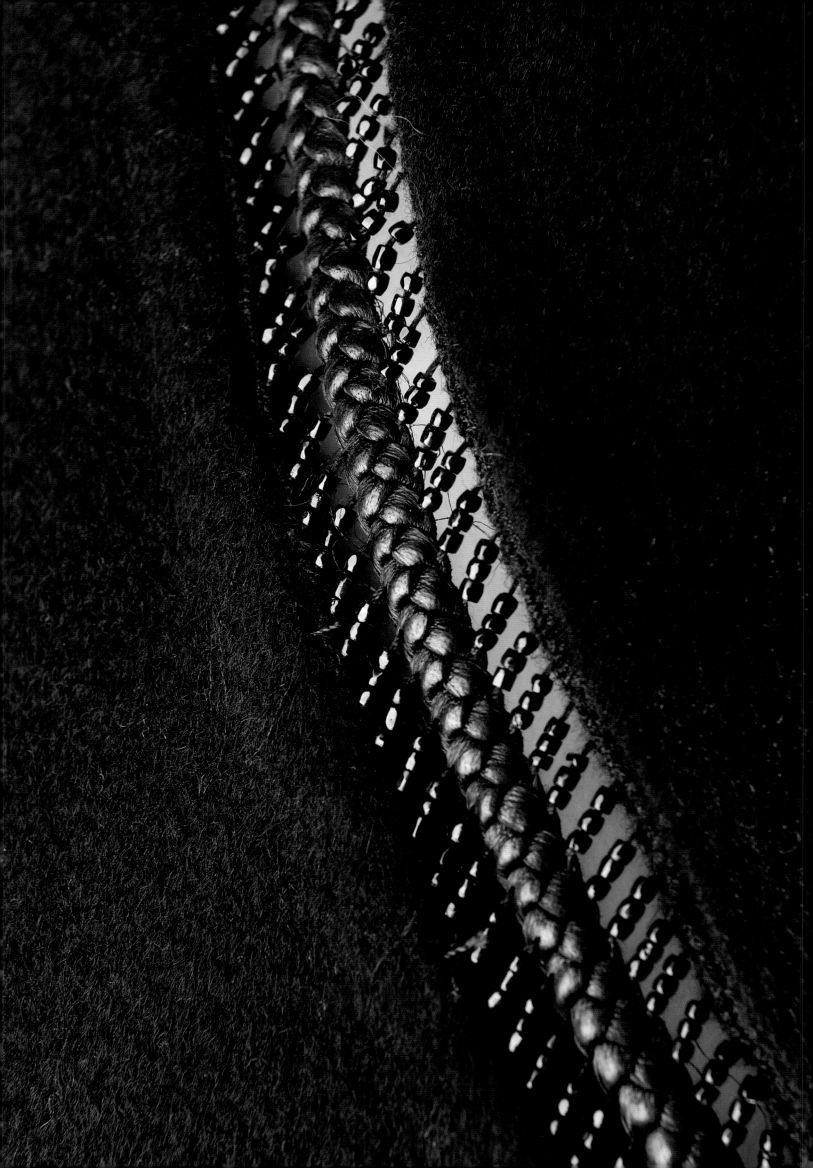

Below: black cashmere suspension
suit, fall/winter 2004 haute couture
collection.
Photograph: William Palmer.

Facing page: detail, braided
leather and glass bead connections
for the cashmere suspension suit.

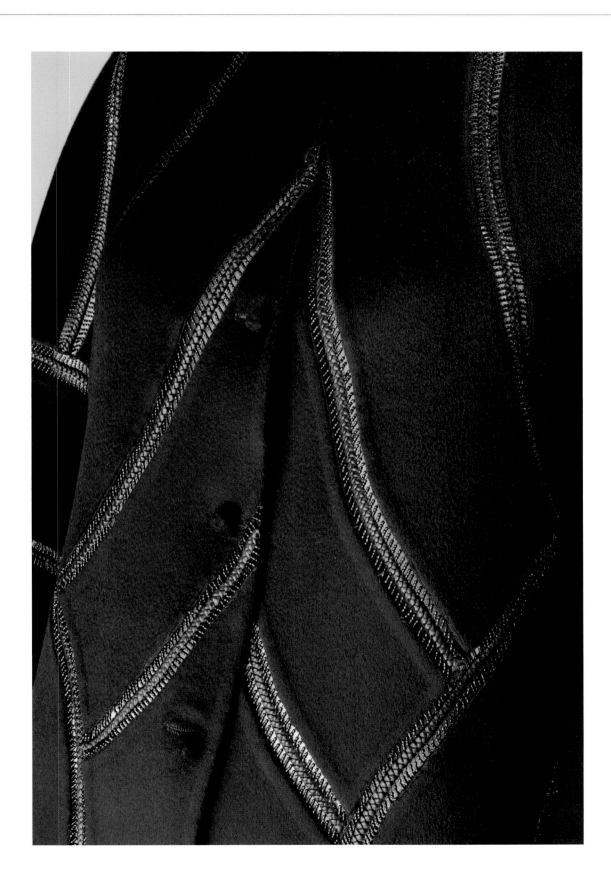

"Twombly Swan" cotton gazar
evening dress inspired by Cy
Twombly, spring/summer 2002
ready-to-wear collection.
Photograph: William Palmer.

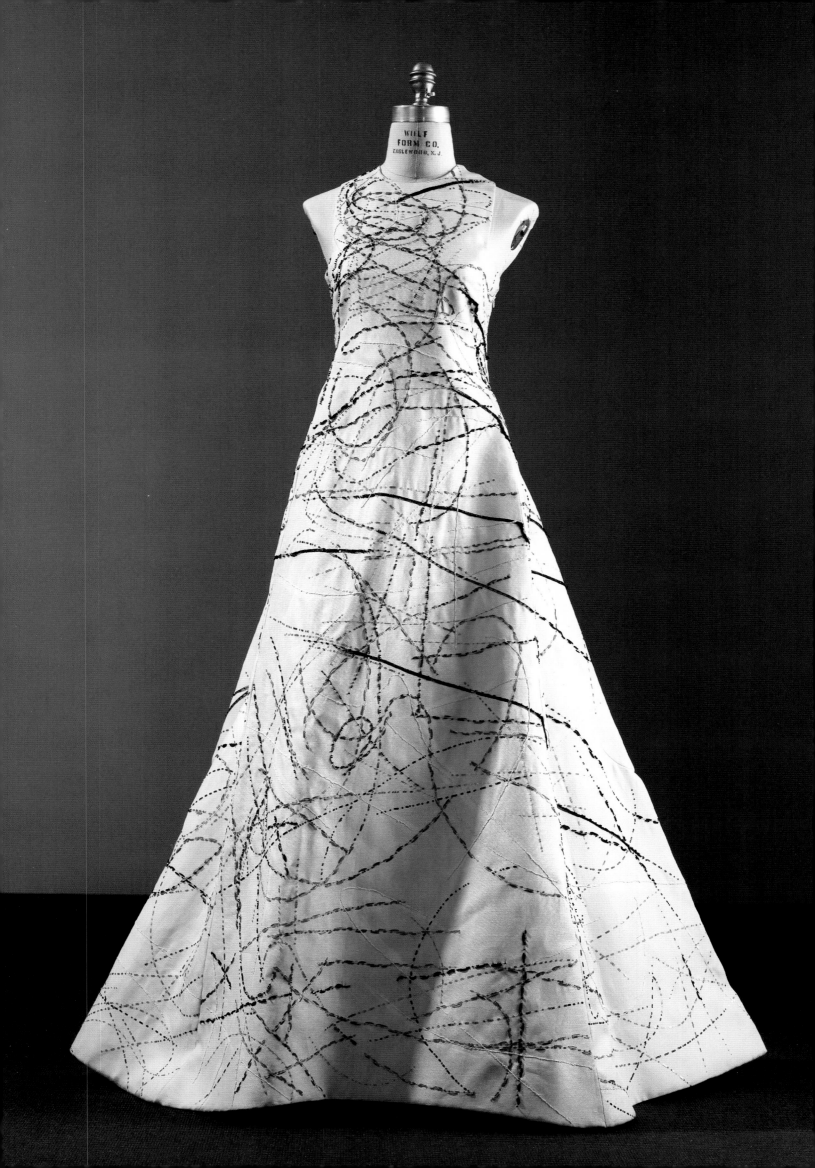

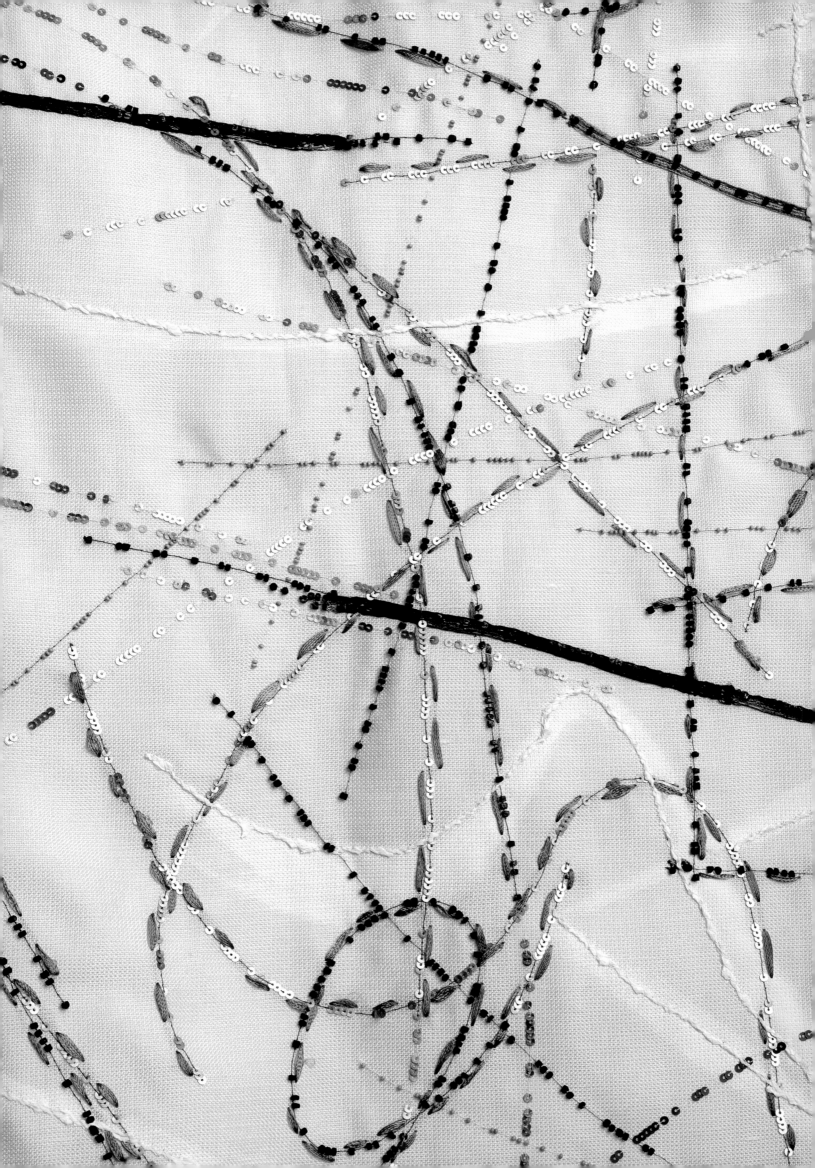

Detail of "Twombly Swan" cotton
gazar evening dress.
Photograph: William Palmer.

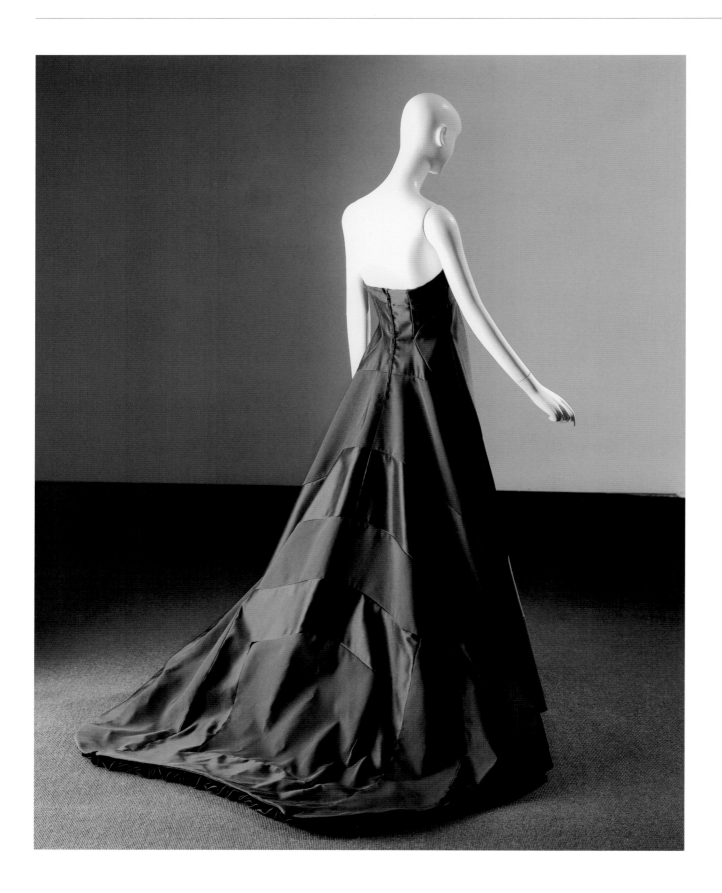

Black duchess satin and faille
"Ripple Effect Infanta" evening
gown, fall/winter 2002
haute couture collection.
Photograph: William Palmer.

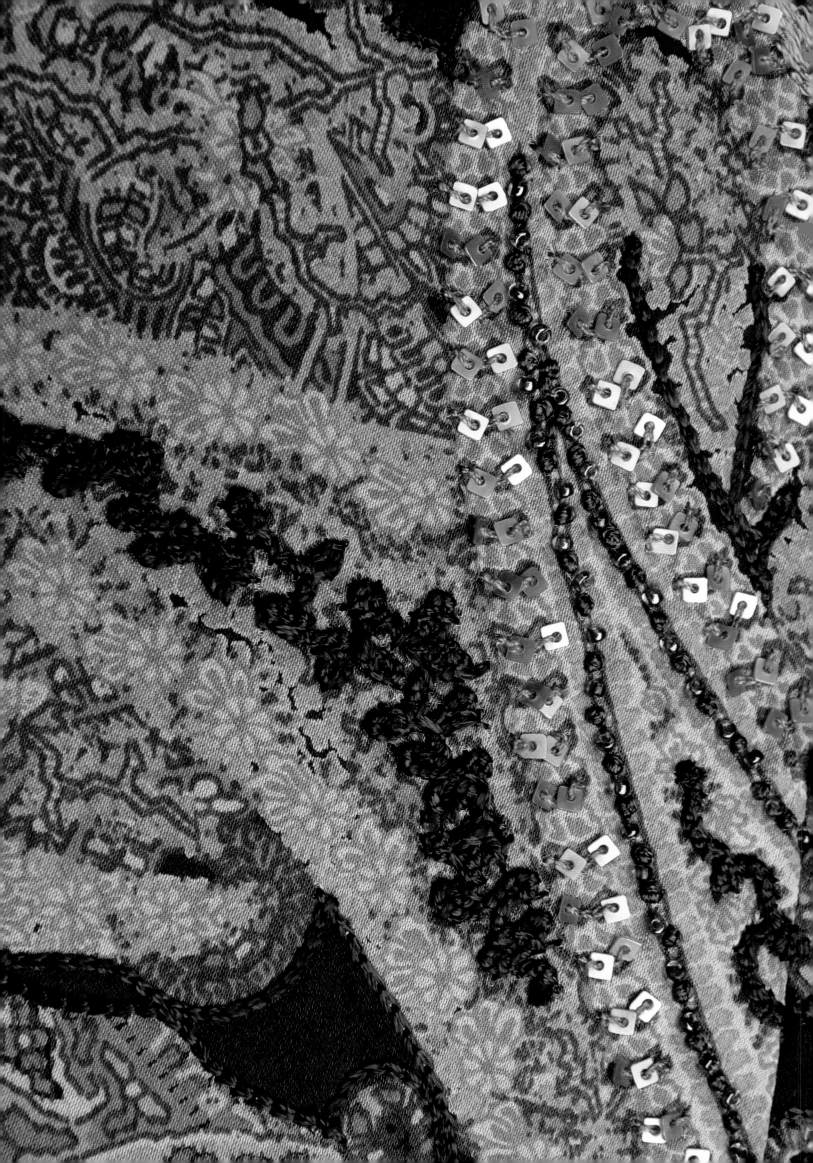

Below: gray cashmere day coat,
fall/winter 2004 haute couture
collection.
Photograph: William Palmer.

Facing page: interior detail,
 gray cashmere coat, printed and
embroidered silk satin.

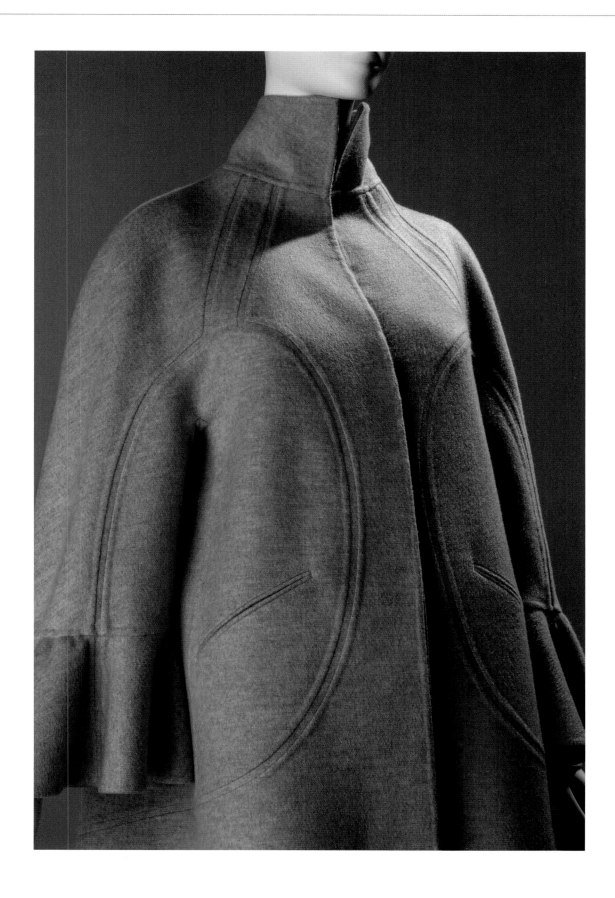

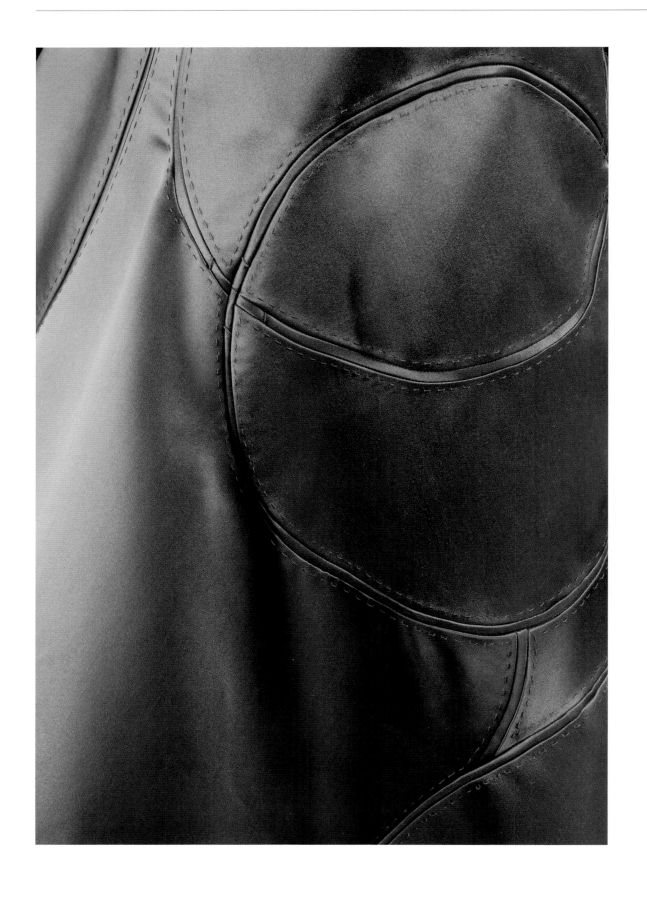

Graphite silk duchess satin
Infanta with circular insets,
fall/winter 2004 haute couture
collection.
Photograph: William Palmer.

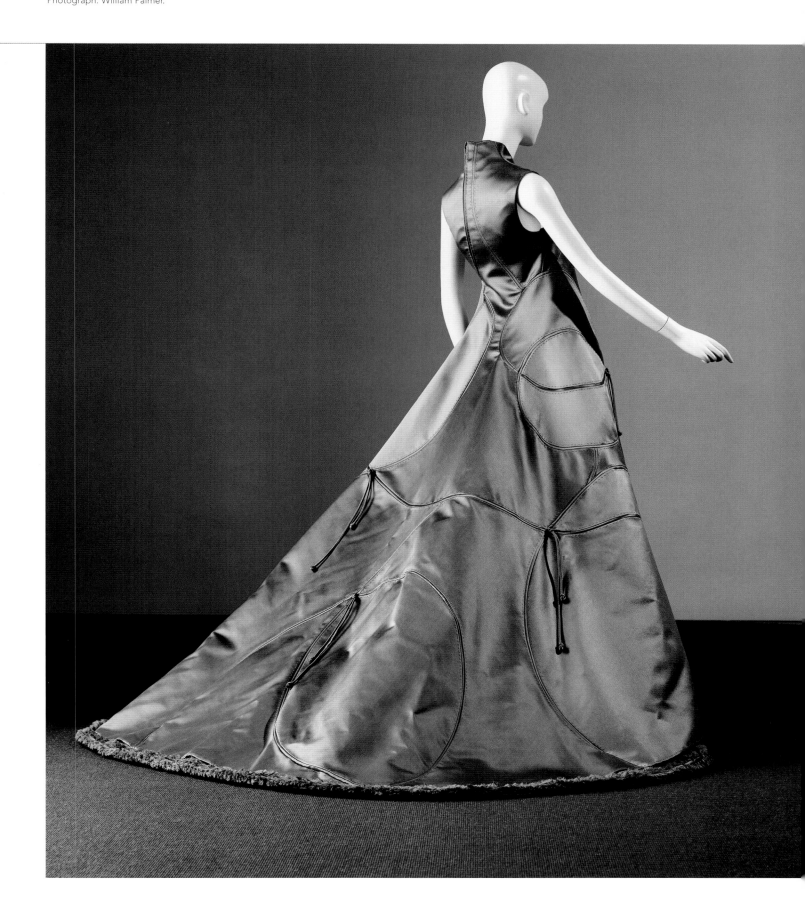

The same quantity of materials is also used for other dramatic versions of the *Infanta*. Made from amethyst purple duchess silk satin, it possesses the dynamism of an African sculpture in that the garment's shape changes dramatically as it is viewed in the round. From the front, the simple Empire, or raised waistline, gives no clue to the broad and erect arch of fabric that spans the shoulders and encases a small roll, or obi, resting between the shoulder blades. The solid surface in front is broken with the inclusion of matching insets of silk faille that gently fracture the smooth, glossy sheen of satin due to the changing interplay of light across its surface.

Another departure in the evolution of the *Infanta* can be seen in the example made entirely of graphite gray duchesse satin for the fall/winter 2004 collection. While the garment is monochromatic, its surface is broken up with arcs and curves that circumnavigate its overall triangular silhouette. Gondek used a multi-step process to create this gown. She began by pinning "style tape" to a dress form to determine the general lines of the circles. Muslin was then draped over the form in order to transfer the lines into a two-dimensional pattern before tracing them onto soft paper. The dimensions were modified and the paper patterns were pieced. This combination of drafting and draping may be repeated several times, often with Rucci's input, until the final design is approved. Gondek works to insure that the grain lines of the fabric are parallel whenever possible so that the seams can be sewn together easily.

One of the most dramatic and imposing of all of Rucci's garments is his "Doges" *Infanta* gown made for his first haute couture collection, fall/winter 2002. Made of ink black silk duchesse satin, the garment has a high neck, long sleeves and is a clear departure from his sleeveless and strapless versions. On the runway, it was ornamented with an ancient stone secured to a black silk cord. He noted in an interview with curator Anne Bissonnette that this *Infanta* was "one of my favorite garments in my career" because it was "just wonderful to state the majestic."[21] The majesty of the gown comes in part from the vast expanse of negated color and its billowing silhouette. Historically, voluminous black clothes moved between academics and monks, widows and nuns, to signal scholarship, piety, and sexual inaccessibility. Black robes, academic or clerical, all but erased the corporeal body.

flou

Ralph Rucci has been criticized in recent years by a number of journalists for too ardently embracing the type of structured garment mentioned above. His silhouettes, though mobile and pliant when worn, appear to be rigid and sharp and give the impression, to some, of a kind of impenetrability. Though this assertion is an oversimplification of the full scope of Rucci's creativity, the designer admits that the power implied in his sculptural pieces does not fit every taste and as such they are not his best sellers.

Perhaps due in part to the kind of constructive criticism he has received in the press, the recent trend for softer gowns, a desire to revisit and refine his early forays with draping in the style of Madame Grès, and a restless desire to expand his creativity, Rucci has been making more and more softly draped dresses. Known as "flou" in French, soft draping is now a staple of each

Rucci collection and can come in the form of gauzy caftans and swing jackets as well as chiffon evening dresses.

Fluting, a lyrical technique of deeply pleating fabric and tacking it to a hidden ground fabric, is most often associated with the couturier Madame Alix Grès, especially when it is executed using matte silk jersey. From the earliest days of Rucci's career, he was hand-rendering his own fluted garments, as seen in a bodice from his archives dating to around 1980. For him, as for Madame Grès, this construction technique is simultaneously decorative and functional. Rucci uses fluting both sparingly and in unexpected ways.

A good example of its judicious use can be seen in a black evening ensemble made for the fall/winter 2003 haute couture collection. It consists of a full, heavy satin skirt emblazoned with bleached streaks topped with a sheer silk jersey bodice. To the latter, Rucci applied a modesty panel of matching fluted fabric that falls in a wide band from the turtleneck, and wraps around the breasts and across one arm.

The concept of fluting was taken in another direction for garments with ornament that is also structural. A brilliant example of this is his alabaster silk knotted jersey evening dress made for the spring/summer 2003 collection. Simple in concept but excruciatingly difficult in execution, the gown is made from seemingly endless but narrow bands of fabric that are sewn to create tubes, then knotted to create a mesh-covered bodice. The knots end at the waistline, where the unfurled fabric is then sewn together to make the voluminous, 117-gored skirt.

Lesser known Rucci *flou* creations are his gowns made from silk chiffon. Many of his chiffon pieces are simple, such as the oversized scarves that accessorize his day and evening clothes. He routinely includes at least one or two significant chiffon dresses in each runway presentation. Among the finest examples of these are the special commissions from one of his leading clients, Tatiana Sorokko, née Ilushkina. The daughter of Nicolai Ilushkin, one of the fathers of the Soviet Union's nuclear weapon program, she found her way onto the Paris runways before marrying art dealer Serge Sorokko and becoming an important couture client and collector.

Sorokko worked with Rucci to modify his strapless chiffon columns by adding fabric to one shoulder as to lend the garment a more classical silhouette and a greater sense of drape. The flow continues with the inclusion of chiffon flowers made with gathered self-fabric strips that are shredded at the ends and placed on the shoulder in single file, cascading down the single back seam. He made several of these chiffons for Sorokko: one was printed with an image of a large falcon taken from a seventeenth-century Japanese painted screen while another one-of-a-kind ombré (or shadow) version was made for the occasion of her husband's fiftieth birthday.

conclusion

Ralph Rucci celebrated his forty-ninth birthday on July 31, 2005. The following year, 2006, marked his twenty-fifth anniversary as a fashion designer. Rucci finds himself at the peak of his powers. He is respected and even revered by the members of the fashion community. His work is noted for its sculptural quality, and, more importantly, the employment of innovative construction techniques that have allowed him to transcend the fickle nature of fashion.

While some may be able to recognize his hallmark pieces, such as the dramatic *Infanta* gowns, the full extent of his contributions remains little-known. The difficulties inherent in interpreting Rucci and his work have caused most fashion reporters to simplify their analysis. He neither sets trends in fashion nor creates novel collections; his work is often considered by many to be free from the dictates and quixotic changes in women's fashion design. Rucci does follow the general look of contemporary fashion, but his responses to the needs of modern life come from something deeper: an emphasis on movement and a desire to highlight the natural female form through the craft of dressmaking.

This may be another reason for the resistance to interpretation inherent in Ralph Rucci and his designs: in his work there is a strong emphasis on clothing construction, one of the most neglected areas in the field of costume study. Just as the history of dress is often treated in a frivolous manner, so the importance of costume design as a valid craft, let alone an art form, is almost entirely ignored. It is in this realm of craftsmanship that Ralph Rucci makes his most important contributions.

Finally, the study of Rucci's work is made most difficult because the world of fashion connoisseurs, women who lived their lives wearing haute couture, is all but gone. The private and silent communication between such ladies no longer informs fashion. It is therefore miraculous that Rucci has created such a powerful statement and found a loyal clientele to express his vision. His garments, like his singular and unwavering artistic vision, cleave to the body, move like clouds around that body, and by extension, allow fashion to transcend the ordinary. A passage of scripture (Matthew 5:8) seems exactly right as a summary of Ralph Rucci's career: "blessed are the pure in heart: for they shall see God." Amen.

1 Kirk Varnedoe, *Cy Twombly: A Retrospective,* New York: The Museum of Modern Art and Harry N. Abrams, 1994, p. 9.

2 *Vogue,* July 1967, pp. 80–81.

3 Harold Koda, "Balenciaga: The Architect of Elegant Clothing," *Threads Magazine,* June 1987, p. 21.

4 Kirk Varnedoe, *Cy Twombly: A Retrospective,* New York: The Museum of Modern Art and Harry N. Abrams, 1994, p. 23.

5 Annarita Cavallini, in interview with the author.

6 Ralph Rucci, in interview with the author.

7 Booth Moore, "His Designs Are Suitable for Framing," *Los Angeles Times.* Saturday, June 4, 2005, p. E1.

8 Ibid.

9 Cathy Horyn, "Mysteries of Inspiration: Spring 2002 in the Making," *New York Times,* 4 September 2001, p. 8b.

10 Annarita Cavallini, in interview with the author.

11 Cathy Horyn, "On Seventh Avenue, the Buzz, the Ropes and the Seams," *New York Times,* 12 September, 2000, p. B11.

12 Ralph Rucci, in interview with the author.

13 Germain Bazin, *Baroque and Rococo Art,* New York: Praeger, Inc. Publishers, 1964, p. 60.

14 *Harper's and Queen,* 1939.

15 It should be noted that the high, tight armhole – contrary to the commonly held belief that it is restrictive – is a very modern couture detail perfected by the famed couturiere, Gabrielle "Coco" Chanel (French, 1885–1972). The small and perfectly fitted armhole actually allows the wearer a full and less restricted range of movement and prevents the bodice from pulling up and being distorted.

16 Gail Gondek, in interview with the author.

17 Ibid.

18 Ibid.

19 Ibid.

20 *V Magazine,* volume 20, November/December 2002, n.p.

21 Anne Bissonnette, *Chado Ralph Rucci,* Kent, Ohio: Kent State University Museum, 2005, p. 33.

Bazin, Germain, *Baroque and Rococo Art*, New York: Praeger, Inc. Publishers, 1964.

Bissonnette, Anne, *Chado Ralph Rucci*, Kent, Ohio: Kent State University Museum, 2005.

Bolton, Andrew, *Wild: Fashion Untamed*, New York: Metropolitan Museum of Art and Yale University Press, 2004.

Burnham, Dorothy, *Cut My Cote*, Toronto: Royal Ontario Museum, 1973.

Cappock, Margarita, *Francis Bacon's Studio*, London: Merrell, 2005.

Coleman, Elizabeth Ann and Brian Rushton, *The Genius of Charles James*, New York: Holt, Rinehart and Winston, 1982.

Fukai, Akiko, "Japonism in Fashion," *Japonism in Fashion*, Kyoto, Japan: Kyoto Costume Institute, 1994.

Horyn, Cathy, "Mysteries of Inspiration: Spring 2002 in the Making," *New York Times*, September 4, 2001.

Horyn, Cathy, "On Seventh Avenue, the Buzz, the Ropes and the Seams," New York Times, September 12, 2000.

Jouve, Marie-Andrée and Jacqueline Demornex, *Balenciaga*, New York: Rizzoli, 1989.

Kirke, Betty, *Madeleine Vionnet*, San Francisco: Chronicle Books, 1998.

Koda, Harold, "Balenciaga: The Architect of Elegant Clothing," *Threads Magazine*, June 1987, pp. 20–25.

JAR, Paris, London: Christies, 2002.

Jones, Jonathan, "A Man for All Seasons: Cy Twombly," *The Guardian*, January 14, 2003.

Les Créateurs de la Mode, Paris: Editions du Figaro, 1910.

Madame Grès: The Sculptress of Fashion, Graduate Thesis, New York: Fashion Institute of Technology, 1993.

Mears, Patricia, *Halston: Modern Is the Only Way to Live*, London: Phaidon, 2001.

Moore, Booth, "His Designs Are Suitable for Framing," *Los Angeles Times*, Saturday, June 4, 2005.

"Of Feathers and Frou-frous," *Utusan* Express, January 21, 2004.

Schaffer, Claire, *Couture Sewing Techniques*, Newton, Connecticut: Taunton Press, 1993.

Sylvester, David, Sam Hunter, Michael Peppiatt, *Francis Bacon: Important Paintings from the Estate*, New York: Tony Shafrazi Gallery, 1998.

Varnedoe, Kirk, *Cy Twombly: A Retrospective*, New York: The Museum of Modern Art and Harry N. Abrams, 1994.

V Magazine, Volume 20, November/December 2002.

Vogue, July 1967, pp. 80–81.

White, Palmer, *Haute Couture Embroidery: The Art of Lesage*, New York: Vendome Press, 1988.

Interviews with the Author

Cavallini, Annarita, July 19, 2006.

Gondek, Gail, August 30, 2006.

Kim, Joon Yeon, July 19, 2006.

Ricat, Jean Francois, August 18, 2006.

Rucci, Ralph, August 23, 2006.

Thill, Robert, Independent Art Historian, July 26, 2006.

Van Natta, Vivian, August 21, 2006.

VonAesch, Christine, July 19, 2006.

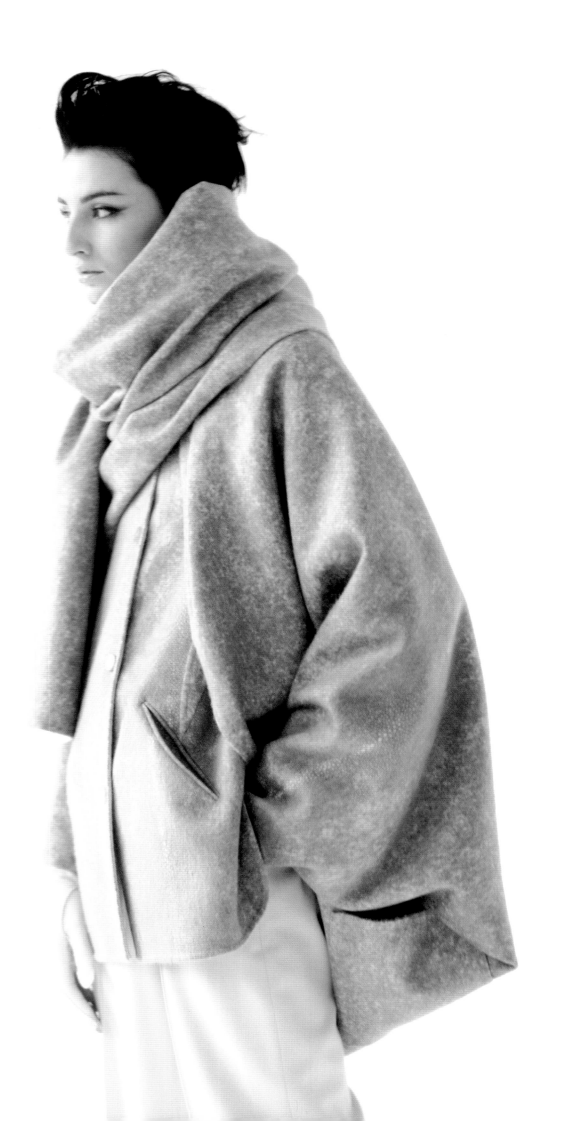

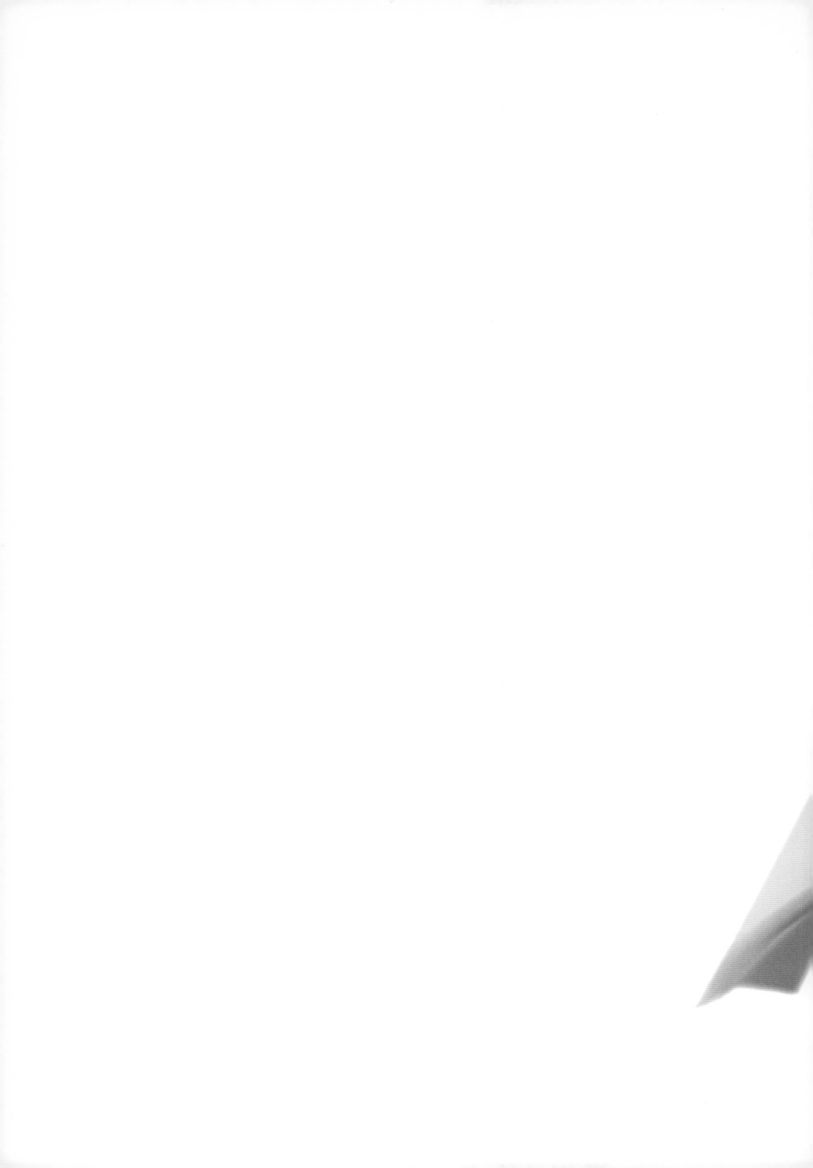

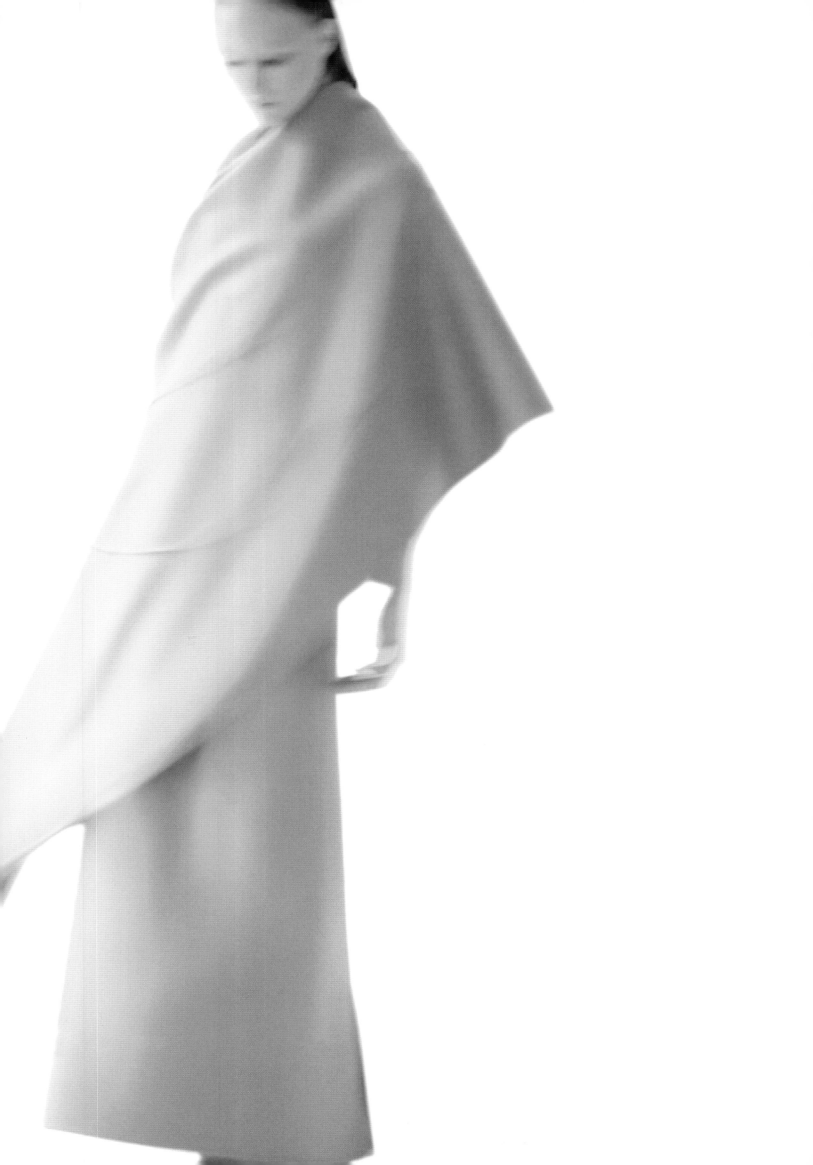

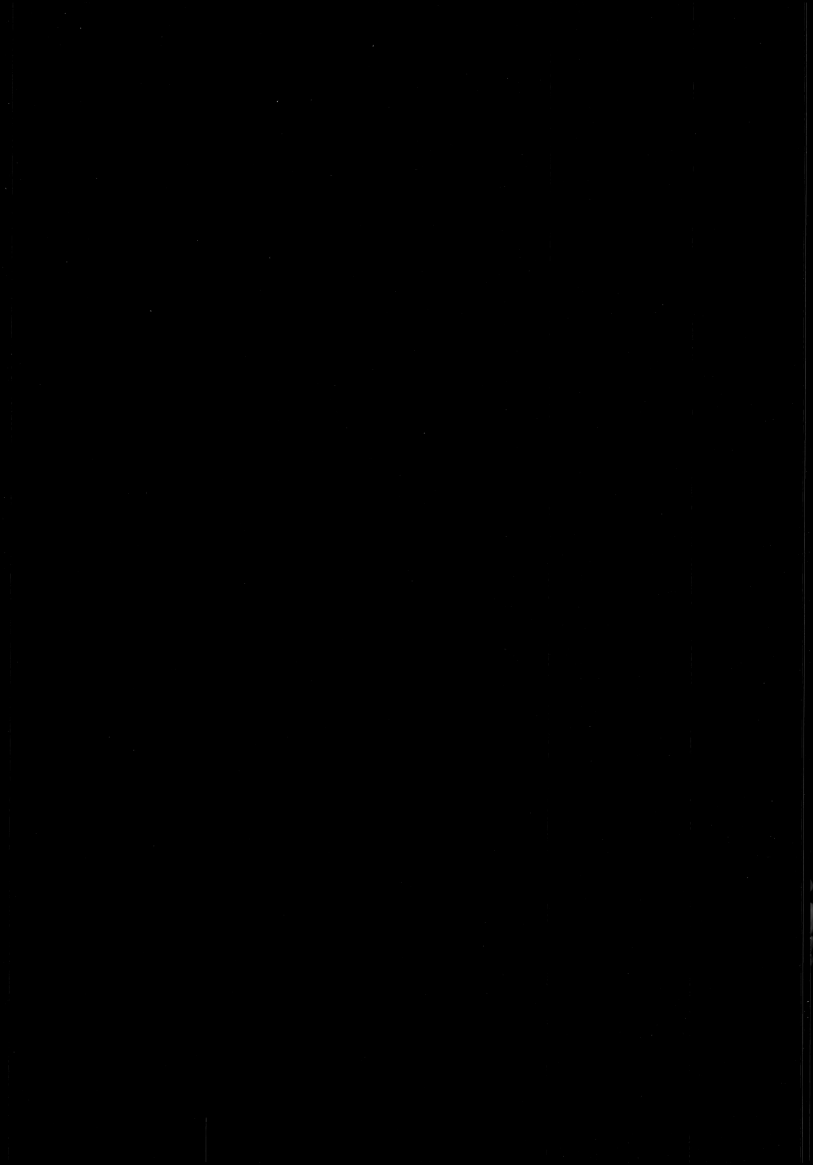

For more than half a century, my métier of embroidery has given me the amazing privilege to meet and work with the greatest masters of Haute Couture, both French and International, and to be an accomplice of their talent. Ralph Rucci, with his culture, his exceptional creativity, and his sense of perfection, holds an important place within this elite group.

I am honored by his friendship.

François Lesage

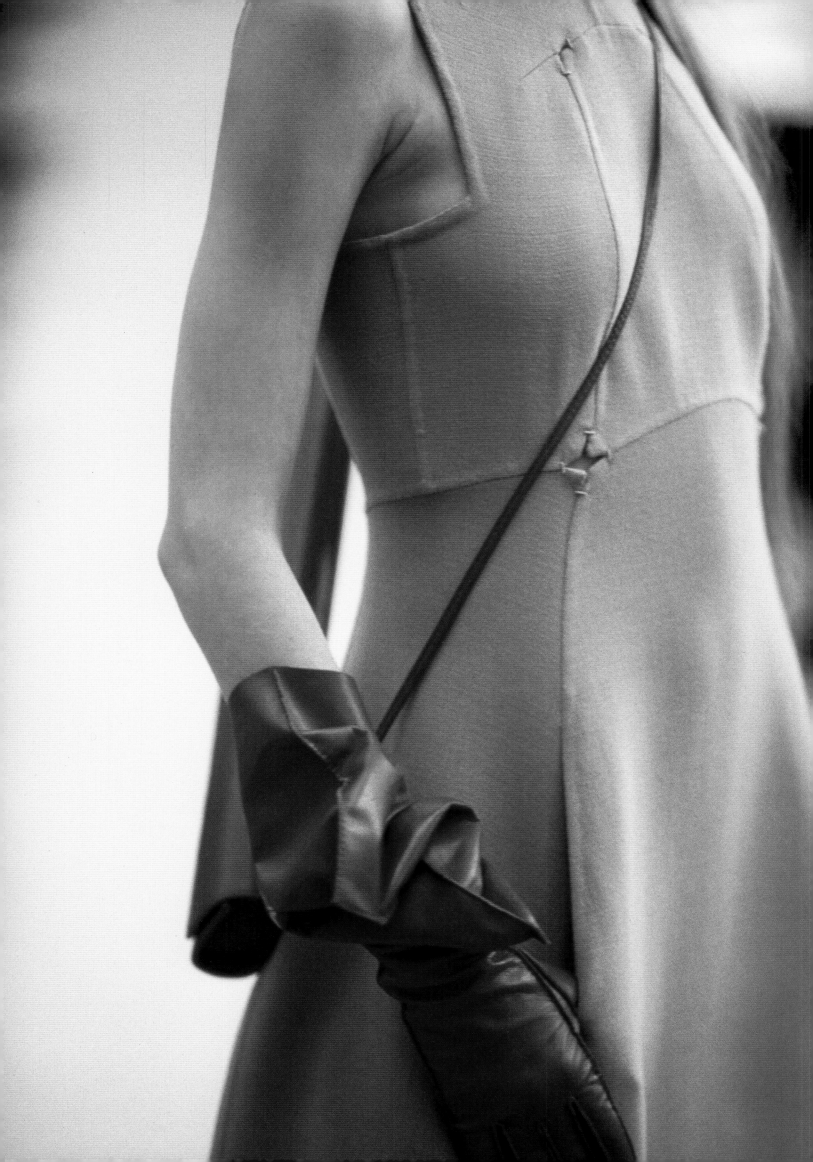

Rather than chasing industry trends, Ralph Rucci has made his mark with refined cuts and luxurious materials, and it is an independent approach that he applies to his accessories as well. In an industry increasingly dependent on accessories, his are designed to enhance but not compete with the garments. Colors and materials are selected in order to co-ordinate harmoniously with the clothes, and materials are frequently shared between garments and accessories. In Rucci's collections it is not unusual for dresses to have leather bodices or insertions that coordinate with the handbags, gloves, and boots.

Rucci dislikes the current trend for over-accessorizing, and believes accessories should have a personal meaning for the wearer. Rather than striving to create the latest "it" bag, the accessories are instead used to set the tone and enhance the quiet sophistication of the garments. Rucci strives for elegance but also a sense of serenity which allows the personality of the wearer to show through. Intelligence and individuality are qualities he especially prizes and, not surprisingly, the consistent Rucci image is one of strength and confidence. He sees his customers as connoisseurs of fashion or "collectors of art."[1] Accordingly, his collections are shown with handcrafted and unusual accessories which emphasize the beauty of the unique and intriguing. The invitation to take a closer look is prevalent throughout Rucci's collections, as things are never as simple as they seem.

This holistic approach is part of a carefully crafted vision which extends even to the hair and makeup of the models. Throughout the collections, the approach to beauty has been consistent, and this has been reflected in the sleek hair, simple makeup and short, neat nails of his models. For the past several years this vision has been carried out by Chrisanne Davis (makeup) and Laurent Philippon (hair). The hairstyles in particular may be considered a metaphor for Rucci's aesthetic sensibility, appearing simple and uncomplicated at first, but revealing an underlying complexity on closer inspection. The hair is carefully braided and coiled into styles that echo the basketry and plaiting prevalent throughout Rucci's work. Laurent Phillipon describes his creations for Rucci as both "minimal" and "architectural" and remarks that his stylistic consistency is remarkably different from other designers. Unlike his peers, Rucci is not interested in trends and obvious sex appeal. While the Rucci woman is sexy she is always elegant and in control, leaving nothing to chance. This is reflected by her sophisticated and controlled approach to beauty.

The shoes and boots seen on the runway have been created by several different designers but most often by Manolo Blahnik, a designer known for his lady-like elegance. While the styles created for Rucci may vary, they all share a minimalist aesthetic. Surface ornamentation is repeatedly eschewed in favor of subdued colors and clean lines. Sandals frequently feature clear strips of vinyl to give the illusion of the bare foot and a longer leg. High boots have also been a Ralph Rucci staple and are most often in suede to co-ordinate with the ensembles, though they also can be of fabrics or exotic skins like alligator. High boots traditionally convey masculine authority and power bvut through Rucci's sleek styling they are able to also project elegance and luxury.

Rucci's handbags are timeless, organic, and refined. Shapes and styles re-occur and are reinvented, an attitude that is markedly anti-"it" bag. (On the heavily decorated and ultra-hyped "it"

Chado Ralph Rucci,
fall/winter 2006.
Photograph courtesy of First View.

Rucci is known for his carefully coordinated acce-
sories. In this ensemble from the Chado Ralph
Rucci collection for fall 2006 the lambskin gloves
and bag are carefully matched to the green cashmere tailleur although an unexpected element is
added with the thigh-high black suede boots.

bags, Rucci remarks enigmatically: "they are perfect for what they are and what they're for."[2]) The handbags, made for Rucci by Carlos Falchi and later Lambertson Truex, feature simple styles and shapes designed by Rucci himself. Practical forms such as stylized backpacks, streamlined totes and shoulder bags appear but are given sophistication through fabric and color. Tubular shapes are frequently used by Rucci, and have been seen slung like an arrow quiver across the back, dangling from a narrow cord (or strap) or cradled in the hand. Not surprisingly, Rucci favors rel-atively simple minaudière styles for evening.

Gloves are a perennial element in Rucci's collections and are created in collaboration with Daniel Storto. Storto's creations for Rucci are simultaneously ladylike and fierce and add the per-fect counterbalance to Ralph Rucci's infantas and cashmere tailleurs. Like Rucci, he is known for his intellectual experiments with shape and form and like Rucci, he pursues perfection witha fer-vour. When asked about their collaborations he replied: "It's a lot of work. I like his approach to design . . . Our tasks are very similar. Every piece must fit like a puzzle. It's a challenge."[3] Not sur-prisingly, interesting and innovative gloves have become a Rucci trademark, and their collabo-rations have produced a variety of styles including the "no-glove" glove which featured, in place of thumbs or fingers, just a simple leather harness.[4] Other experiments have included thumb guards with decorative ties that wrap around the wrist and a buttery-soft lambskin with attached gloves.

Rucci's jewelry can be delicate or massive, but is always unexpected. Dean Harris, who spe-cializes in organic forms and materials, provides these jewels for Rucci. His handcrafted pieces are noted for both their gracefulness and drama; typical of his work are a baroque pearl on a slender chain and large nugget style rings. Dean Harris works with Rucci to develop pieces for the collection and often begins with an inspirational material like red jasper or black diamonds.

Other accessories are used sparingly and are selected for the greatest effect. Belts, which have been produced for Rucci by Daniel Storto or Kleinberg Sherrill, are used to delineate the waistline and usually consist of a braided leather tie or sash. Often these belts are integral to the overall design of the garment and cannot be removed without spoiling the intended silhouette. Millinery rarely appears in Ralph Rucci's collections, but is used to set a mood, as in the collec-tion for spring 2005, when he sent eight models down the catwalk in similar ensembles in a vari-ety of colors. The hats, by Susan Van der Linde, a New York milliner popular with New York's elite, finished the look and reinforced the feeling of repetition and uniformity. Fur hats, wraps, and muffs also are used to great effect and are created by famed furrier Pologeorgis Furs.

While the Rucci aesthetic is constantly evolving, several dominant themes emerge and recur throughout his collections. As the name "Chado" suggests, the influence of Asian culture is pro-nounced and deliberate. While this can clearly be seen in the kimono sleeves and necklines of the garments, it can also be seen in the unconventional accessories. In the past, Rucci has used antique bamboo baskets as handbags as well as small antique birdcages as necklaces. As a col-lector of arts and antiques, Rucci acknowledges the beauty of age, patina, and imperfections. This approach to imperfect beauty is one prevalent in Japanese art and unusual in fashion.

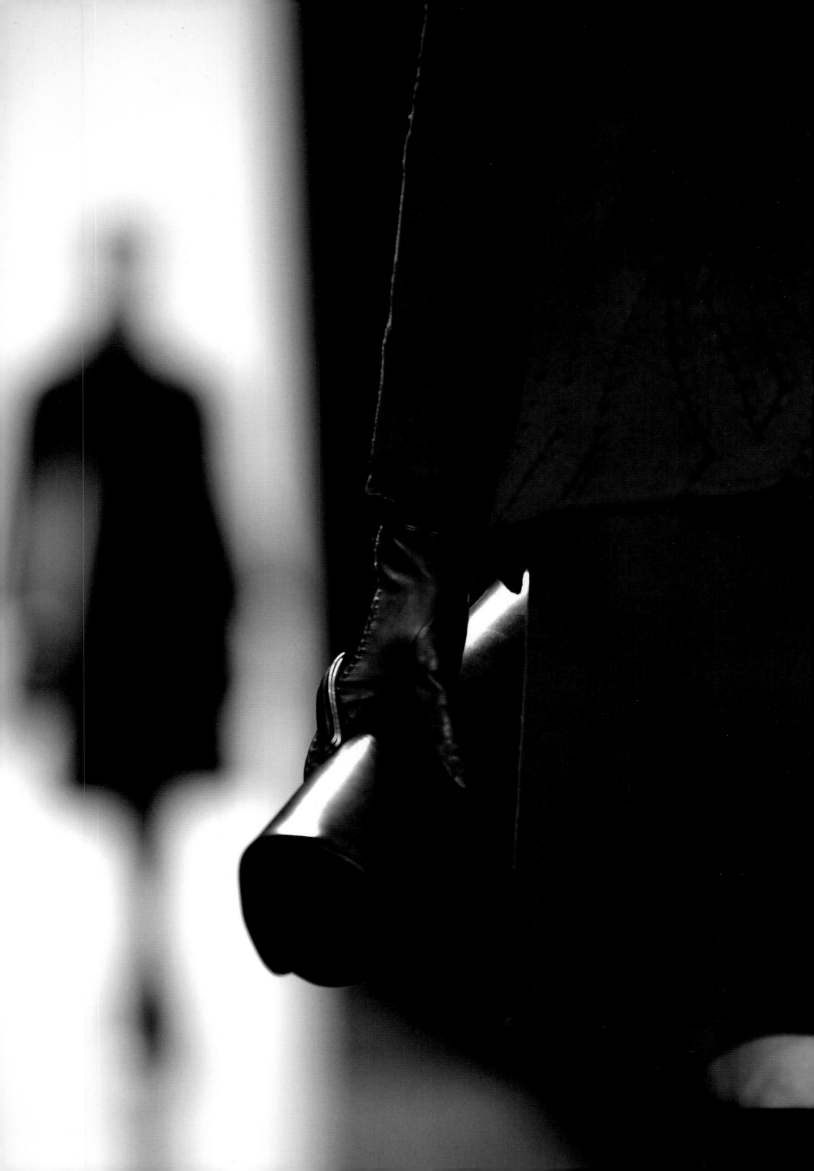

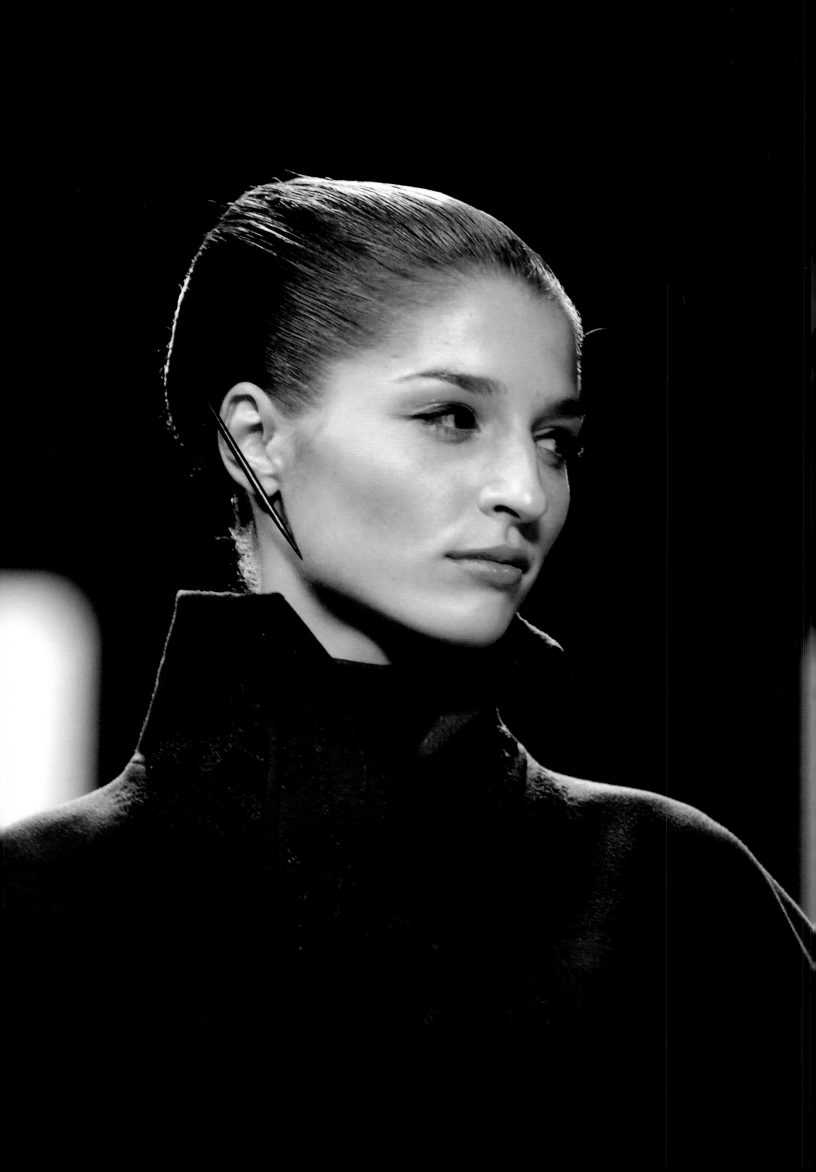

Rucci is clearly influenced by his love of art and architecture, proudly naming his dresses after great twentieth-century artists like Cy Twombly. Rucci is an artist himself, and his printed textiles are often based on his own paintings. Painterly motifs reccur throughout his work and add an intellectual aspect to his designs. This influence is most marked in his garments but can also be seen in accessories such as the obituary gloves. The clean lines of modern architecture are also an inspiration, and with The Four Seasons Hotel in New York said to be the idea behind the quill jewelry produced for the fall 2006 collection.

Despite his love of luxury and opulence, Ralph Rucci is also a minimalist. Rucci is an advocate of clean, uncluttered silhouettes and selective adornment. His preference for clean lines and geometry can be seen in simple shapes of the accessories, particularly the soft tubular "roll" bags and the slouchy gloves constructed from unusual geometric shapes. The minimalist aesthetic is also seen with selection of shoes, narrow leather belts as well as the stacked rings of semi-precious stone.

The beauty of nature, and the inherent opulence of natural materials is the also an important theme. Rucci's use of furs and exotic skins is unapologetic in this age of political correctness and a bold stance on luxury. The materials are frequently left undisguised from their original form and lend a certain raw element to the luxury. This is most obvious in the skins used for assortment of gloves, handbags and boots but is also a recurring theme in the jewelry. Past collections have included necklaces and earrings crafted from porcupine quills and a necklace made from a prehistoric fossilized tooth. This raw glamour evokes an image of a modern warrior goddess and projects confidence and strength.

Ralph Rucci's evolutionary approach to fashion and accessories is unusual and courageous in the trend-driven world of fashion. Instead of drowning his collections with accessories, his judicious selection instead serves to highlight his sleek silhouettes and serene beauty. In Rucci's holistic vision every detail is meaningful and nothing is left to chance. The accessories, although they are always secondary to the garments, play an important role in defining the Rucci aesthetic.

1   Webber, Kathleen Nicholson, "Ralph Rucci Honored by Drexel University," *Women's Wear Daily*, May 26, 2005.

2   Kirschner, Marilyn, "Ralph Rucci: 'Prince' of the City," www.fashionlines.com, June 5, 2006.

3   Suppes, Christine, *Daniel Storto, Master Glove Maker*, www.fashionlines.com, December 1, 2003.

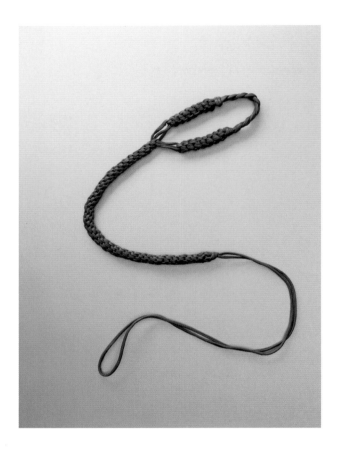

Braided leather belt,
Daniel Storto for Chado Ralph Rucci,
fall/winter 2003.
Photograph: William Palmer.

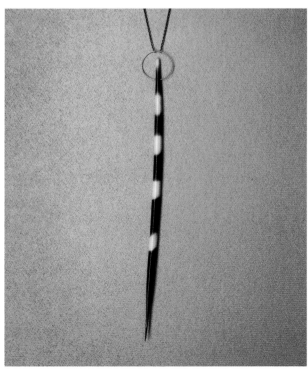

Porcupine quill necklace,
Dean Harris for Chado Ralph Rucci,
fall/winter 2006.
Photograph: William Palmer.

For the Chado Ralph Rucci fall/winter 2006
collection, Dean Harris created several unusual
pieces of jewelry fashioned from porcupine quills.
While the porcupine quill has a long history in
traditional dress and adornment, the jewelry's
refinement makes it equally modern and
timeless.

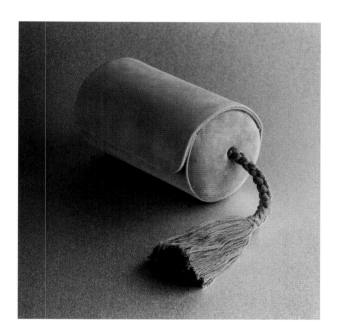

"Roll" bag,
Carlos Falchi for Chado Ralph Rucci,
spring 2006.
Photograph: William Palmer.

Rucci is known for interesting handbags but is
extremely judicious in their selection. He finds
simple forms like binocular cases endlessly chic
and inspirational. The roll bag deliberately
echoes styles favored by Halston during his
heyday, although the soft color and braided
tassel are typically Chado.

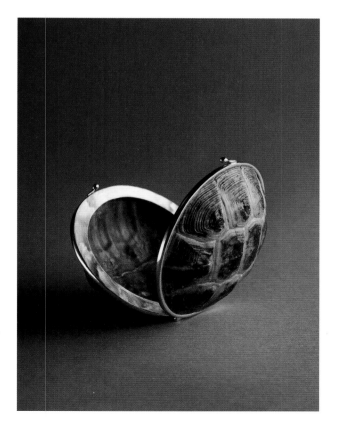

Tortoise minaudière,
Chado Ralph Rucci, fall/winter 2006.
Photograph: William Palmer.

Minaudière and reticule purses handcrafted from
tortoise shells made an appearance on the runway
for Chado Ralph Rucci for fall/winter 2006.
The effect is both sumptuous and dramatic; a fresh
take on traditional luxury.

...leads to

...contradiction...

...goodness is in

...freedom can be

...is that space and

...architecture the...

...space and silence

...then...

...we can...

...which is totality

Detail, handpainted leather "Obituary" gloves,
Daniel Storto for Chado Ralph Rucci, fall/winter 2004.
Photograph: William Palmer.

Although he can no longer recall whose obituary was used,
these gloves are an exploration of the power of the written
word to give meaning to objects and stimulate the
imagination. They recall, both in appearance and in intent,
Cy Twombly's impassioned scribbles.

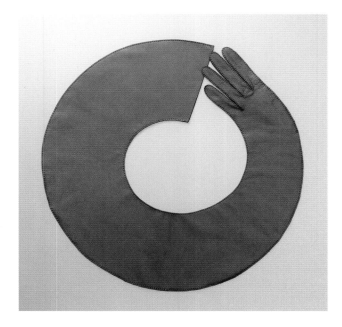

Circular glove,
Daniel Storto for Ralph Rucci Chado, fall 2002.
Photograph: William Palmer.

Daniel Storto's gloves play an important role in the
presentation of for Ralph Rucci's collections. Although gloves
are traditionally associated with the staid and ladylike, Stortos
creations combine quiet elegance with the avant-garde. His
experimental approach was apparent is his creations for the
first couture collection of 2002 which featured circular and
rectangular gloves. These gloves were designed
deliberately to slouch down the arm and were paired with
tubular bags slung across the chest like a quiver.

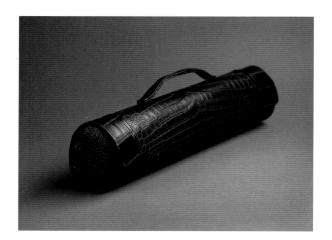

Alligator handbag,
Carlos Falchi for Chado Ralph Rucci,
fall/winter 2006.
Photograph: William Palmer.

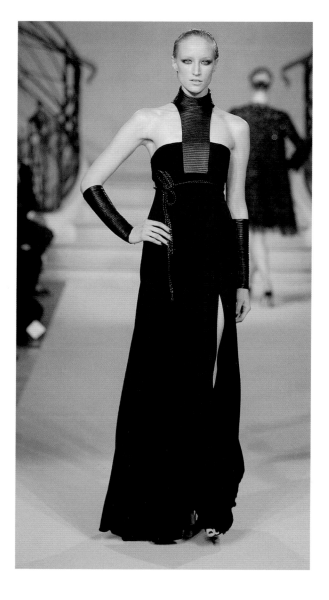

Chado Ralph Rucci,
fall/winter 2005.
Photograph: Dan Lecca.

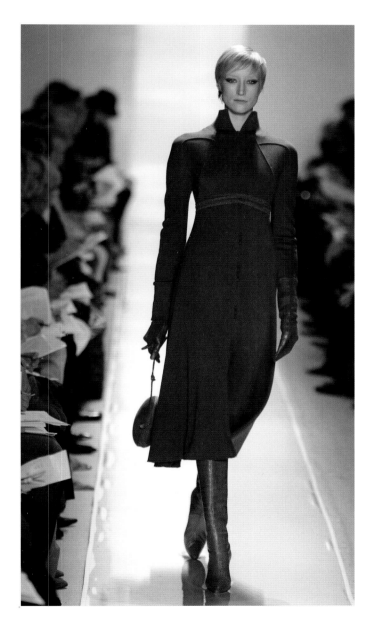

Chado Ralph Rucci,
fall/winter 2005.
Photograph: Dan Lecca.

A perfect example of Rucci's holistic approach to fashion is this ensemble from the Chado Ralph Rucci fall/winter 2005 collection. Constructed of heather-gray wool jersey with olive-green alligator insertions, it was accessorized with pieced wool jersey and alligator gloves, an alligator belt, olive-green lambskin "egg" bag and knee-high lizard boots.

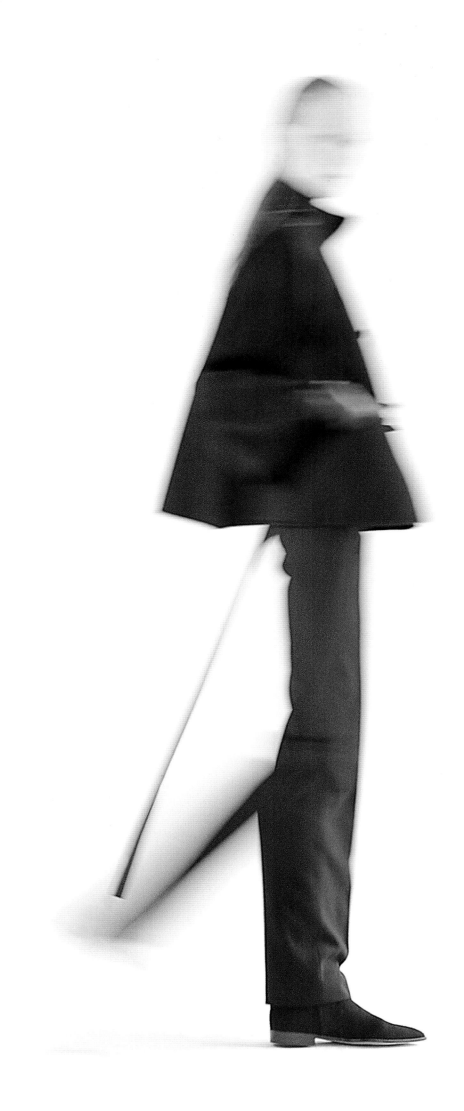

In fashion as in life, perfection is often sought and almost never achieved. That is, of course, unless the seeker is Ralph Rucci. In an industry known for its visionaries, he is a virtuoso. His tailoring is master class, but the one thing Ralph Rucci never cuts is corners. Mr. Rucci is personally involved in every step of his design process from conception to catwalk. He works with the world's most prestigious mills to select only the finest cashmere, silk, and embroidery, and is constantly innovating ways to make his creations move in harmony with the body.

Mr. Rucci is known for his exquisite fabrications and immaculate attention to detail – reminiscent of Chado, the intricate and graceful Japanese tea ceremony from which he has taken his company's name. His sculptural pieces are revered for the pared-down elegance that keeps them feeling modern and chic season after season. He is the first American designer since Mainbocher to be invited to present his collection at the exclusive Paris couture shows and has a dedicated clientele of celebrities, socialites, and fashion industry professionals that grows in number and devotion with each passing year.

Mr. Rucci's signature precision and passion for beauty elevates fashion to an art form. Like the artist Cy Twombly, whom he admires, his work is also profoundly architectural, with an emphasis on craftsmanship, construction, and creativity. In Ralph Rucci's hands, minimalism is transformed to mastery, and simplicity to the sublime.

Glenda Bailey

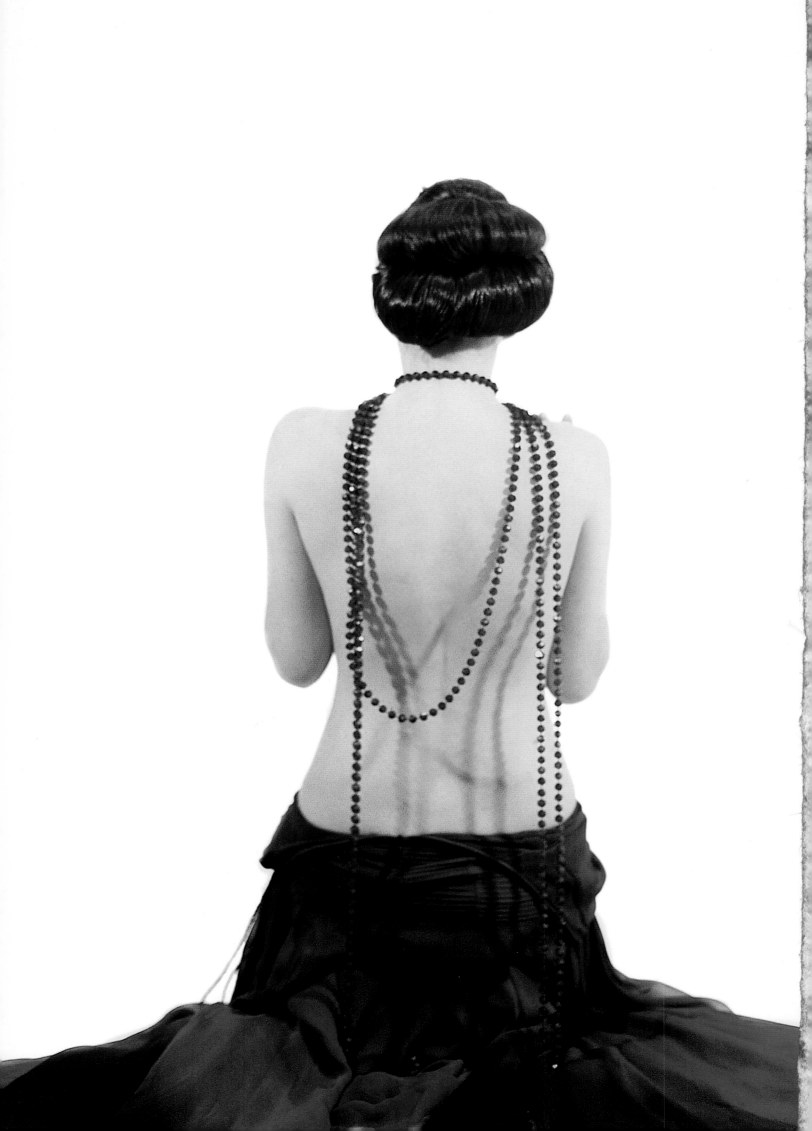

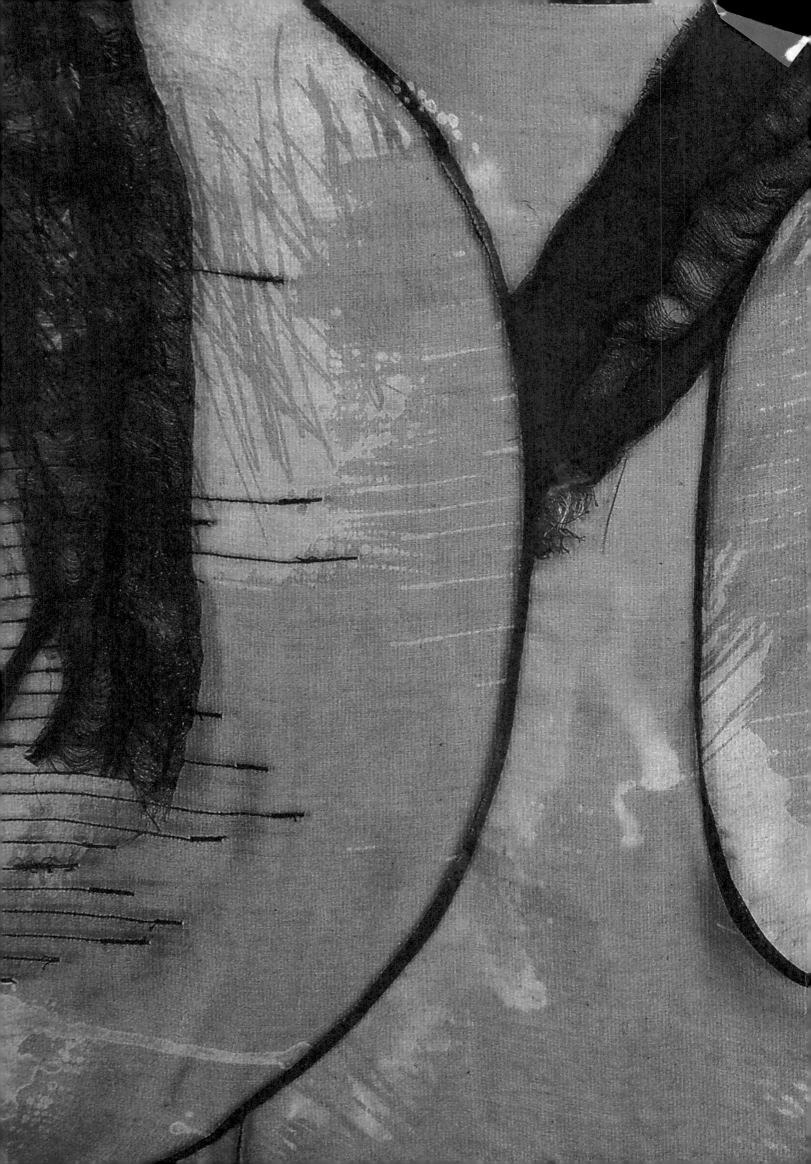